T0357775

WHEN THE GOING
WAS GOOD

WHEN THE GOING WAS GOOD

An Editor's Adventures During the
Last Golden Age of Magazines

GRAYDON CARTER

WITH JAMES FOX

Illustrations by Eric Hanson

PENGUIN PRESS | NEW YORK | 2025

PENGUIN PRESS
An imprint of Penguin Random House LLC
1745 Broadway, New York, NY 10019
penguinrandomhouse.com

Copyright © 2025 by Graydon Carter
Penguin Random House values and supports copyright. Copyright fuels
creativity, encourages diverse voices, promotes free speech, and creates a
vibrant culture. Thank you for buying an authorized edition of this book
and for complying with copyright laws by not reproducing, scanning, or
distributing any part of it in any form without permission. You are
supporting writers and allowing Penguin Random House to continue to
publish books for every reader. Please note that no part of this book may be
used or reproduced in any manner for the purpose of training artificial
intelligence technologies or systems.

PP colophon is a registered trademark of Penguin Random House LLC.

Illustrations copyright © 2025 by Eric Hanson

Designed by Amanda Dewey

LIBRARY OF CONGRESS CONTROL NUMBER: 2024035644
ISBN 9780593655900 (hardcover)
ISBN 9780593655917 (ebook)

Printed in the United States of America
1st Printing

The authorized representative in the EU for product safety and compliance
is Penguin Random House Ireland, Morrison Chambers, 32 Nassau
Street, Dublin D02 YH68, Ireland, https://eu-contact.penguin.ie.

*For the centers of my existence, my extraordinary wife, Anna;
my five equally extraordinary children, Ash, Max, Spike,
Bron, and Izzy; and our dachshund, Charley*

CONTENTS

WHEN THE GOING
WAS GOOD

One Big Scoop and a Wedding

May 2005

This could so easily have been where it all ended.

My wife, Anna, and I were on our way back to New York from the Bahamas. We'd spent ten days at the Ocean Club on our honeymoon and it was time to get back to work—or "the coffee cup" as we say in the Carter household.

I'm not what you would call the most relaxed flyer, and I tend to get to airports early because I don't want to compound the stress by having to rush to the gate. At the airport, while I fretted about the flight ahead, Anna's cell phone rang. I didn't have a mobile back then, and calling Anna's was the only way my kids or the office could get in touch with me. In those days I never left the house without a few quarters in my pocket for pay phones, along with a handkerchief (more about that later). Anna answered the call and handed me the phone. She whispered the words "David Friend!"

David, one of my deputies at *Vanity Fair,* where I'd been the editor for more than a decade, was indeed on the line. In the euphoria of marriage and honeymoon and all that, it had utterly slipped my mind that at ten thirty that morning *Vanity Fair* had released an article we'd been working on for the past two years. It revealed the identity of "Deep Throat," the highly secret source Bob Woodward relied on during his Watergate reporting with Carl Bernstein. As the *Post* itself had noted, the identity of Deep Throat was "among the most compelling questions of modern American history, dissected in books, in films, on the internet, and in thousands of articles and hundreds of television programs."

Two years of work and worry over a major story—at the time, the Holy Grail of journalism scoops—and here I was stuck on the day of its release in the tiny departure lounge of Nassau International Airport. I mouthed the words "Holy fuck!" to Anna. She mouthed back, "What?" David reminded me that, as we'd planned before my departure, he had called both Bob and Carl that morning at around nine thirty to tell them we were faxing them advance copies of our story naming Mark Felt, the former deputy director of the FBI, as Deep Throat. I asked what their reaction had been. David said they had thus far made no comment, but that word was trickling out and the phone lines at *Vanity Fair* were already jammed.

A more confident editor would probably have been elated at the news. I am not made of such vibrant stuff. My foremost worry was one that I'd had the whole time we were working on the article: that we had somehow gotten it wrong. The fact of the matter was, we weren't 100 percent sure we had the right man. A mistake of such magnitude becomes the stuff of legend and winds up in the first paragraph of your obituary. Also, this was a rough period for journalists. It was during the George W. Bush administration, and if you got something wrong, armies of righteous nitpickers on the right—and the left—would descend to lay waste to your career and possibly your livelihood. Our main worry was that there was in fact no Deep

Throat: that it had been a journalistic device, a composite of several sources—perhaps ginned up, some even said, by Alice Mayhew, who was Woodward and Bernstein's editor at Simon & Schuster, to move the plot along in *All the President's Men*. I never bought into that rumor. Alice was the preeminent nonfiction editor of political books in the nation. And an aboveboard and formidable person in every way. I had played tennis with her as her doubles partner a few times out on Long Island, and whenever I missed a shot, she wouldn't say a word. She'd just give me a look that could have de-strung a racket on the other side of the court.

—

Ten days earlier, Anna and I had stood at the altar of a small Episcopalian church a short walk from our home in Connecticut, about to get married. It was, as it is for so many grooms, aside from the birth of my children, one of the happiest days of my life. I felt incredibly fortunate to be marrying this smart, beautiful woman before my kids and our relatives and friends. There were a number of hymns, including "Jerusalem," which I was told later had confused a number of our Jewish friends who were surprised to hear a hymn with that name in an Episcopalian service. Anna, in addition to having Scott as a surname, is a Scot, and her father, Sir Kenneth Scott, a distinguished former diplomat, and her brother Andrew both wore kilts. For the walk to our house, we thought bagpipers would be a nice touch and hired a group associated with the New York City Police Department. Along the way, Harry Benson, a Glaswegian whom I had worked with at *Life* and *Vanity Fair*, was taking some snaps. At one point he whispered to me that some of the tunes weren't Scottish at all. They were IRA anthems.

The weather was decent, and the wedding party had assembled

on our terrace and spilled out into the garden. After dinner, we made our way to our barn, which conveniently had a stage. There, Tom Freston and John Mellencamp had an incredible wedding gift for us: Otis Day and the Knights of "Shama Lama Ding Dong" and "Shout" fame, the band that had performed so memorably in the movie *Animal House*. When the night was winding down, Anna and I were about to drive off to the Mayflower Inn, not far from us, for the first night of our marriage when we found Fran Lebowitz sitting beside our driver in the front seat. Fran was a big part of our lives. We had first met in the men's department of Bergdorf Goodman years earlier when she asked my advice on a tie she was buying for her father. A friendship developed and Fran became an integral part of our family, joining us for Christmas dinners as well as any number of trips to Los Angeles. But this was a bit more togetherness than we expected. It seemed that her ride to a friend's house, a town away, had left early, and so Fran was hitching a ride with us. In the boisterous delirium of the moment, and with the need to get us to the Inn and Fran to her destination, the office and our big scoop seemed a million miles away.

—

The identity of Deep Throat had been a guessing game in Washington and journalism circles for years. Everyone from Henry Kissinger to Diane Sawyer had been proposed as Woodward and Bernstein's secret informant. Our evidence that Felt was Deep Throat was, we believed, close to conclusive, but it came from secondhand sources. We were 95 percent sure—but that last 5 percent was unnerving, the difference between great success and humbling failure. If we were incorrect, it wouldn't quite be on a par with the London *Sunday Times*'s 1983 publication of the fake Hitler diaries, an episode that its editor, Frank Giles, never lived down. But it would be close. After David's update, I realized I simply could not get on that plane unless I knew one way or another if we had the right man.

The journey to this moment had begun two years earlier, when I got a call from John O'Connor, a San Francisco–based lawyer. He said that he represented the man who was Deep Throat and that he and his client wanted the story to break in *Vanity Fair.* You get a lot of crank calls when you're an editor of a magazine, but I had a general policy of always taking the calls and looking into leads when they presented themselves. O'Connor and I talked for a time. He wouldn't reveal who his client was. But I was intrigued enough to say, "Let me have someone get back to you." I asked David if he was free and if he could come down to my office. We had worked together at *Life* in the mid-1980s and I'd brought him to *Vanity Fair* a few years after joining it myself. David had sort of an oddball role at the magazine. Unlike the other editors there, he had few fixed writers. He was listed on the masthead as editor of creative development, a title I must have given him, though I was never sure what it meant. I'm not sure he did either. But David was a dogged hand and, more important, because he wasn't always closing stories for the current issue, he was available. I told him about the phone call with O'Connor, gave him the number, and asked him to follow up.

Their conversations dribbled on for a few months. Eventually, we had a name: Mark Felt. Neither of us had ever heard of him. We learned that he had once been number two at the FBI. David and I would meet every few days about the story, but we had our doubts. Chief among them was Felt himself. He was in his early nineties by this time, he had suffered a stroke two years earlier, and he was starting to show signs of dementia. The evidence supporting his claim was strong but essentially circumstantial. He had said nothing about the matter for more than three decades. He had only acknowledged the truth to his family a year or so before O'Connor called me, after family members, having put various clues together, had confronted him. He admitted to them that, yes, he was Deep Throat, but he was reluctant to go public with the information. Felt was proud of his part in exposing the corruption and obstruction of justice he saw in Nixon's White House during the Watergate cover-up, but he also remained loyal to the men and women of the agency.

When David flew out to San Francisco to meet Felt in person, he found him in a diminished state. This meant we had to work around him to firm up the story. All we had to go on were sources at one remove: Felt's daughter, a college teacher; his grandson, who had gone to school with O'Connor's daughter; and O'Connor himself. They all confirmed earlier conversations in which Felt had described his role as Deep Throat. There was also Felt's autobiography, published in 1979, which contained a number of subtle clues, as well as noncommittal but suggestive phone calls between Felt and Woodward. Felt's daughter remembered that someone called Bob Woodward, whose name she didn't recognize at the time, had come to visit her father in 1999, on the twenty-fifth anniversary of Nixon's resignation.

After about a year and a half of back-and-forth, we felt we had hit a wall. Then we came up with an idea that would allow us to publish Felt's claims without the sort of guaranteed proof you want when you are wading into such a potential mess. We figured that O'Connor, like so many lawyers, might be a closeted writer. So we offered the story to him. We believed that it would give us a slight, gossamer layer of cover. O'Connor agreed and turned in an article that, after a number of rounds of editing, we thought worked. At that point, only a handful of people knew of the assignment: me; David; Chris Garrett, our managing editor, who had to sign off on the plan; and Robert Walsh, our legal editor.

We soon brought Susan White, the director of photography, in on the secret. In order to keep the circle as small as possible, she sent her husband, Gasper Tringale, a photographer, to San Francisco to shoot Felt. (I later got an earful from Annie Leibovitz, *Vanity Fair*'s principal photographer, who thought she should have shot it. I couldn't disagree with her—although I did admire Gasper's picture.) We set up a special room at the magazine, an office within the office. We papered the glass doors and kept it locked when not in use. We also put the story on a separate server, one that wouldn't be accessible to anyone at Condé Nast, the parent company of *Vanity Fair* and a score of other magazines—and competitors—including *Vogue*, *GQ*, and *The New Yorker*. David Harris, our art director, joined the Felt gang. So did John Banta, our head of research, who oversaw fact-checking.

With our doubts continuing to linger—as doubts have a habit of doing in journalism—I knew that I could have settled the matter with a phone call to either Bob, who was still at *The Washington Post*, or Carl, who was on our masthead. I figured that if I called Carl, he'd call Bob, and Bob would get the revelation into the next day's *Post*. And obviously if I called Bob, we'd get the same result. By this time, a dozen and a half *Vanity Fair* staff members were in on the plan. We had all worked together for more than a decade and the trust between us was rock-solid. We held the secret as closely as Bob and Carl had done since the early 1970s. The big trouble here was the lead time. This was before magazines had digital editions, so we had to edit the story, photograph the story, lay out the story, check the story, print the issue, ship the issue, and then wait for newsstand people all around the world to open their boxes of the magazine and start selling copies. With a monthly magazine, you have ten days to two weeks between the time it leaves the printer and when it appears on newsstands. During this period, the issue is completely out of our control, and we'd had problems before with printers tipping off someone else to a hot story. We'd also heard that *The Washington Post* had gotten wind of what we were up to. We couldn't afford to wait until the magazine hit the newsstands, so we decided to release the story even before we shipped it to the printers.

In advance of printing and shipping any issue, the various top editors at Condé Nast were required to deliver a summary of each issue of their magazine at a grim affair called Print Order. Si Newhouse, the chairman, would be there. As would the president of the company and the heads of three or four departments. The editors stood at one end of the conference table with their publisher and anxiously tap-danced their way through a draft copy of their new issue. The publisher then reported on how many pages of advertising had been sold in the issue compared with the same month the previous year. The number of copies that were printed for each issue was dependent on the quality of the issue that was presented that day. Well, not quality so much as the perceived newsstand salability. I left the Mark Felt story out of my presentation for the July 2005 issue. I told Si after the meeting that it might be wise to print more copies than the look of the issue warranted. He nodded without asking a question.

In those days, you didn't announce news with a tweet. You released it in successive waves to selected press outlets. Or you released it all at once and wide to the wire services, newspapers, and television news divisions. Which is what we did with our Deep Throat story. Just before we released it to the wire services, Beth Kseniak, our head of communications, gave the scoop to ABC News, which broke into regular programming with the story. By the following day, it was front-page news around the world. For the first seven or eight hours of that first day, though, all through the rollout, there was still no confirmation from Bob or Carl that Felt was indeed Deep Throat.

When David had told them about *Vanity Fair*'s plans to name Felt, they'd been cool, giving nothing away. What we learned later was that Carl had flown from New York to Washington to meet up with Bob and Ben Bradlee, their editor during the Watergate investigations. Ben was eighty-three and retired but still a dynamic force of nature. He called a meeting to decide how to respond. The three men were joined by Leonard Downie Jr., *The Washington Post*'s executive editor, who had been at a management retreat on the Maryland shore when he got the call to return to the office.

According to a front-page story in *The New York Times*, written by Todd Purdum and Jim Rutenberg, Bob and Carl stalled. They didn't want to give their story away by simply confirming our reporting. And who could fault them? They'd kept the secret for three decades. (I suspect, though, that Carl might have shared it with his ex-wife, Nora Ephron; in *Heartburn*, her novel based on the breakup of their marriage, the husband is named Mark Feldman.) Ben spent all day trying to persuade Bob and Carl to confirm the news. Bob kept pushing back, because he had made a promise to Felt that he wouldn't release his name until after Felt's death or upon his request to do so. Bob questioned whether Felt was mentally capable of making the decision to go public and whether he was fit enough to release him and Carl from their promise. It turned out that Bob had a book ready to publish after Felt died, and our story would have doubly scooped him. Ben put his foot down. As Carl later recalled, Ben said, "Not even a close call. No way to go but to confirm it. We got beat on our own story." Ben himself told *The Times*: "That story laid it all out, and it's silly to say you have no comment and won't even say whether the goddamn thing is right, when you know it's right."

I knew none of this that afternoon as the call for boarding was announced at the airport in Nassau. Anna and I kept moving to the back of the line, waiting for word about Bob and Carl's statement. To make matters more stressful, the battery on Anna's phone was about to die. After letting pretty much everyone else move into line ahead of us, we finally had to make our way toward the gate. Just as we were about to hand the boarding agent our tickets, David called.

"Please tell me something good," I said.

He obliged: "Woodward and Bernstein just confirmed it was Mark Felt."

Anna would later say she detected a tear in my eye.

Beth, meanwhile, was in the ABC News studios. She had booked O'Connor for *Nightline*, then the network's premier late news show. Ted Koppel was the anchor. And he was a tough interrogator, badgering poor O'Connor with questions about how he could possibly know for sure that Felt was Deep Throat. Beth felt so sorry for O'Connor that she almost cut the interview short. As Koppel continued his questioning, her phone rang, and she got the news about Bob and Carl's confirmation. Her eyes, too, began to water, both from relief and from the general tension of the days and months leading up to the moment. She watched as Koppel was informed of the news. He had been taping the show as if it was live; now he had only fifteen minutes left. Beth noticed that his manner changed dramatically: gone was the haughty, suspicious inquisitor. Koppel spent his remaining time trying to get all the questions out that he had avoided during the first part of his interview. Beth pulled O'Connor when the fifteen minutes were up and rushed him over to *The NewsHour with Jim Lehrer* on PBS. The next day, she rotated him among all three morning shows—a feat people in her trade consider a major trifecta. It was a wonderful moment for the staff and a great thing for a monthly magazine that was approaching its centenary.

I spoke to both Bob and Carl that week, and they could not have been more gracious. In the end, the Deep Throat revelation proved good for them too. Bob finished the book on Felt he had been working on, and *The Secret Man* was published that summer. Bob and Carl's victory lap of the news cycle in the days that followed the *Vanity Fair* revelation was like seeing the journalistic equivalent of Watson and Crick, Martin and Lewis, or Brad and Jen back together, however briefly.

Chapter 2.

Bitter Winters and
a Lot of Hockey

Growing up, I worried at times that I was destined to become little more than one of those faceless, nameless men in the scenery of someone else's better life. I was decent at sports, but nobody would have ever called me a jock. I read everything I could get my hands on, but nobody would have ever called me a scholar. I was clever, but nobody would have ever called me a brainiac. I was reasonably good-looking and could talk to girls and make them laugh, but nobody would have ever called me a Casanova. I had dreams, but nobody would have ever called me ambitious. Everything was impulse driven: toward sports, music, cars, books, films, and girls. It could also be said that my parents, and indeed a good number of my friends, thought that life, in the professional sense, had little in store for me.

As I regularly tell my kids, few people learn from success. A worthwhile professional life is built over a boneyard of failures. Early failures, as opposed to successes, are instructive. The trick is to keep them minor. And to figure out what went wrong and why. There is no school for editing, like there is for dentistry, cooking, or even real estate sales. Journalism is a lead-from-your-instinct business. You just have to be really curious, and care, about everything.

And so, somehow, in my case, with a lot of mishaps and a dollop of good luck along the way, things just worked out. It wasn't easy all the time, but step by step I managed to achieve the four things the twenty-five-year-old me thought would bring me happiness in my adult years:

1. Living in New York. Greenwich Village specifically.
2. Becoming the editor of a big, general-interest magazine.
3. Being one half of a wonderful marriage.
4. Having a large, happy family and a dog.

All this came in time. But I'm getting ahead of myself.

—

In the early 1950s, my parents packed up me and my younger brother, Gary, and we sailed from Canada to Southampton on an ocean liner, the RMS *Scythia*. It had been a Cunard Line workhorse during the war, serving as a troop and supply ship. Transatlantic flight was still relatively new back then, and most ocean crossings were done by sea. From Southampton we went to stay with my uncle Wallace, an otherworldly eccentric who lived on D'Oyly Carte Island, a family property on the Thames. We got there by means of a flat-bottomed skiff that was hauled across a bend in the river by chain. The house itself was enormous and dark and teeming with cats. Peter Cushing would have felt right at home. My uncle was, my mother told us later, a distant relation to Richard D'Oyly Carte himself, the producer of the Gilbert and Sullivan comic operas.

After a few weeks there, and then a stopover in London, we decamped to Zweibrücken, a small German town about an hour from the Luxembourg border. This would be our home for the next four years. My father was there with the Royal Canadian Air Force, training young pilots, and my mother had her hands full with my brother, who was not yet one. I was four years older and was on my own a lot of the time. I played in abandoned bunkers, learned a smattering of German, and spent hours with my Britains toy soldiers, the Fleischmann HO gauge model train I got for Christmas one year, and a small toy Royal Canadian Mountie. All of which I still have. We traveled constantly, and even though I was a kid, I remember the sight of European cities and towns that had been devastated by war. In the winter, my parents would head off to Chamonix and Méribel to ski, leaving us with our housekeeper, Frau Fleigga, a smoker of Promethean might. I had few close friends, and my brother was too young to be of much use to me, but I remember those days with great fondness. I was sorry to return home to Canada. Which we did, the year I turned seven.

Life in Canada for a boy pretty much revolved around skiing and hockey in the winter and fishing, canoeing, street hockey, and goofing off in the summer. There was little of the surfboard, bikini, and hot-rod glamour that American kids seemed to swirl around in. Family vacations were endurance contests that pitted inattentive yet restrictive parents against their captive children. Sitting in the back seat of a two-tone '57 Chrysler—the one with some of the biggest tailfins Detroit ever put on a car—on a long, hot road trip with both parents smoking up front, and Perry Como and Percy Faith on the radio, was nobody's idea of heaven.

My father had a number of skills, few of which could be turned to financial advantage. For example, he had the determination (and, as it happened, the bladder) to drive a full day in the car without a single stop. In the front seat he carried an empty mickey bottle that once held rye whiskey. This was for emergencies. When my brother or I had to go to the bathroom, he would hold on to the wheel with one hand and distractedly pass the bottle to the back seat with the other. We'd gingerly try to stick our little penises in through the neck to relieve ourselves. In most instances, there were some false starts, and when we were done, we'd screw the top back on, wipe our hands on our jeans, and pass the bottle up to the front seat. Peanut-butter-and-jam sandwiches that had been made by my mother before we hit the road were generally eaten before 11:00 a.m. On one trip, to Niagara Falls, my father broke with tradition and decided to pull over to a roadside diner for lunch. By this time the mickey bottle was already full. My mother wanted to empty it in the bushes. But my father was starved and said he'd do it after we'd eaten. It was a hot day, so we left the windows rolled down and went in to eat. When we got back to the car after lunch, the bottle was gone.

Aside from his determination (and ability) to drive hours on end without peeing, my father's abiding passion was wood. In all its forms. Especially firewood. Canadian winters are interminable and bitterly cold, and my father prided himself, as many Canadian dads did, on his way of being able to turn a crumpled-up page of newsprint, a bit of kindling, and a single match into a roaring inferno. He was also not one to part with a dollar unless he absolutely had to, and so the cost of firewood was a constant source of frustration for him. When we ran low, he'd wait until the sun went down and then throw my brother and me into the back of the car and venture out into the night.

My father would head directly for the wooded areas controlled by the National Capital Commission, the agency responsible for tending to the parklands around the capital city of Ottawa. The

NCC's woodsmen regularly cut up fallen trees and piled the logs by the roadside. My father had a big Coleman spotlight that he'd hold against the roof of the car to scan the side of the road for some freshly cut wood, much the way coast guard skippers do when they're looking for survivors of a boating accident.

Once, as we skidded around a corner on the icy road, something caught his eye. "Now, that's a yule log!" he shouted. And indeed it was. There in the snow by the side of the road was the log of my father's dreams. It must have been a foot and a half in diameter and three feet long. We pulled onto the shoulder and padded into the snowbank. It took a while to chip away at the snow and ice.

Finally, we could fully see the prize. I was maybe ten at the time, and prying that log away from the snow was like getting a corpse out of the frozen ground. It was a bitterly cold night, and I could barely feel my fingers or toes. After a half dozen or so attempts, we dislodged the log and lugged it to the back of the car. My father opened the trunk and the three of us somehow managed to get it in, not without a fair amount of inventive blasphemy on his part. There were also a dozen or so smaller logs, and one by one we added them to the haul. Like moonshiners, we did all this in the near dark, with just the jerky movements of my father's spotlight casting an eerie silent-movie aspect to the agony. By the time we were finished, the trunk wouldn't close. My father pulled a length of twine out of his pocket and tied the latch under the trunk to the bumper. We jumped into the car after the heist, but the weight in the trunk brought the bumper almost to the road and our '57 Chrysler fishtailed off into the night with the front wheels barely touching the ground.

Only another Canadian can begin to understand the level of cold experienced during the long winters of a 1950s childhood. This was before the days of goose-down jackets and fleece-lined boots. Winter uniforms both for sports and regular wear were composed of wool, flannel, and unforgivingly hard leather. It snowed for about five months of the year. After some storms, the snow almost covered the ground-floor windows of our house. My father would regularly howl at the heating bills that came in during the long winter months. At night, he would turn the thermostat down to 45 degrees. On particularly cold mornings, my brother and our sister, Cathy, and I would wake up with frost on the *inside* of our bedroom windows. Everyone had a frostbite story. My father used to say that he was skiing once with a man whose frostbitten ear had fallen off during a tumble. We were never quite certain whether that was true, but it went a long way toward ensuring that we always wore woolen caps outside. (Canadians call them *toques*. For you non-Canadians, we pronounce it "toooks.") Most cars had electric heating coils that had to be plugged in at night to keep the engine blocks from freezing.

Hockey was everything—in part because there wasn't much of anything else. We listened to hockey on the radio on Saturday nights, and on Sunday nights, we had dinner listening to *Our Miss Brooks* with Eve Arden. When we finally got a television, things changed, but only marginally. The addition of American programs like *The Ed Sullivan Show* and *Bonanza* sparkled up Sunday nights considerably. There was only one Canadian channel for much of my early years. Far and away the most popular show was *Hockey Night in Canada*. The evenings it was on, streets would be all but deserted. In the winter, we played ice hockey, and in the spring and summer, we played ball hockey, with a tennis ball instead of a puck. What baseball cards were to American kids, hockey cards were to Canadians. Americans had heroes like Mickey Mantle, Roger Maris, and Whitey Ford. Canadian boys had Gump Worsley, Maurice "Rocket" Richard, and Terry Sawchuk. At our Pee Wee league annual dinner one year, the great Detroit Red Wings forward Gordie Howe showed up to sign our sticks. The film *Slap Shot*, with Paul Newman, came out in 1977 and ran in Ottawa for months—much like *The Rocky Horror Picture Show* did at the 8th Street Playhouse in New York's Greenwich Village.

The hockey rinks that most kids played on were outside and had sheds with potbellied stoves where players went to change or just warm their fingers and toes. Spending hours on the ice in the leather skates of the time could be a punishing ordeal. I still have a pair from those days and a young person who spotted them hanging on the wall of our garage not long ago referred to them as "vintage"!

Hockey was for weekdays. On weekends, we would go skiing at a club in Quebec about a half-hour's drive away called Camp Fortune. It had been established before the war and had seen few updates since. There was a rotary wooden wall phone in the warming shed, and the only way to get up the hill was on a rope line powered by an old truck engine. Our skis were all wood, with primitive leather and metal bindings. Ski boots were low-cut and made of floppy leather and had less support than an average pair of basketball shoes does now.

I played organized hockey until I was about thirteen. There were no helmets or mouthguards then—no protection at all above the collarbone. And there was a lot of checking and roughhousing on the ice. Everyone I knew who played in their later teens was missing at least a few teeth. And something in the back of my mind told me that, whatever I was going to be doing in life, a complete set of teeth would be part of what I needed to get ahead.

—

As I said, my father was a bit tight. For reasons that have always escaped me, we never had a pencil sharpener in the house. Pencils were sharpened with a penknife. At one point, my father decided that my brother, sister, and I were drinking too much milk.

We switched to powdered milk for a few months. It was foul and undrinkable. My mother put an end to it simply because she thought we'd get rickets. Through my entire childhood, my father refused to buy a base for the Christmas tree. So every December we'd go out and chip away at the snow to find rocks that we would put in a pail that my father would arrange to hold the tree in place.

One year the government department where my father later worked after his spell in the air force decided to upgrade its storage system. In the course of this, they threw out hundreds of plywood shelves. This was old-fashioned plywood—as dense and as heavy as marble. The boards were about three feet long, two feet wide, and an inch thick. Two-inch notches were cut out of each of the four corners. Every day after work my father would bring four or five of these shelves home in his car, and then he and I would carry them downstairs to the basement. In the end, we must have had a hundred of them stored away. He had no real plan for them. He just loved the idea of having all that wood at hand.

I was in my early teens by this time, that brittle period when anything your parents said, did, or wore brought on serial waves of mortification. My father was oblivious to the embarrassment he caused me. In the summer he wore his World War II–era wide-legged khaki shorts. But he was rake thin, and even in my youngest years I knew that he didn't have the legs for them. My mother and I would beg him to buy some newer Bermuda shorts, but he would have none of it. He was, it could only be said, also charmingly incompetent. In my father's eyes, he was a misunderstood creator who could whip up anything on short notice. One Saturday morning, my mother came to my room, her face flushed and her eyes welling with tears. "Gray, Gray, you've got to come quickly! It's your father!" I got out of bed and raced to the front door behind her. I don't know what

I expected. But what I saw was so unsettling that it caused me to hold my hand over my mouth.

It seemed that my father was feeling particularly expressive that morning and had decided to build a fence in our front yard. And for his fence he was using the shelves we had lugged down to the basement every day for the past few months. But he hadn't dug holes for the uprights, or used a level or a plumb bob, or laid out the fence with a string guide, or done anything that a professional fence builder would do. With absolutely no planning or expertise in carpentry, he just hammered upright posts into the ground using a brick, and then nailed the shelves between them together one after another, the way you'd connect playing cards at their ends with a spot of glue. It was crooked and wobbly and went up and down with the terrain and just looked horrible. My mother and I stood there speechless. Neighbors began to stop their cars. Then other kids on the street came by. But my father kept at it, nailing one piece of plywood to another. Sometime before noon, he decided to take a break and went inside to get himself a beer. He brought a garden chair around to the front and sat there admiring his work. My mother and I hid inside and watched the scene through a break in the curtains.

A wind started to pick up and it got stronger. The first board broke away from the one it was attached to and fell to the ground. And then, without that as support, the second board broke and fell. And then the third and the fourth. And on it went, like dominoes. In a matter of minutes, the whole contraption had collapsed. One neighbor honked his horn as if in victory. Kids my age who were watching the scene simply lost control. I just closed my eyes at the shame of it all. My father was silent at the loss of his beloved fence. He sat there for a while and then went inside and up to bed. An hour later he emerged and called me and my brother to the front of the house. For the next two hours, before an audience of cheering neighbors and schoolmates, we lugged those heavy shelves back to their old resting spot in the basement, our legs ragged with scrapes from the open nails.

My father was good-looking in the way of David Niven. He was slim and had a wartime mustache that he kept his entire life. He was born in Moose Jaw, Saskatchewan. His father had been an engineer in London who'd read Jack London's *The Call of the Wild* and upped and moved his family to western Canada in order to go into business trapping beavers and selling their pelts. In time he had built up a decent-sized trading post. And that is where my father grew up, the brother of three older sisters. He was seventeen when he enlisted in the Royal Canadian Air Force at the outbreak of the Second World War and became a pilot, first flying Spitfires and then Lancasters, the British version of the American Flying Fortress. His mastery of these great warplanes at such an age gives credence to the adage that wars are fought by teenagers. Like a lot of his friends who signed up, he grew a mustache to look older. The rookies had another trick. They would sand down the collars of their light blue shirts to make it look as if they had been flying longer than they had. He loved to tell the story of a night of homemade entertainment during the war. A singing group that billed itself as the Four Redskins was to come out carrying signs with the words THE, FOUR, RED, and SKINS. But they got a bit discombobulated, and the signs came out reading THE RED FOUR SKINS. Not surprisingly, it brought the house down.

My mother, Margaret, had grown up in a leafy area of Toronto called Forest Hill Village. Her father owned a midsize industrial-soap company, and the family lived reasonably well. By reasonably well, I mean they had two Packards, a maid, and a summer lodge in the Muskokas, the lake district north of Toronto. My mother went to Havergal College, the private school for girls. And her brother went to Upper Canada College, the private school for boys. My mother was attractive and was going out with the captain of the University of Toronto football team when she met my father. Something clicked, and they began to see each other. One time, during the war, when he was home on leave, they went to the local movie house. As the theater began filling with young women and their dates—most of them in uniform—my parents found seats in the middle. They spotted friends here and there and waved. All of a sudden, my father broke wind. He did it so loudly that people in front of them turned around. He stood up immediately, turned to my mother, and said, "Oh, Margaret!" and proceeded to make his way across the other people to the aisle and left the theater.

My mother, bless her heart, found this incredibly funny and joined him outside. They got married soon after. My father was a great whistler and a great farter, and he could carry a tune from either end. He swore to friends that he could fart the "Colonel Bogey March"—the theme song from *The Bridge on the River Kwai*. He never performed that feat in my presence, but he did have a way of letting off air in the most unfortunate of public circumstances. My mother would just shrug, with an exasperated "Your father!" The one time she put her foot down was when he wanted to name our thirty-six-foot sloop *Passing Wind*.

When the war ended, my father opened a shop selling Parker pens. He shared the space with a man who made hand-rolled balls of rat poison. My father was a man of endless unambition and was simply not cut out for the world of high commerce, and the shop lasted a year. My father's only real professional skill was as a pilot. And he loved flying. So he eventually reenlisted in the air force and stayed there for a good part of his career.

After returning from Europe, we had settled in Ottawa, Canada's capital. Our neighborhood was called Manor Park, not far from the center of town. Only later did I realize how pretentious Manor Park sounded. And the roads there all had names redolent of English aristocracy: Arundel, Blenheim, Lonsdale, and the like. Canadian names were ripe for ridicule from non-Canadians. The name Avenue Road in Toronto even then seemed slightly ridiculous. (Years later, when I was working at *Time*, John Leo, one of the magazine's columnists, loved to rib me over the fact that there were nine professional football teams in Canada, and that two of them were called Rough Riders—something he attributed to a national lack of imagination.) But we were happy in Manor Park. Kids left the house after breakfast and just monkeyed around until dinnertime. My parents weren't alone in essentially letting their kids loose on the world with little in the way of supervision. After the war, many of them just did what they were supposed to do: come back, get married, get educated, and drop a few kids to replace them when and if. Childhood was not the spectator sport that it is today. If today's parents can be labeled helicopter parents, '50s-era parents were largely submarine parents: there, but not really in evidence. I played all manner of sports when I was in school—football, basketball, track, hockey—and not once do I ever remember my mother or my father showing up for a game or a meet. I didn't hold it against them. Nobody's parents came to watch their kids.

Ottawa itself was a quiet, post-Edwardian capital of moody stone-and-brick government buildings. The main department store, Ogilvy's, sold thick clothing, and almost all of it was in tartan. There were few restaurants, and when a pizza parlor opened, the news of its arrival made the local paper. Kids rode their bicycles everywhere. Weather aside, it was a comfortable place for servicemen to settle after the war and raise their families. There were really only two major movie theaters, the Elgin and the Capitol, and these were where my friends and I would flock to on Saturdays for matinee showings of the latest David Lean epic, one of the *Carry On* or Ealing Studios comedies, or the first Bond films.

My parents' life revolved largely around skiing, playing golf, sailing, and weekly bridge games with their best friends, Ian and Nina Maclennan, who lived not far from us. Ian and Nina were a big part of our family life. Ian had been a decorated flying ace during the war and then had become a leading architect in Canada. Nina was an eccentric English beauty. Their son Bruce was and still is one of my closest friends. The Maclennans were more sophisticated than us, more glamorous than us, more worldly than us. Our house was filled with modern Swedish furniture. Theirs was cooler and more bohemian. They had something on their walls that nobody I knew had—modern art. On bridge nights, my dad and Ian wore jackets and ties and my mom and Nina wore cocktail dresses and pearls. They would have highballs, then dinner, and then the card table would come out. Mantovani might be on the hi-fi. When Chubby Checker came out with "The Twist," I remember looking over the banister and seeing my parents and the Maclennans dancing this new dance. I thought it all was the most glamorous existence in the world.

On evenings when others would come over for dinner, my father, who had limited interest in late nights, would make his way over to my mother at about 10:00 p.m. and whisper just loud enough for others to hear, "Marg, we really can't keep these good people any longer." He had a way of shaking hands at the door that gently steered guests toward their cars. Because he was charming and funny, other men adored him and women were tickled by his attention. When he was at the Maclennans and needed to refill his drink, he'd ask Ian where he should put his empty glass. If he harbored any professional dreams, he never displayed them, and he seemed content and relatively happy for most of his life. He was devoted to my mother, and never, to be honest, showed any particular interest in his kids. Like many parents of their generation, mine were benign and largely absentee.

And also like many of his friends, my father enjoyed a glass of rye whiskey at the end of the day. He mixed his rye with ginger ale. When I reached drinking age—actually, before I reached drinking age—I began to siphon off his rye into a hip flask. My father liked to mark his bottles with chalk, and when the surface of the whiskey dropped below the chalk line, I simply filled it up to the level with ginger ale. My thinking, such as it was, was that since he mixed it with ginger ale anyway, he wouldn't notice the dilution. The result was that my father was drinking seriously watered-down cocktails at home. One night my parents went out to a dinner party and the next morning my mother said that my father had gotten so woozy that he almost drove into a tree on the way home. She said that she couldn't understand it, because he didn't have any more to drink than usual. I realized that he had become so accustomed to drinking my concoction that he could no longer handle the real thing. I put my own alcohol consumption on hold until I could buy the stuff myself.

In high school, I was a dreadful student. Constantly distracted, constantly daydreaming, and always just following my own interests. If *Beowulf* was being taught in class, I was reading Hemingway. Or *Mad*. If science homework was assigned, I spent the evening reading comics or building small models of Buckminster Fuller's geodesic dome out of balsa-wood sticks, rubber tubing, and tiny nuts and bolts. I read a lot—just not what I was supposed to. In those days, kids watched TV lying on the floor on their stomachs. I always had a book on the floor with me—a rare case of being able to multitask.

On the learning front, I had a problem then that I still have now: spoken instructions for just about anything come at me like random words. I can only describe it as a form of oral dyslexia. In order to absorb anything, I have to read it. I am also unable to follow a map or follow any sort of simple directions. I simply panic. I re-member getting lost up near Lenox Hill Hospital, in Manhattan, one day. Even though the streets and avenues run in a grid pattern and are numbered, I simply couldn't find my way to Lexington Ave-nue and the subway.

I listened to rock 'n' roll like any kid my age, but my true pas-sions were jazz and folk music. There was a coffeehouse in Ottawa called Le Hibou, and my great friend Dave Caldbick and I would sneak out of our homes with jackets and ties under our arms. We'd put them on outside and would then talk our way into Le Hibou to listen to musicians like Ian & Sylvia and Buffy Sainte-Marie—always in a haze of cigarette smoke. Dave was a friend I carried through into adulthood. His father was the Queen's doctor when she visited Canada. And Dave and I would spend hours poring over his medical books, terrified always by pictures of men who had con-tracted elephantiasis that caused their scrotums to swell up to the size of duffel bags. Bedtime until I was into my mid-teens was 9:00 p.m. I would regularly stretch it an hour, reading under the covers with a flashlight.

My family loved watching football on the weekends in the fall, although our local team, the Ottawa Rough Riders—not to be con-fused with the Saskatchewan Roughriders—specialized in dashing the hopes of its fans. Hockey was, as I have mentioned, a serious passion. As was boxing. On weeknights when there was a major prizefight, I'd listen to the bouts on the radio. Westerns were domi-nant in the '50s and '60s, and I watched them all. But my true love was *The Phil Silvers Show*, which was centered around a motor pool run by Ernie Bilko at an out-of-the-way U.S. Army base called Fort Baxter. I tell my kids that everything I learned about parenting or running an office, I learned from Bilko.

Decades later, when Tom Freston was the head of MTV, a network called TV Land that ran old programs from the '50s and '60s fell under his direction. The Bilko show was on the network until research showed that it was largely being watched by retired servicemen—not the ideal demographic for advertisers. Tom sent over a gift that became a part of the Carter lifestyle—a complete set of Bilko videocassettes. We had a stone fishing camp on Lake Waramaug, up in Connecticut, by that time. There was no cable, so I set up an old twelve-inch television in the living room by the huge fireplace and connected it to our videocassette player. For the next two decades, anytime one of the kids or I wanted to watch television at the camp, the only thing to watch was Bilko.

Bruce Maclennan and I and all the other boys we knew looked much the same—especially in the summer: checked short-sleeved shirts, blue jeans, and brush cuts with butch wax to make the fringe at the front stand on end. Bruce accessorized this look with a face full of freckles. When we were eight or nine, he and I would take the bus downtown to the YMCA to go swimming. Bus tickets were made of thin, red cardboard and were the size of postage stamps. They cost a quarter for a sheet of four. We'd gingerly split the tickets in two and with a black pen mimic the design on the other side. This way we got eight rides for the price of four. Swimming at the Y was not for the faint of heart. This was largely because we had to swim naked—along with all the other men, who ranged in age from teens to ancient. We saw hair in places we'd never seen hair before. Afterward we'd go to the Y cafeteria and, with the money saved from the bus tickets, get large bowls of french fries that we would drown in salt and vinegar. By the time we left, our lips were swollen and blue.

If we could scrape together fifty cents, we would go swimming at the Château Laurier, the big railroad hotel in the center of town. At the Château's pool, we were allowed to wear bathing suits—which was a major part of its appeal. The Château Laurier was home to the studio of Yousuf Karsh, an Armenian photographer who had settled in Ottawa before the war. He shot mostly in black-and-white and took a number of iconic portraits of the celebrated figures of the day, including Winston Churchill, Mother Teresa, George Bernard Shaw, and Ernest Hemingway. Karsh was not just Ottawa famous to us. He was world famous.

My mother was a gifted Sunday painter and she urged me to paint and draw, which I did and continue to do to this day. As it happens, my ability to draw people would lead by chance to the beginning of something that became my professional life. I was eager without being particularly ambitious, if that makes any sense, about not only art but about what I wanted to do in life. I wanted to become something, but I had no idea what to become or how to become it. When I was about fourteen, my mother gave me two books she thought I'd like. The first was Moss Hart's theater memoir, *Act One*. No book has ever touched me quite the same way. It showed me that you could achieve your dream if you found out what your dream was— and were blessed with a bit of talent and good fortune. The other book was *Youngblood Hawke*, Herman Wouk's massive novel about a young writer trying to make it in New York after the war. Both had familiar themes of yearning. And yearning along with daydreaming were two things I excelled in. They were pretty much all I did.

After reading *Act One* and *Youngblood Hawke*, I knew that I wanted my adult life to be in New York, in the world of magazines or the theater. The city, that shimmering vessel of opportunity and reward, was where I wanted to be. It figured large in the movies I loved, like *Sweet Smell of Success, The Naked City,* and God knows how many screwball comedies. In those days before videocassettes and streaming, movies would be shown during the day a few times a week on television.

I would scan the newspaper to see what was playing. When

something caught my eye—*His Girl Friday*, say, or *Double Indemnity*—I'd plot out my operation to stay at home. A gentle "cough" would arrive the night before. In the morning, I would be listless. My mother would jam a thermometer in my mouth at the slightest indication of sickness. On those mornings, when she left the room, I'd put the thermometer against a light bulb, checking it regularly until the temperature read just above 100 degrees. She'd come back in, check it, and suggest I spend the day in bed. Movies and the magazines I read were my guideposts to the more glamorous world outside our frosted, snowy windows. I wanted an adult life of cocktails, cigarettes, bridge games, witty banter, and clothes that weren't tartan.

My one taste of being in charge of anything ended up in flames. And I don't mean that in a figurative way. Pretty much every year, from the age of ten onward, I was shipped off to Camp Pontiac, a Canadian summer camp run by the Anglican Church. This camp, like so many others in those days, was intentionally austere—a mess hall with bad food; a tuck shop that sold thin, colored plastic cord that could be woven together to make key fobs and bracelets for parents; and bunks with scratchy bedding. When I turned sixteen, I was made a counselor, in charge of a bunkhouse with a dozen or so twelve-year-old boys. I was settling in on the first day of my first job and found a copy of *Mayfair* magazine from the summer before tucked under my mattress. *Mayfair* was a distant English sibling to *Playboy*. The women were a bit pastier and more fully dressed than the wholesome, otherworldly naked creatures in *Playboy*, but because there were almost no articles, there were more pictures. One of the kids spotted the magazine and asked if I could tear out a page for him. Which I did. Word spread, and by the end of the first day, the magazine was down to a few ads and photos of women in actual clothing. I used these semipornographic pages to keep control. Anyone stepping out of line got theirs confiscated for a day.

As I have said, I had modeled my management skills on those of Ernie Bilko. Strict, fair, but conspiratorial—that was the Tao of Bilko. I was a model of leadership command through the first few weeks. But a surprise announcement of a thorough bunk inspection on the penultimate day of camp threw me off my mark and into a panic. This was a Christian summer camp, after all, and I thought the fathers would be horrified by my housewarming gifts for the boys. I worried that I'd be thrown out of camp, my parents would be livid, and it would be a black mark on my record into adulthood. I gathered my charges and told them that they'd have to return the pages. The first kid I had given one to—who fancied himself a card and had clearly become the leader—said he'd give it back, but that it would cost me a dollar. I huffed a bit but paid him, and then one after another, the others came to me with their tattered pages in return for a dollar. By the end, I was down $12 and had a pile of photos and nowhere to hide them. I couldn't put them in the trash—someone would find them and turn me in. Even if I tore them up and threw them away, anyone, even an Anglican priest, would know in a second what they were.

I crumpled them up, put them in a pile, and with a match set them on fire. God knows what I was thinking. Within seconds, the flames were half a foot high and I could see that the fire was beginning to char the bunkhouse floor. I stamped it out. A few of the boys looked on in horror. The rest, led by camper number one, were enjoying the whole performance. I managed to sweep the ashes out of the bunkhouse. I found some sandpaper and got rid of the singed area. The next morning, there was some sort of drama in another part of the camp and the inspection was called off.

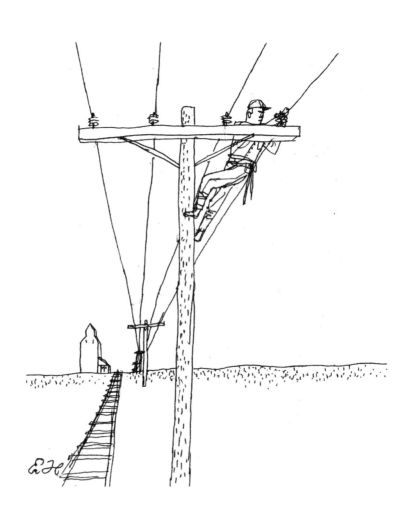

Chapter 3.

A Lineman for
the Railroad

Decades ago, and probably extending well before that, there was a custom among middle-class Canadian families in the East to send their sons out West to work on the railroad for a spell. The parents' intention was not only to get the boys out of their hair for a while but also to toughen them up and introduce them to the ways of the world outside their comfort zones. As it happened, one of my father's sisters, Aunt Irene, was a vice president of the Canadian National Railway, a sprawling transportation network of trains, steamships, and grand hotels. It was as much a part of the national identity as the actor Lorne Greene, the star of *Bonanza,* and *Hockey Night in Canada.* Aunt Irene was a tall, thin, dignified woman. I don't think I ever saw her when she wasn't wearing a twinset and pearls. Family lore had it that during the final chapter of World War II, she had been the wire operator who sent word of Hitler's death to news organizations across Canada.

Afterward, she went to work for the Canadian National Railway, also as a wire operator, and rose through the ranks. I was just out of high school. Egged on by my parents, I wrote to her, asking for a job. As she described it in her letter back to me, there were two types of positions available. I could be a groundman at $2.20 an hour. Or I could be a lineman at $2.80 an hour. Like any sane person, I had a fear of heights and said that I'd like to get a groundman's job, which I was told entailed lugging equipment to the linemen, who would be climbing telegraph poles all day. She told me to report to the Symington Yard in Winnipeg. And with few prospects for the future, little in the way of resources, and only a dim idea of what I was about to get into, I found myself on a train heading thirteen hundred miles west to the capital of Manitoba.

I stayed with my aunt the first night and reported to the railroad's headquarters at 7:00 the next morning with a duffel bag of my belongings: a few pairs of shorts, jeans, a jacket, a couple of shirts, a pair of Kodiak work boots, and some Richard Brautigan and Jack Kerouac books, acceptable reading matter for a pseudo-sophisticate of the time. The Symington Yard was a vast complex, one of the largest rail yards in the world. On some days it held more than seven thousand boxcars. Half that many moved in and out on a single day. Like other young men my age, I was slim, unmuscled, and soft. In the hall where they interviewed and inspected the candidates for line work, I blanched as I looked over a large poster that showed the outline of a male body and the prices the railroad paid if you lost a part of it. As I recall, legs brought you $750 each. Arms were $500. A foot brought a mere $250. In Canadian dollars.

There were about ten of us, and we were led to a room where a severe-looking nurse peered down our throats, checked our hearts, and then asked for urine samples. I filled the beaker to the very top by accident and when the nurse attempted to pick it up off the table, she couldn't help but spill a bit down her hand. Two of the tougher-looking recruits behind me thought this was funny and one patted me on the back.

By the afternoon, I was on a train to a small town out on the endless Saskatchewan prairie—my head leaning against the window, my stomach aching from hunger—trying to figure out a way that I could get out of this in a few weeks and get home. This was my parents' idea of what I should be doing. Certainly not mine. A man with the big, meaty hands of someone who used them in taxing labor was sitting beside me. He had brought his own food, and out of a small pouch he pulled a roll that had been wrapped in waxed paper. His sandwich was like nothing I had ever seen before.

To me, a sandwich was something made of white Wonder bread, with baloney or peanut butter and jam inside. But this was a round, soft roll and the meat was thick and breaded. The man noticed me looking at the sandwich and quietly brought another one out of his pouch. He indicated that I should take it. I made a gesture to say, *No, no, I couldn't*. But he just smiled and put it into my hand. I wasn't sure if he spoke English. I unwrapped the waxed paper and bit in. To this day, I don't think anything I have ever eaten was as welcome or delicious. It was breaded chicken on a roll with a glorious sauce. I thanked him profusely over and over and he just kept nodding and smiling.

We pulled up to a siding where the conductor said I had to get off. I did as I was told and stood by the tracks as the train pulled away. When it was gone, I looked around. The land was as flat as a billiard table and stretched for miles in every direction. On the siding was a collection of boxcars. A man waved to me in a menacing manner, indicating that I should get over to him chop-chop-ish. I looked behind me and then turned back to him and gave a *Who me?* gesture. He nodded and I hurried over and introduced myself. He said nothing. He was in his midforties and built like a refrigerator.

His blond hair was short on the scalp. Enormous veins ran down his forehead and around his nose. He had terrifying bright blue eyes and hands the size of catchers' mitts. His incisors were pointed, and one of his uppers was enameled in gold. He looked through me, pointed to one of the boxcars with windows on the side, and left. I walked over to the boxcar, climbed the steps, and opened the door.

It was a Saturday, not only the day off but also the day of new arrivals. Men of various ages and sizes were stretched out on the wooden bunks or settling in. There were eight beds on one side of the door and eight on the other. Nobody said a word, but a fellow who was lying down pointed a nicotine-stained finger in the direction of a bottom bunk at the back of the car. I thanked him and sat on the bed and looked around. I was the youngest in the group. Everybody was smoking. Everyone had a mustache. And everyone looked a lot tougher than people I was used to. The bed was as hard as the floor. There was a single pillow and a gray, worn blanket that lay folded at the foot of the bed. As I was to learn in the coming days, all but one of the men had some sort of record—breaking and entering being on the bottom rung of achievement and grand theft auto at the top. Petty thievery and criminal mischief were almost entry-level accolades. Working on the railroad may have been a way to toughen up doughy middle-class boys; for others it was a sort of French Foreign Legion waystation between prison gates and semi-civilized society.

We ate in the reefer car, which was broken up into three parts. One part was the cold box, where ice and frozen meat and other provisions were stored; one part housed the kitchen; and the last part held a long communal dining table. I sat down at the end of the table and was joined by a tall, fair-skinned fellow with curly red hair and a decent mustache. His name was Craig Walls. He wanted to be a writer and was taking a year off to pay for his tuition at the University of Winnipeg. Canadian kids in those days tended to pay their own way through school. Annual college tuition was in the $1,200 range, and therefore within striking distance if you worked in construction or the railroad during the summer. There was a certain pride in the deepness of the blue in the blue-collar job you took to pay for school. Construction was good. The railroad was better. Working in the oil fields of northern Alberta was the deepest blue of all.

Two others at our end of the bunk car became part of our circle, if you could call it that. One was a short, funny, wiry kid named Ernie, who had grand theft auto on his résumé. And the other was Errol, a darkly handsome lady-killer. He had syphilis and said that it required him to have a small whisk device inserted into his penis at regular intervals to remove the thin scabs that formed there. I don't know if he was kidding or not, but when he told us this, Walls and Ernie and I could barely speak. But it did make Errol seem awfully cosmopolitan to us.

The next morning, the new arrivals were called out by the fellow who had waved to me from the siding. He never announced the fact, but he was the foreman, and his name was Herb Harzbeck. He was German and there was some talk among the vets on the crew that he had been in the war—on which side was up for debate. The vets called him "squarehead" behind his back.

On the ground were piles of equipment for the newcomers. We were told to grab a set each. There wasn't much to the gear. There was a big leather belt about four inches wide with slots for tools. There were also spikes attached to braces with leather straps to hold them to your legs. These were called pole gaffs. The braces went from the instep to just below the knee. They strapped around the top of the calf and at the ankle, and there was a leather strap that went under the boot. After a few false starts, we managed to get the pole gaffs on and hobbled around a bit, the way skiers do with a new pair of boots. There was a pile of leather gloves with long gauntlets that came up almost to the elbow. We sifted through the lot trying to find a pair that matched and fit. When we were suited up, Herb brought us over to one of the telegraph poles to show us how to climb. Hands on either side of the pole, lean back, but not too far. And then drive the first spike into the wood. When that was set, drive the next spike in a little higher. Then the next one, and so forth. He was essentially walking up the pole, but vertically. He made it look easy.

It was anything but. I'd seen telephone repairmen back home climbing poles that had metal footholds all the way up, almost like ladders. But they wore safety belts that allowed them to lean back and fix whatever needed fixing. Here there were no foot grips. I asked Herb where the safety belts were, and he gave me a dismissive look. There were no safety belts. We took turns trying to climb the pole. There were a number of false starts and tumbles. I could get up maybe three steps before my arms gave out or one of my spikes didn't dig in deep enough and I fell to the ground. This was all a terrible mistake, I kept thinking to myself. At the end of the demonstration and my own feeble attempts, I worked my way over to Herb and said that there had been some sort of error—that I had signed on to be a groundman. "No groundmen," he barked. "Just linemen."

Over the next couple of days, my general fear of heights and my more specific fear of falling off a telegraph pole began to subside. I managed to climb a twenty-foot pole. And then a thirty-foot pole. I began to get cocky, and in an attempt to scramble up one of the higher poles, I slipped near the top and shot straight down. In my shock and embarrassment, I hadn't noticed it at first, but I had torn the front of my shirt and ripped big patches of skin off my chest. One of the patches held the few chest hairs I had grown by this point in my life. Herb took me to the reefer car. He cleaned off the blood and put a block of ice on my chest, which eased the pain. Then he wrapped my chest in a bandage. The skin began to heal in a couple of weeks, and within months was back to normal. And, lo, where there had been a few sprigs, something approaching actual chest hair began to appear.

That summer, I had been trying to grow my hair long. I wanted to be a hippie—or at least look like one. But one day, Herb motioned to me and Walls and made us sit down in front of him. He pulled an electric shaver out of his vest and shaved us to the scalp. So much for my dream of being a Canadian Abbie Hoffman. Aside from the lack of a criminal record, which in this group was like working in a hospital without a medical degree, I wanted to stand out. There is nothing more parochial or bland than being a soft, white Anglican kid from Ottawa. I feigned being something of a Jewish intellectual. In this crowd, the mere fact that I had brought books singled me out as a great thinker. A few of the tougher hands took to calling me "professor."

~

Those telegraph poles you see alongside train tracks served two purposes back then. One was for actually sending telegrams. The other was to enable dispatchers to know where the trains were at any given moment. The telegraph wires would eventually wear out, and our job as linemen was to haul fresh wire up the pole on our shoulders, remove the old wire, let it drop to the ground, and then connect the new wire to the glass insulators on the horizontal wooden arms or spars. Once we had mastered the fine art of climbing, we were ready to be put to use. We were awake at 5:00 a.m., and after breakfast we suited up and stood around anxiously. Even in late spring, it was cold on a Canadian prairie morning, a few degrees above freezing. We would wear two or three layers on top to stay warm. A group of us would climb onto a motorcar—not one of those contraptions from silent movies, with hand-operated seesaw locomotion, but a motorized cart with benches big enough for five or six men on either side. We would be dropped off a half mile apart, on the assumption that we could each cover a half mile of track before lunch.

On that first morning, I jumped off the motorcar. There was already a climber a half mile behind me. And in minutes, one would be deposited a half mile in front of me. Other than that, where I was, it was just me and an endless ocean of prairie. The new telegraph line had been laid out alongside the track. The poles up ahead looked to be no taller than twenty feet. It took me two or three attempts to make it to the top of the first pole. Like all the others, it was covered in creosote, a black, sticky, coal-tar coating that preserved the wood but stuck to gloves, jeans, and skin. I survived the first pole. I survived the second pole. In four hours, I made it to the spot about a half mile up where the next climber had been dropped off earlier in the day. The temperature had climbed thirty degrees between sunrise and noon, and I had started gradually to remove layers of clothing.

The motorcar appeared in the distance and came my way. It stopped to pick up other climbers, and then every few hundred yards or so, we'd stop and grab the clothes we had all discarded as the temperature rose. This was in the days before bottled water, and by the time we were picked up, we were parched. There was a big cooler on the motorcar and a ladle. I opened the top and saw that it indeed contained water, but not just water. The surface was awash with dead flies and bits of grass. I dipped the ladle into the cooler and gingerly managed to get it out without picking up any extras. The water was warm and fetid. But it was wet, and I learned to appreciate it. We returned to the railcars for lunch, then went back out for another four hours.

One morning Herb threw a bunch of canvas hats on the ground. "Take them," he said. We each grabbed one. The hats came with a fine mesh that fell from the brim onto our shoulders. They were mosquito hats. We were heading into a patch where the black flies were horrendous. Black flies are not like house flies. Canadian black flies are the size of a thumb tip and they bite. For three days we lived in those hats. We never took them off. We lifted the netting when we were eating to make way for food. We slept with them on too. At night, the sound of black flies smacking against the mesh screens was unnerving.

Evenings were spent smoking, drinking, playing cards, and reading. Then the whole ordeal started again the next morning. Weekends were different. At sundown on Friday, we were given passes on the Canadian National trains and could travel as far as we wanted, as long as we were back at work and ready to climb at 5:00 a.m. sharp Monday. On one of the first weekends off, Walls and I decided we'd try to make it to Winnipeg, about six hundred miles to the east. I decided to clean up, and resolved to take a shower before leaving. The routine for this was highly labor-intensive. It involved chipping off a chunk of ice about half the size of a cinder block from the reefer car and carrying it to the bath car. You put the block of ice in a pail and then onto a stove to melt it. Then you took the pail and poured the water into a contraption that looked like a watering can and hooked it on the ceiling over the shower area. You pulled the nozzle down a bit, wetted yourself, soaped, and prayed there'd be enough water left to rinse off.

There were no sleepers available on that trip to Winnipeg, so they put us in the mail car near the end of the train. We slept on sacks with the Royal Mail Canada logo on them. Old locomotives in those days had bunks right in the engine, and on a subsequent trip, Walls and I were allowed to sleep there. Meals were taken in the dining car. We were a pretty scruffy lot, so they usually sat us in the back, near the kitchen, where big muscular men cooked up meals on long grills heated by gas jets.

By most Fridays, though, we were too worn out to travel on the weekend. Saturdays were for writing home, reading, and the occasional water fight. The siding was equipped with dozens of fire extinguishers. They were big red canisters that you filled with water and then strapped to your back. There was a pump that you compressed with one hand, and a hose for the other hand. We'd load them up with water and divide into teams. Often it would escalate. During one fight, we climbed to the roof of the boxcars and scampered across the tops the way gunfighters did in old Westerns.

During one such water battle, we noticed an enormous machine off in the distance. As it approached along the track, we realized that it was a vehicle maybe two stories high and two or three times as long as a boxcar. It crept ahead slowly, deliberately, replacing old track with new track. Half of its very large crew loosened the rails in front of the machine. And the other half tightened the new rails down in its wake. As the machine got closer, it became apparent that this was a much rougher-looking crew than ours. We put away our water cannons and just watched as this army made its way slowly by us. In the distance, I thought I saw someone I knew, and as he got closer, I shouted out, "Bruce! Bruce!" He looked my way and ran over. It was Bruce Maclennan. We had only a few minutes to chat before he was called back to his crew. I was lonely for home by this time. Seeing Bruce and then watching as he headed back off gave me a lump in my throat—although knowing someone on this much-tougher line gang gave me a certain amount of cred among my own bunkmates.

The water cannons were always filled for emergency use. Often this involved putting out brush fires that started in the midday sun when what were called "hot boxes" went by. These were engines that spewed burning oil and accidentally set the brush on fire. We'd be sent out on motorcars to extinguish the flames. On my first fire call, a wind picked up and the flames licked skyward and singed my eyebrows down to almost nothing. They grew back, but never as thickly as they had been before the fire.

We were advised to stand well clear of the ditches that border the rails when the Super Continental, the railroad's gleaming passenger train, whisked by every day. One rookie hadn't heard this bit of useful information, and on his first day, as the train sped through, he got too close. He was soaked and a bit more: someone had flushed a toilet. Back then, there were no holding tanks on trains; when you flushed, the waste just emptied onto the tracks. The Super Continental came by at the same time every day. Often we'd make a pact to have our pants pulled down and moon the passengers.

Our cook got sick at one point and was sent home to Saskatoon. Herb announced that we'd each take turns cooking a meal. We had complained about the food when the cook was there. But with him gone, it deteriorated rapidly. I had never cooked a thing in my life. When my time came, I went to the reefer car to scout the provisions. There was a large leg of something, so I brought it to the kitchen. A coating of green covered parts of it, and I cut those sections off with a knife. And then I put the meat in the oven. I had no idea what temperature to set the oven at or how long to leave it in there. I didn't want to burn it, so I set the oven at medium heat and left it for three hours. I told Walls about this, and he told me I was out of my mind. We raced to the kitchen and opened the oven door. The meat had barely cooked at all. And given that it was about a foot thick, he told me that we would need another four or five hours at high heat. Dinner was late that night, and as we picked through the stringy, under-cooked meat, I kept my head low to avoid the looks coming my way from my fellow diners.

Our pal Errol had a habit of heading into town to pick up local girls. One night he returned a bit drunk and fell into his bunk. The lights were out and he drifted off to sleep. Sometime in the middle of the night, the door to the bunk car was kicked open and all of us inside were jolted awake. Three men stormed in with flashlights, going from bunk to bunk. When the light shone into my eyes, I covered them with my hand. The men continued to move down the car until they got to Errol's bunk. Two of them grabbed him and hauled him outside. We couldn't see much in the dark, but clearly they were working Errol over pretty badly. Then they left, screaming obscenities, and made their way, flashlights in hand, across the open field. Walls and I ran outside to see if Errol was okay. He was. But just. He had a broken rib and a black eye and was bleeding from the head. We woke Herb and he came and bandaged him up. In the morning, we heard the backstory. It seems that Errol had tried to pick up one of the men's girlfriends and she was up for his affections. He left the crew a few days later and we never heard from him again.

I had signed on for six months, and as my tour of duty was coming to an end, I was still unsure about what I was going to do with my life. I'd had other minor jobs before, but none like this. My parents weren't alone in making sure their kids got busy during the summer, working at something, anything. "Allowances" were a thing we read about in American books and magazines. As a result, I was always digging around for pocket money. During winters, I had worked as a ski instructor at a local club and sorted mail at the Central Post Office over the Christmas break. In the summers I worked as a camp counselor and canoe instructor. I worked as an unarmed bank guard one hot summer, and I pumped gas. I gave guitar lessons for a number of years. This occupation was cut short when a kid a good ten years younger than me said he could use some tips. I asked him to show me what he could do, and he proceeded to play "Classical Gas," a legendary guitar masterpiece, almost as well as the man who composed it, Mason Williams. I gave the kid his money back and gave up the guitar-lesson game.

Nothing I had done before, or pretty much after, could match the sense of accomplishment and sheer exhilaration of that half year on the railroad. I liked being around the crew, most of whom had endured hardscrabble childhoods and had just naturally got into a bit of trouble in their teens and twenties. When my stint was done, I packed my gear into my duffel bag and said my goodbyes to the other fellows. Walls and I kept in touch for a while, but in the days before the internet, this was never an easy option. One day a letter I had sent him came back with a stamp saying he had moved. A decade or so ago, I heard from a friend of his that Walls had died, which saddened me terribly.

Out on the line on one of my last days, just before dusk, I was preparing to get picked up by the motorcar for the trip back to the bunkhouse when I saw the Super Continental in the distance. I clambered up to a field beside the tracks to watch it go by. It was traveling slowly, and in the pink late-afternoon light I could see into the dining car. There was a young couple seated inside. They were nicely dressed and looked to be having a good time in the amber glow of the table lamp by the window. Lonely, tired, and dirty, I felt a million miles away from the attractive couple. It was then that I resolved, whatever I did, I was done with showering at the end of the week rather than the beginning of the day. It was time to get on with the life I envisioned for myself. I wasn't completely sure what that was going to be. But I knew one thing: I wanted to be on the other side of that window.

Chapter 4.

A College Magazine
to the Rescue

I returned too late from my job on the railroad to begin college in the fall. I went looking for work. I had no marketable skills and so was quickly scooped up by the Canadian government. The people in charge thought I was a promising leadership candidate, and I was assigned to a consultant's position in the department that looked after paying all the other federal government employees. Bob Hixt, a fellow consultant a few years older than me who had actually gone to business school, took me under his wing and we became inseparable.

As it happened, there were real consultants roaming around the offices, important-looking people from the New York firm Peat Marwick Mitchell. Everyone in the office was expected to meet with them and tell them what they did during the day and why they did it. Bob and I were in a twist, because we had absolutely nothing to do. We wore jackets and ties to the office in order to look professional, but once we got there, we read newspapers and books, talked to friends on the phone, goofed off, and attempted to look like men on the go. One day, out of sheer boredom, we decided to invent our own Peat Marwick efficiency expert. We called him Winston Purdy and we'd drop his name constantly. We gave our fellow wage apes the impression that Purdy had entrusted us with all the information he had been gathering on everyone else. It got to a point where others in the office were referring to something Purdy had said in a meeting or repeating ribald stories that he had told over lunch.

Near the end of my blighted tenure in service to the good people of Canada, I was asked to research and write a report on the computer system that handled payments for employees, pensioners, and others reliant on the government's dime. I had not only never worked on a computer, I'd never seen one before. The one I was supposed to assess was a room-sized IBM into which information was fed with punch cards. For four months, I researched and pulled together a detailed description of the system's payment method along with an explanation of how it could be streamlined. Bob coached me in the finer points of PERT charts, something I had never heard of, but which he told me stood for Program Evaluation and Review Technique. Once I heard the expression, I used it a lot in conversation with superiors. The finished opus ran to a couple of hundred pages. Bob referred to it around the office as "the Carter Report." Soon others did as well. I left shortly after the assignment was completed, and sometimes I lay awake at night wondering if I had made a mistake that would mean government employees or aging veterans wouldn't get their checks at all.

———

B ruce Maclennan's father, Ian, the architect, was one of those electrifying, driving forces who tend to ignite sparks in a young man. I wanted to be like him, and because he was a celebrated architect I got it into my teenage head that I, too, should be an architect. I could draw fairly well, and I had a reasonable sense of design, but I was hopeless at math and engineering. I lasted a single year studying the subject. Not knowing what else to do, I drifted over to the political science department at the University of Ottawa, a Jesuit school downtown. I had an interest in political science but no particular passion for making it a career.

About a month or two in, I passed an open-plan office in the liberal arts building that was filled with young people, desks, and typewriters. I poked my head in and introduced myself to the two people who appeared to be the ringleaders of this small pack, Graham Pomeroy and Mike Segal. Graham was an expansive chatterbox and appeared to be mature beyond his years. He was clearly the head man. He told me they were starting a literary and poetry publication called *The Canadian Review*. They'd received a grant from the university and use of the offices we were sitting in. I didn't have much time for contemporary poetry, but I was interested in the literary bit. I asked if they needed help and Graham said that they could use an art director. I told them I could draw, and so the job was mine.

I didn't mention this at the time, but what I also had in my favor was a reasonable knowledge of past magazines. I had spent hours at the public library studying them. There was one I thought we could model ourselves after—*Scribner's Magazine*, which had been started in New York in the late nineteenth century by the Scribner's publishing house. It became noted for its groundbreaking articles, including Jacob Riis's "How the Other Half Lives" and a serialization of Hemingway's *A Farewell to Arms*, which was banned in Boston at one point on grounds of immorality. Theodore Roosevelt wrote for the magazine. So did Edith Wharton, John Galsworthy, and the great war correspondent Richard Harding Davis. The magazine's covers were designed by Rockwell Kent and inside were the works of a pantheon of artists of the time, including Maxfield Parrish, Frederic Remington, and Howard Chandler Christy.

I suggested that we mimic their look as best we could and designed a cover template for *The Canadian Review* modeled on that of *Scribner's*, using classic typefaces and an ornate border. In those days, covers were often set in hot type, the antique process where individual letters are placed in troughs on printers' plates. There were no computers. Layouts were done by hand using a waxer to glue sheets of type onto layout boards. Color printing was expensive, and so aside from the cover, almost all the images inside were black and white. Nobody really knew what they were doing.

Oh, and I got married to a lovely young woman named Marie Williams. Her father owned a farm across the Gatineau River that looked out over Ottawa. Her uncle had been my boss during my illustrious government career and she and I just sort of hit it off. It was a spur-of-the-moment marriage, and we were happy at first. But the more I got involved with the magazine, the less time I spent at home. I would leave our place at dawn and return sometime after dinner. It was no way to treat a marriage, and Marie and I drifted apart. It was completely my fault. There wasn't much to divide up and we used the same lawyer for the divorce agreement. Marie went on to a successful career in the Canadian museum system.

As at any small magazine, there were constant tensions. Graham was dedicated to the poetry in *The Canadian Review*, and I was more interested in the literary stories we were doing. As for my studies, I rarely went to class. I simply didn't have time. A number of my professors wrote for us, and they did their best to cover for me on the classroom front. It was chaotic and exhilarating.

I thought more political coverage was what the magazine needed.

And so our deputy editor, Jonathan Webb, and I decided to go to the Democratic National Convention, in New York, in 1976. We arranged for credentials and booked a room with twin beds at the Statler Hilton, which had once been the Hotel Pennsylvania. I got a bit excited when I saw on the rotary phone that the number was PEnnsylvania 6-5000—the same number as in the Glenn Miller song. The hotel rooms had compartments in the doors called Servidors that could be opened both from inside the room and from the hallway. A little sticker on it informed guests that if they put their shoes in it, they would be returned shined the next morning. I wanted to look crisp and professional among all the real journalists at the convention, and so I put my shoes in the compartment. The next morning, when I opened it, the compartment was empty. I called downstairs and was told that the Servidors hadn't been operational for years. It was the only pair I had brought and so I had to walk down 34th Street in my socks to a shoe store to get replacements.

A year or so in, Graham got either bored or tired of the interoffice squabbling and departed, leaving me as the de facto editor. The staff at that point was firmly in his corner. Never underestimate the bickering that can take place within the walls of a little magazine. Our political editor, a Frenchman named Guy Charpentier, was obsessed with coverage of General Augusto Pinochet, who had just staged a military coup in Chile. Patrick Esmonde-White, who was English and served as our "foreign correspondent"—a grand title for someone who rarely left the office—was obsessed with the horrors being committed by the Tontons Macoutes, the Haitian secret police.

And then there was the poetry, which made up a sizable portion of the over-the-transom submissions. I like poetry, but of the old-fashioned, classic variety. Robert Service; Robert Browning; Alfred,

Lord Tennyson; Lord Byron; Samuel Taylor Coleridge—that sort of thing. The non-rhyming gibberish that flowed into our offices on a daily basis was something else. I would shovel this compostable rot unopened into the wastebasket. The pro-poetry contingent caught me in the act one day and revolted, leaving en masse.

By that time I was going out with a classmate, Kate White. She was a tall, auburn-haired beauty and was about the smartest person I had ever met. She came in to lend a hand and steered me toward *Harper's*, which until recently was being run in New York by Willie Morris. We slowly began mimicking it, and *The Canadian Review* did end up looking a bit like Morris's magazine—as put out by a handful of college students who had no idea what they were doing. Then John Watts showed up at our door. He was a Swiss Army knife of a man, able to lend his hand to just about anything. He wrote, edited, and became our art director. (He would go on to build a sailboat and take his family on a yearslong voyage around the world.) On the business side, my mother and her close friend Doreen Buckles came in to handle subscription "fulfillment," which in those pre-digital days involved keeping tabs on readers with index cards. Doreen wore Chanel suits to the office and looked wildly out of place. A few years later, she became sick and my mother would visit her every day. The whole ordeal so upset her that every time she visited Doreen in the hospital, she'd stop at the gift shop for some cookies. And she put on weight. On Doreen's final day, my mother asked if there was anything she could do. Doreen, who could barely speak by then, pulled my mother down to her and whispered, "Yes, Marg. You can go out and buy a whole new wardrobe one size larger."

Once I became the editor, I changed my byline to E. Graydon Carter. The *E* is for Edward. Although I was Gray to my family and friends, I thought that with my full name and the added *E*, readers would assume that I was older and more established. (I held onto that *E* right up into my thirties. By that time, I *was* older, and figured I could do without it.)

Despite the exit of the pro-verse contingent, poetry remained a constant frustration. Canadian writers in those days churned the stuff out in heartbreaking volume. One day a young woman came in and asked if we could use someone to reply to the poetry submissions. I hemmed and hawed a bit. Then she said that she didn't want to be paid. I hired her immediately. When the magazine was in the long, tragic process of folding, I was called by someone in local government, informing me that this woman, our poetry editor, was suing me for two years' back wages. I had to show up at a hearing, and despite my protestations that this had been a volunteer job, I lost the case. This did little to enhance my esteem for modern verse.

———

About three years after we started the magazine, the University of Ottawa announced that, beginning with the next term, all classes would largely be taught in French. What with my spotty attendance and lackluster grades, I was having enough trouble studying in English. So I switched over to the school across town, Carleton University. I tried to transfer to the undergraduate journalism program, but they wouldn't have me. Years later, when I was at *Vanity Fair*, I was sent the mock-up for the journalism school's new website. At the forefront was a gallery of the program's more prominent alumni. Including me. I called the office of the dean of the school to explain I was most flattered by my inclusion in their pantheon but that the school had rejected my application.

Carleton didn't have office space for *The Canadian Review*, so we rented offices in Cooper House, a handsome old brick building downtown that had once been the headquarters of the Canadian

Liberal Party. The building was incredibly grand, and I had a huge office with bookshelves, a long leather couch, and a fireplace. I spent so much time here—so thrilled to be living the magazine life—that my irregular attendance at Carleton dribbled away to the occasional cameo. I was about to start my final year when I got a call from the school suggesting that I not come back. I simply had too many "incompletes" to ever graduate. And thus ended my academic career. I wasn't even a college dropout—by then an almost fashionable career appendage. I was a college discard.

The Canadian Review was printed by *The Montreal Gazette*, a big city daily that took on outside printing jobs when its presses were down. With a small magazine, your printer is in part your banker. They print your magazine, and then you pay them once you've recovered your meager rewards from newsstand sales, subscriptions, and advertising. We were constantly late in our payments. I also had a *real* banker, who had given *The Canadian Review* a loan. I had a bit of money and had signed personally to guarantee it. The one condition was that I had to stop off each day for a chat with the branch manager. He was an easygoing fellow, or at least as easygoing as a bank branch manager can be. We would chat for a few minutes and when I got up to leave, he'd say to me in the cheeriest fashion he could manage, "You know, Graydon, you're going to go out of business." That was how I started every day.

Some help came via Tom Van Dusen, who had been a political aide to former prime minister John Diefenbaker and was an esteemed journalist in town. I was friends with a number of his kids, and he had taken a shine to me. Tom was called in to help Prime Minister Pierre Trudeau during a period of stubborn inflation. Trudeau's office needed some hands to draft speeches for him and his cabinet ministers to deliver on how the government was handling the economy. Although I knew practically nothing about economics—

and was completely up front about this lack of knowledge—Tom urged the fellow in Trudeau's office who was in charge to hire me. I was paid the then astronomical rate of $500 per speech. A researcher would send notes and statistics over and I would pour a thousand words into a set of remarks. This money went right into *The Canadian Review*. I'm not sure that anything I wrote was ever used. But the fees were welcome.

At the other end of our floor in Cooper House, John Doran, whom I knew glancingly from childhood, was in the process of starting a business that would go on to renovate much of Ottawa's old downtown area. John was a great sounding board on business matters—an area I had little scholarship in. John Watts and Kate and I would go out to lunch on a regular basis and conspire about how we were going to get money. No idea was too crackpot. The pope was coming to North America and John had a thought. Old Spice's Soap on a Rope was a popular thing then. It was a bar of soap with a loop of rope embedded into it. You hung it on one of the shower taps. John's idea was Pope on a Rope, with the soap being in the shape of the pontiff. (We didn't do anything with it, but a few years later, someone else did.) We also thought of taking out ads for a "solar clothes dryer"—which would be nothing more than a clothesline.

Knowing of our dwindling resources, Bruce came over one day and suggested that we change the title to *The Canadian Revue*, with pictures of naked women. Bruce also read about a government program that offered employers two years' salary if you hired someone with disabilities. We applied, and one day a man turned up. He was in his mid-fifties—more than thirty years older than the rest of us. We were never quite sure what his disability was. But his name was Peter Chow, and he was to be our accountant. He spoke limited English and the first thing he did was put an abacus on his desk. From that day on, our accounts were calculated this way. Every morning,

Peter would perform twenty minutes of tai chi exercises in the center of the office and then get to work on his abacus, tallying our demise.

Which came soon enough. I had depleted not only my bank account but also my credibility with my banker, my printer, and my landlord. The strange thing was, the magazine had a substantial circulation of fifty thousand, which was enormous in a country a tenth the size of the United States. But after four years of scrambling, the money had just run out. We sold the mailing list to our closest competitor, a far more illustrious magazine called *Saturday Night*. On the last day, having given away the office furnishings, I left with an old calendar from the Royal Bank of Canada that I had bought at an antique store some years earlier. It was metal and had large number cards that you changed every day. It traveled with me to *Time*, to *Life*, to *Spy*, to *The New York Observer*, to *Vanity Fair*, and to where I am now, *Air Mail*. I've had it for more than half a century, and it's a cherished talisman that ties me to that tiny, failed magazine that changed my life forever.

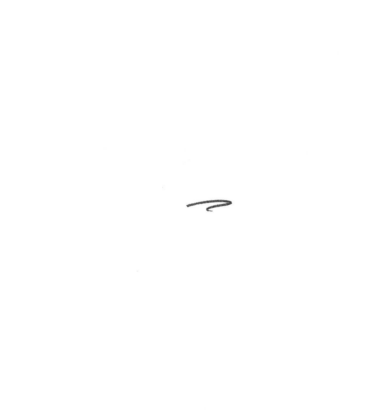

Chapter 5.

Candide in New York

The summer after *The Canadian Review* folded, I was at a complete loss for what I would do next. I had essentially given up my college education for the magazine and now I didn't even have that. In *The Canadian Review's* waning days, I read about a new English-language newspaper that had been started in Paris by two young American journalists, Tom Moore and Harry Stein. It was called *The Paris Metro* and was Berliner-sized, with a logo that was a takeoff on the Art Nouveau typeface of the city's Metropolitan underground. Tom had worked at *Life,* where he had written a story about a botched bank holdup in New York that became the basis for the Sidney Lumet film *Dog Day Afternoon.* Harry was the son of Joseph Stein, who wrote the book for the musicals *Zorba* and *Fiddler on the Roof.* I wrote to Tom and asked if I could have a job. I told him I'd be up for doing pretty much anything. He wrote back and said to come and see him if ever I was in Paris. I wasn't planning on a trip, but I made arrangements to stay with a family friend and bought a plane ticket. I had enough money for a three-day stay, and figured I had to make some sort of haste.

I got to Paris and headed to the paper's offices fresh off the plane, with my suitcase. I found Tom there and he claimed to remember me writing him. Tom was a tall, charismatic fellow and the sort of person you wanted to work for. The office bustled with what looked to be a few young college grads. When Tom explained the state of the paper's salary rations—no pay—I was heartbroken. I told him thank you and said that I needed a proper job. Two days later I was flying back to Canada.

My résumé was now seemingly one failure after another. Aside from Tom at *The Paris Metro*, whom I had met once, I knew nobody in the magazine business outside of Canada. The Ottawa correspondent for *Newsweek* lived down the street from my parents—but such was the reverence I held for someone in such an esteemed position that I never had the nerve to even say hello to him on the street. I still had a bit of money from the sale of *The Canadian Review* to *Saturday Night* and with it I rented a small clapboard cottage overlooking the Gatineau River, about twenty minutes outside Ottawa. I went there with Kate. Sundays we would drive into the city, buy the out-of-town papers, and bring them back to the cottage to read.

One morning she was leafing through the Sunday *New York Times* and noticed an ad for a publishing program at Sarah Lawrence College, just outside New York City. "You should think about this, Gray," she said. I thought it might provide a way into something in New York. I sent in a letter of application, and they accepted me. I arrived at Sarah Lawrence and settled in. It was a five-week program, and I was assigned to a mock-Tudor dorm called Titsworth. As I lay in bed that first night, I was almost feverish in the knowledge that less than twenty miles south, Manhattan—and everything it had to offer—was humming in all its glory and promise.

The publishing program brought in the editors of many of the major magazines of the day. There was Carll Tucker, the editor of *Saturday Review*, a liberal monthly that had been founded in the mid-1920s and for a long stretch had been edited by Norman Cousins, one of the giants of journalism, commentary, and criticism. Gordon Lish, the legendary Knopf fiction editor came. So did Lewis Lapham, the editor of *Harper's*, and Otto Friedrich, the editor of the Nation section of *Time*. Otto was a remarkable person, as I was to learn later. His father, it was said, had been instrumental in drafting the West German constitution following World War II. Otto had been summa cum laude at Harvard and was the last editor of the fabled *Saturday Evening Post*. After returning to Ottawa, I wrote to each one of the speakers and asked if I could come and see them in New York. And every one of them said yes.

I arrived in Manhattan in the middle of a July heat wave. You got off a plane in those days by walking down the boarding stairs onto the tarmac. When the plane door opened, I almost fainted. I had never felt such heat. The jacket I was wearing certainly didn't help. It was a massively thick Harris Tweed sports coat—one of the only two that I owned. The other one was a navy blazer as thick as a camp blanket. Lewis Lapham was my first port of call. I dropped my bags with a friend I was staying with. She had a fifth-floor walk-up on West 14th Street above a shop that cashed checks for workers who didn't have bank accounts. I then headed to the *Harper's* offices on lower Park Avenue.

By this time, I was positively drenched in sweat. About a half hour before my meeting, I slipped into the old Sheraton Russell Hotel, a few blocks north of the *Harper's* offices, and made for the men's room. I did my best to mop up my sweat and then walked over for my appointment in the searing heat. Lewis heard me out and said that, alas, he had nothing available. He did say that he had heard that *Foreign Affairs* magazine had an assistant's job open, and that he would call over there for me. I asked how much he thought the job would pay. "Oh, somewhere between $12,000 and $15,000." I told Lewis how much I appreciated his offer, but that I had no money and figured I would need at least $20,000 a year to survive. He said that he had a meeting to go to but, glancing at the sweat stains on my shirt, offered to let me sit in front of the air conditioner for a half hour or so. Which I did.

On my last day in New York, I went to see Otto and through him I met Ray Cave, the top editor at *Time*. I had no proper writing clips. But I had brought copies of *The Canadian Review* with me and Ray politely leafed through them. I was driven by the knowledge that a job wasn't an option. It was a necessity. This was my last interview in New York. And I think that my desire for the job, fueled by quiet desperation, might have made a difference. Decisions on hiring, Ray said, take six months; they might have something for me then. When I heard this, I did something I've never done before. I put my hand on Ray's arm and said, "No, no, I need a job now." I don't think he quite knew what to do with that gesture. *Time* was a pretty buttoned-down affair, and I'm sure that sort of tactile response was a no-no.

In any event, I returned to the fifth-floor walk-up to pick up my things for the trip back to Ottawa. As I got to the top of the stairs, the phone was ringing. I managed to get in to answer the call. It was Ray's number two, Jason McManus. "I don't know what you said to Ray, Graydon," he said. "But we're prepared to offer you a job as a writer. Can you start on Monday?" My heart almost stopped. I blurted out, "Thank you so much, Mr. McManus, but I need a week to fly home and gather my things." Jason said, "Fine, we'll see you a week from Monday."

When I returned to Ottawa, I went to my parents' slightly down-at-heel sailing club for lunch. They made no mention of my trip to New York and never asked how it went. I was about to leave in a huff, when my mother said, "Oh dear, we didn't want to say anything, because this came for you, and we opened it by mistake." She handed me a rejection letter from the personnel department of Time Inc. that had been mailed out before my meeting with Ray. The letter said that the magazine had no openings. When I told her about the job, my mother almost wilted with happiness.

—

I packed up my possessions in preparation for my move. Kate had sold my papers and my meager collection of manuscripts to the University of Calgary. We split the money and with my share I bought an old red 1972 BMW 2002 that had been buried under a snowbank for the winter. I threw my clothes and a tennis racket into the car and drove to what I was hoping would be my destiny. I didn't have an apartment, so for those first few weeks I stayed at the Prince George Hotel on East 27th. The room was paneled in fake wood and didn't have a phone. In those days there were maybe five television stations in New York, and they all went off the air sometime after midnight. But even those weren't available to me. The room had an old TV set, but it burned out after my second day and the hotel never bothered to replace it. I had told the fellow at the front desk that I was in college, so that I could get the student room rate of $22 a day. The trouble was, I had to look like a student when I was in the lobby, so I rolled up my jacket and tie and carried them out in a plastic bag, then put them on once on the street. I reversed this on my return.

New York in the summer of 1978 was a festering pot of arson, stabbings, prostitution, and graffiti, all of it chronicled in trademark hysterics by the *New York Post*, which had been bought by Rupert Murdoch two years earlier. Ed Koch had recently defeated a slew of Democratic rivals to become the city's new mayor. The Son of Sam serial killer had just been sentenced to life in prison. In a few months, Sid Vicious would kill his girlfriend Nancy Spungen in the Chelsea Hotel. The murder rate was through the roof. There were burned-out abandoned cars everywhere. Stewardesses lived in the East Thirties to be nearer to the tunnels taking them to LaGuardia and JFK. Bankers, lawyers, and debutantes lived on the Upper East Side. Writers lived in Greenwich Village and the Upper West Side, about the only places they could afford. There were bodegas and head shops on almost every block. And the city was filthy and sweltering. I can't recall when I had ever been so happy.

New York was always a magazine city for me. Growing up in Canada, magazines—*Life, Look, Esquire, The New Yorker, New Times,* and *Time*—more than anything else, told me the story of the city, its industry, its might, and the people who made it the center of just about everything I was interested in. Magazines even had their own buildings. There was the Time & Life Building on Sixth Avenue. Over on Madison there was the Condé Nast Building, and farther uptown, the Newsweek Building and the Hearst Building. There was a huge billboard in the main concourse of Grand Central, and from time to time one of the newsweeklies booked it. Lining the train platforms were smaller billboards for *Time* and *Newsweek* and magazines I'd never heard of, such as *Grit* (an agricultural supplement that was included in the weekend section of rural newspapers). My guess was that those billboards were intended to catch the eye of advertising agency account executives for brands such as Chesterfield cigarettes and J&B scotch as they headed home to Greenwich and Westport and other bedroom communities. And here I was, about to become part of it all. I could not believe my good fortune.

I had no new clothes—no New York clothes, anyway. I only had my Harris Tweed and my battered old blazer with a club crest on it. I wore it to a meeting in one of those early weeks and someone asked if I moonlighted as a doorman. I went back to my hotel room that night and with a razor blade cut through the stitches of the crest and took it off. The fabric under the crest was considerably darker than the rest of the jacket. I managed to look even more ridiculous. I had absolutely no money. When I got an apartment, I used Joy, my dishwashing soap, to wash my hair. But I had to do something about my wardrobe. I went out and, on credit, bought a lightweight tan gabardine suit at Paul Stuart on Madison. On the first morning I wore it, a fight broke out on the subway between two people over a container of Chinese noodles. Veterans of the subway quickly but discreetly moved to the far end of the car. I was the last to move and, just then, one of the two people threw the food container. The other person ducked, and it hit me square on the back.

There was an in-house Time Inc. newsletter called *FYI*, which, among other things, ran ads for sublets of apartments belonging to correspondents who had been posted out of the city or the country. I got my apartment this way. It was on the ground floor of a town house in Greenwich Village, down the block from Café Loup. It had high ceilings, a loft bed, and a wall of leaded-glass windows that looked out over a garden. It was glorious. The one thing that made me feel more like a true New Yorker than anything else came in the mail that first month. It was the Brooks Brothers credit card I had applied for.

Considering the digital husk that it now is, it's difficult for the most recent arrivals to this planet to fathom just how mighty *Time* magazine once was. It was the 1923 brainchild of Briton Hadden and Henry Luce, who had been classmates at Yale. Their new magazine was designed as a weekly that would sum up the news of the day for people such as themselves: educated, upwardly mobile, and on the go. The cover of *Time* was a singular totem of American success (Franklin D. Roosevelt) and failure (Richard Nixon). The magazine's circulation when I got there was over four million copies every week. I have no idea what it is now. But it's not that.

When I first walked through the doors of the Time & Life Building on Sixth Avenue, it was still the *Time* magazine of yore, the weekly that could move the market and influence presidential elections. I thought of the Time & Life Building like a vertical university. Different floors were devoted to each of the magazines: *Sports Illustrated*, *People*, *Life*, *Fortune*, and assorted lesser titles. Kenneth Fearing, the poet and novelist, created a similar subject-per-floor empire in his murder mystery *The Big Clock*, later made into a great film with Charles Laughton and Ray Milland. The *Time* magazine floors represented the inner temple, though.

The magazine had not only its august history but a stable of writers that no other magazine of the period could match. I was inserted into a staff consisting almost entirely of Ivy Leaguers, Rhodes scholars, and assorted other overachievers. Even the fact-checkers seemed to have master's degrees or doctorates. *Time* was in the process of being restocked with more than a dozen young people my age—many of them future stars. There was Walter Isaacson, later *Time*'s editor and the biographer of Albert Einstein and Steve Jobs; Jim Kelly, another writer who rose to become editor of the magazine; Rick Stengel, a third future *Time* editor; and Steve Smith, who became the editor of *U.S. News & World Report*. There were a number of Pulitzer Prize winners-to-be, including Michiko Kakutani, who would spend much of her career as the chief book critic of *The New York Times*, and Maureen Dowd, who is still a celebrated columnist at the paper. Frank Rich, later to become the chief theater critic at *The Times* (and, more recently, a hugely successful producer at HBO), was there. So was Evan Thomas, who went on to become a noted historian and biographer. Tom Sancton, a Rhodes scholar, was considered one of the great clarinetists in the country; he became the magazine's Paris bureau chief and eventually settled there, turning out a series of well-received nonfiction books. There was Annalyn Swan, a lovely arts writer who married her crosstown rival at *Newsweek*. They went on to coauthor a Pulitzer Prize–winning biography of Willem de Kooning, among other books.

Two of my future partners were also at the magazine: Kurt Andersen, whom I later teamed up with to start *Spy* magazine, and Alessandra Stanley. Alessandra had spent part of her childhood in Paris, knew the city and the language, and got a job at *The Paris Metro* right out of Harvard. She wrote beautifully. Even then, though, she had her eye on covering the world outside America's borders. She would later join *The New York Times*, where she traveled the globe as a correspondent and bureau chief. Along the way, she picked up four languages and one (now former) husband, the writer Michael Specter.

Life in New York in the late '70s was dangerous but exhilarating. Rents were cheap—my apartment in the Village cost me $220 a month. The heating was spotty and one night my friend Steve Probyn, who was staying with me, slept in his Canadian winter great coat on the sofa. Restaurants were largely mom-and-pop affairs, with red-checkered tablecloths and candles in the necks of wicker-clad Chianti bottles.

On the floor above me lived Sheila Cooley, an attractive young medical student. I asked her if she'd like to go out to dinner. We went to one of the few restaurants I'd heard of—"21." We must have been given a decent table, because not far across the room, Walter

Cronkite, the revered CBS anchorman, and Harry Reasoner, the *60 Minutes* correspondent, were also having dinner. At one point, Sheila pulled out a cigarette. The restaurant had porcelain ashtrays with a holder for matchboxes in the center. "Here, let me do that," I said in the suavest voice I could muster. The trouble was, rather than striking the rough side of the box, the match caught on the bottom, and the box went flying in the air, spraying matches everywhere. Sheila was courteous after that when she saw me in the building, but no more than just courteous.

New York was unlike Ottawa in so many ways. For one thing, famous people lived there. My first month at *Time* I had two sightings of stars. The first was in the cafeteria. I was getting a sandwich and there across the room was Bruce Gordon, a beefy actor who played the mobster Frank Nitti in the 1960s TV series *The Untouchables*. I raced upstairs to tell someone. I can't remember who I told, but they looked at me as if I was a hick. A few weeks later, I saw Cary Grant walking up Sixth Avenue. Cary Grant! I later learned that he was probably on his way to the offices of Fabergé, the cologne company where he was a "creative consultant."

For many of the new wave of younger writers—we were all in our twenties—it was our first taste of expense-account life. The older writers who had been there for decades schooled the new recruits in the ways of expense-account artistry. The general feeling was that everybody there could be making more elsewhere—a theory I did not subscribe to—but the expense-account life made up for some of that shortage. Indeed, extreme expense-account creativity was looked upon with the same sort of reverence as writing a particularly fine story.

One writer, a friend of mine, was called into the office of Ed Jamieson, the executive editor. The pope was coming to America and the religion correspondent had fallen ill. My friend, whose chief qualification for the assignment was that he was a practicing Catholic, was enlisted to take his place. But he didn't want to go. On the spot, he made up a story about how he had planned to take his family on a fall vacation to Maine for the week. Ed thought about this for a moment and then said, "Look, you go cover the pope and send your family on the vacation. You can expense the cost of their holiday." After my friend got back from the pope's visit and filed his story, he had some receipt forms printed up with letterhead that said "Whispering Pines" or something like that, and with a fictitious Maine address. Then he created, in granular detail, the bills for his family's imaginary vacation. He submitted them on his next expense report, and they were duly paid. Sometime later, he was cleaning out his desk when he found the receipt from the printer that had produced the fake letterhead and hotel bills. He submitted that as well. And it was paid. There was also a cash window at *Time* where you could get an advance on your paycheck. Inasmuch as I ran pretty close to the bone financially, I stopped off almost every Friday to get some cash for the weekend.

For a long period, I served as a "floater," someone who would fill in when another writer in a department was on vacation or out sick. It was the sort of position you put someone in when you didn't really know what to do with them. (Calvin Trillin, who had once worked at *Time*, wrote a novel about the job, and called it *Floater.*) I wrote for almost every section. None of my stories were memorable. And then I was assigned the People page, which was a compilation of amusing stories about the well known or the infamous. The job involved writing crisp, funny shorts—something that I found came easily. It was a backwater, though, and about the only thing that gave me some sense of place was that the People page ran in every issue and therefore my name was on something that was sold in pretty much every town and city in the world. I thought, *Well, this is pretty cool.*

—

*T*ime worked in ways that few other magazines did. It was a miracle of organization and layered reporting, writing, and editing. Stories were decided on Mondays. Telexes went out to far-flung correspondents who then filed their reports on the subject. Researchers meanwhile gathered pertinent facts for the writers. Tuesdays were, for writers, days of relative rest. I made regular visits to the telex room, where big machines rattled off AP and UPI dispatches of breaking news. The soft-paneled ceilings of the offices of the older hands were decorated with pencils that had been thrown upward in acts of fury or sheer boredom. In due time, the younger writers like me copied them and enhanced our own ceilings with dozens of 2H yellow pencils.

I regularly snuck out to the Guild, a jewel of a movie house tucked into one of the buildings in Rockefeller Center. I saw a lot of matinees on those Tuesdays. I also perfected the art of the afternoon nap—a momentary pause in activity that I continue to this day. At *Time*, I'd slide the office door shut and just pray that those above me figured I was researching my story of the week. I would lay my head on my desk for twenty minutes and wake up feeling completely refreshed. As it says in Ecclesiastes, "The sleep of a laboring man is sweet." I can sleep almost anywhere as a result and can fall off pretty much instantly.

On Wednesday, Thursday, and Friday, writers wrote stories based on the research and they filed dispatches on giant typewriters sturdy enough to handle five copies with four sheets of carbon paper between them. Editors would often assign a story with a breezy "It writes itself!" It most certainly didn't. At least not for me. A finished story would be walked down to a wall of Lamson pneumatic tubes on each floor to be distributed throughout the building. Then layer upon layer of editors chiseled the copy into rigorous, data-filled, adjective-heavy *Time*-ese. Fact-checkers fact-checked what survived of all this journalistic engineering. They had to place dots over every word they checked and many of them referred to themselves as "dotters." Three major errors and the head of research would come down to inform the unfortunate soul that their days at this great institution were numbered. I was a deskbound writer, and every once in a while, my heart would skip a beat when I'd read a published piece and recognize a phrase I'd written. Only later did I understand the irony and humiliation of the first drafts that I and my fellow writers produced. They were stamped with the words *Writer's Version*.

Time was a weekly, and on Friday closing nights, staff in uniforms brought dinner (with wine) to writers' offices on tea trolleys. There was a bar at the end of each corridor. I went five years without ever turning on my oven. There were a number of French restaurants a few blocks west of the office, on 50th and 51st Streets, and we often congregated at Tout Va Bien, Café des Sports, Chez Napoléon, or René Pujol. Some of the restaurants, like René Pujol and Tout Va Bien, were popular with the *Life* crowd. (The wrestler André the Giant was a frequent customer at the latter.) Chez Napoléon, or Chez Nap, as we called it, was a certified *Time* hangout. Lunches generally involved splitting a bottle of wine and could be brought in for $25 for two people. These were expensed. Almost all dinners out were similarly expensed, generally on the flimsiest of pretexts: "dinner with source," "meeting with source." And these were the expenses of writers, who did almost no reporting.

There was a magical realism to *Time* in those days. And for most of us, it was all a revelation. There was a person for every conceivable need. Nurses. Doctors. Psychiatrists. Long-distance phone calls could be made for free. Bureau chiefs overseas lived as well as U.S. ambassadors. Cars took you home every Friday evening after the issue was closed. During summers, a group of us rented the filmmaker D.A. Pennebaker's rambling colonial in Sag Harbor, so that's where the cars took us on a ninety-mile trip after the issue closed on Fridays. Another group rented a house up the street. It was a '50s-era bungalow and on every available surface ceramic mice were displayed. We called it "the Mouse House." Through the night, packs of yellow Checker cabs would wend their way over the hills and dunes to homes out on the tip of Long Island.

Jim Kelly and I had the Pennebaker house and Walter Isaacson was a member of the Mouse House group. He took little time in getting the lay of the land, career-wise. Walter signed up for the celebrated Artists & Writers softball league, where big names from *Time*, *The Times*, Simon & Schuster, and the network news operations played on Saturday mornings. At one point he put a phone list on the Mouse House refrigerator. The names included prominent columnists, bureau chiefs, and television anchors. At the bottom was a listing for "the other house." When I saw it, I drew up our own list, with comically esteemed names like Sir Isaiah Berlin and Yehudi Menuhin, and at the bottom, the phone number for "the other house."

One of our housemates was Annie Plumb, who had worked at a number of downtown galleries. She pulled me aside one day and said that I should buy some of Keith Haring's work. She said, "Graydon, you can buy his pictures for, like, five hundred dollars." I was so out of it, I really didn't know what his art looked like. When Annie showed me, I just didn't get it. "I could do that myself" was my reply. Goodness knows how much those pictures would fetch now. Still, my reaction was in keeping with my opinion around the same time after seeing a one-bedroom apartment in the Café des Artistes building, just off Central Park West: I thought it was impossible that an apartment could be worth what the owners wanted. The asking price was $43,000.

One night Adam Zagorin, a talented writer for *Time*'s Nation section, and I were pitted against Walter and Arianna Stassinopoulos (later Huffington) in a game of bridge. My grandparents and parents were terrific bridge players and I had played a bit during college. I was good, but not great. Adam and I went into the game thinking we were doomed. And we were at first. But then things picked up a bit, and on the last two hands of the game, we won by bidding and then making first a small slam and then a grand slam. This won't mean anything to people who don't play bridge, but for those who do, it's something you never forget.

For *Time* writers, there were rooms at the Chateau Marmont or Beverly Hills Hotel during visits to Los Angeles. It was rare that I would travel to do any sort of reporting. That's what the correspondents were for. On the few occasions I was permitted to interview someone in California, I'd also make an appointment to talk to someone at one of the studios—Paramount, Warners, or Fox, preferably—and then just walk around purposefully after the chat so I could soak in the studio-lot atmosphere from the days when the writers' bungalows were filled with the likes of Billy Wilder, Ben Hecht, and Raymond Chandler. Correspondents, who did travel a lot, regularly brought clothes that needed to be dry-cleaned. These they'd get done at whatever hotel they were staying at. An English friend on the magazine's writing staff would regularly have lunch at a pub-like restaurant on the West Side called Cheshire Cheese. He would ask for a couple dozen bangers to be put on his bill to be expensed. They would be eaten by him and his family at breakfast for the next week or so.

I never had much interest in fashion, but I do love clothes. *Time* writers and editors wore suits and ties to the office, and although I wasn't in any way a successful member of the staff, I thought it might not be a bad idea to at least look like one. On a trip to London, I decided to get a suit made. My thinking was that even though a Savile Row suit might cost five or six times what an off-the-peg American one would, I could amortize it by wearing it pretty much every day for years. I had read about Anderson & Sheppard in a magazine. It was founded in 1906 and suited the sort of elegant men that other men drool over: Cary Grant, Noël Coward, Gary Cooper, Fred Astaire, and, much later, dapper fellows like Bryan Ferry and Tom Ford.

I had called ahead, and although tradition had it that you must be recommended by an existing client, I waved the *Time* magazine credential and was given an appointment. I had imagined what this esteemed temple to fine tailoring might look like: clubby and with sample jackets and suits on mannequins. It was nothing like that. It was somber and dark, with wooden floors and long tables stacked high with bolts of fabric. There were no samples to choose from. You basically just started from scratch—but within Anderson & Sheppard's strict guidelines. Norman Halsey—"Mr. Halsey," as he was to me over the next decades, as I was "Mr. Carter" to him—was there to meet me. Mr. Halsey was about the most elegant man I had ever met. He was tall and silvery and, it goes without saying, exquisitely dressed. He went all the way back to the days when both Mr. Anderson and Mr. Sheppard were at the firm. He told me once that Mr. Sheppard always wore a new suit out in a light rain on first wearing. He said it would fit better after that. I once asked Mr.

Halsey if he could cut a jacket in a way that would make me look a bit thinner. He turned a withering eye on me and said, "We're only tailors, sir."

On that first visit, I went through the bolts and wound up with an order for a nailhead-gray suit and a tweed jacket. I alternated them on a daily basis for years. And I still have them. As I do the overcoats, jackets, and suits I have had made since then. Years later, I had suits made for my two oldest sons, Ash and Max. Which they both still have. Anderson & Sheppard was taken over in 2004 by Anda Rowland, who freshened things up a bit and added a cheery haberdashery shop around the corner. When it came time to produce a book celebrating Anderson & Sheppard's centenary, Anda asked if I would edit it. I was honored. I roped in Cullen Murphy, a top editor at *Vanity Fair* and, soon, another Anderson & Sheppard customer. I also corralled the photographer Jonathan Becker and the writer David Kamp, two clotheshorses also from *Vanity Fair*—and my oldest son, Ash.

About thirty years ago, Fran Lebowitz asked me if I thought they could make some suits for her. I told her it was a long shot, given the hidebound nature of the enterprise. I called and said that I'd like to bring her in for a fitting and reminded them that they had made clothes for Marlene Dietrich back in the 1930s. They equivocated a bit but finally said yes. And so began a long relationship between Fran and the Anderson & Sheppard tailors, who would gingerly measure her before each suit or jacket was made. Fran and I owned a number of Anderson & Sheppard jackets that were almost identical. And if we were going out somewhere together I would call her ahead of time to make sure we didn't show up wearing the same one.

But I've gone off-piste. Back to *Time*. The magazine's offices were spread over three floors. There was a series of long hallways, with the writers' offices along the window side and the researchers' offices on the inside. At one end sat the editor (they were generally men) and his secretary. The other end was where the bar appeared at the end of the week. Many of the researchers were debutantes or heiresses, who spent a few years fact-checking stories while waiting for their future husbands or their inheritances. In general, you were assigned a researcher who sort of stuck with you, Sancho Panza–style, for months or years. It was their job to do miscellaneous bits of reporting and prop your stories up with interesting tidbits they picked up in the course of their research.

My social life revolved around the other new writers at the magazine. Lunches were generally shared with a combination of Jim Kelly, Kurt Andersen, Walter Isaacson, Michiko Kakutani, and Tom Sancton. At one point, Michi and another colleague, Lydia Chávez, and I tried to stave off boredom on our Friday nights as we waited for edits by hatching a plot for a novel based on the relationship between two women who had gone through the anti-war marches in the '60s and found themselves slightly adrift in the libertine '70s. We were each going to write alternate chapters. The idea for multiple writers had come from a saucy novel published a decade earlier called *Naked Came the Stranger.* It was the fruit of two dozen journalists at *Newsday,* who took turns writing parts of the book. Our grand quest for bestsellerdom was abandoned when Michi left *Time* for *The New York Times.*

As my days in the city continued, my relationship with my girlfriend Kate in Ottawa suffered. Long-distance romances are difficult during the best of times, and this was in the days before texts and email. Also, neither of us had any money, and so regular travel back and forth between New York and Ottawa was all but impossible. We broke up, and Kate later got married, had kids, and went on to become a force in the Canadian nonprofit world. We continue to correspond. In time, I had a steady girlfriend, Deb Thomson, who worked for American Ballet Theatre and then made an abrupt career change and became a producer for CBS News. Our relationship was short-lived, but our friendship has never wavered.

Jim Kelly had started at the magazine a week before me, and I'd first met him when Libby Waite, the secretary to Ed Jamieson, called and suggested that I have lunch with him. She thought we'd get along. She also suggested that we both open accounts at East River Savings, a small bank in Rockefeller Center. We did that and then we went to lunch at a nearby restaurant called Charley O's. Jim was the son of a New York City cop. He had gone to Regis, the Catholic school on the Upper East Side for academically gifted boys, and then on to Princeton. He had a big thatch of curly hair and loved so many of the things I loved: New York, magazines, cornball television hosts, washed-up crooners, old movies, and show-business schmaltz. From that day forward, we began spending a ridiculous amount of time together. And still do. We'd regularly have dinner somewhere and then prowl the stacks at the Shakespeare & Co. bookstore on the West Side, or hang out at Colony Records, the vast vinyl emporium on Forty-Ninth and Broadway. At *Spy*, Bruce Handy labeled it "loser nightlife."

When I was growing up in Ottawa, we had a few hometown Canadianisms that I carried with me to New York. When kids I knew met up, the first thing we would say to each other was "How's the boy." This was instead of "Hi" or "Hello." And our shorthand way of saying we didn't do much during a particular period was that we "fucked the dog." Don't ask me where that came from. It certainly wasn't literal. The whole time I was growing up, I never thought about how the phrase would sound to others not indoctrinated into our childhood Canadian patois. Early in my days at *Time*, I bumped into Jim on the elevator on a Monday morning. It was filled with editors and writers, all conservatively dressed in Brooks Brothers and Paul Stuart suits with button-down shirts and rep ties. Jim asked me what I did over the weekend and without thinking I just said, "Oh, fucked the dog." I felt the chill on the elevator, realized how it all sounded, and retired forever that particularly floral Canadianism.

When Jim was about to turn thirty, I organized a surprise dinner for him at my apartment. We were all big into black tie back then, so I made it formal and invited about a dozen of our colleagues from *Time*. I had to get Jim there, though, and in a dinner jacket. I needed a convincing cover. So I told him that we were going to a small affair for Laurence Olivier at Lincoln Center, but that we should have a cocktail at my place before heading out. Everyone else gathered at 6:30. Jim arrived at 7:00. It was a wonderfully funny, boozy night, with gifts and speeches, but I could tell that something was off with Jim. As he was leaving at the end of the evening, I asked him if everything was okay. "Did you have a good time?" He said sure, but then he paused and added, "Does this mean no Larry Olivier?"

Everyone smoked in those days—in the office, in restaurants, in elevators, in men's rooms, everywhere. And we drank. You could go an entire week without buying food, not only because of the expense accounts, but also because of the spreads put on at events we got invited to. And since we worked at *Time*, then still a huge force in American journalism and opinion forming, we had incredible access to all that New York had to offer. I once took Walter Isaacson and a *Playboy* Playmate I had met at a dinner to Studio 54. I dated a Rockette. There were old-fashioned nightclubs back then, with floor shows and women who danced in skimpy costumes. I dated one of the showgirls from a seedy spot on the East Side called Club Ibis.

In early 1981, Jim said that he was going to bring a friend over for dinner. When they arrived, I asked her what she'd like to drink. "Campari and soda," she said. I didn't have that. "What about some white wine?" I didn't have that either. I had a bottle of bourbon on my pathetic excuse for a bar and some vodka in the freezer. She passed on both. Dinner went considerably better than the cocktail hour. Her name was Cynthia Williamson. She was the daughter of an American CIA officer and had spent much of her life in Africa. I was to discover later that she had been a legendary beauty at St. Paul's, where she had gone to boarding school, and later at the University of Virginia. She dressed in classic clothes, twinsets, and pearls. I liked that. She read Proust and Jane Austen. I liked that too. She was unlike any young woman I had met before. And I think that after a steady stream of smart, good-looking preppie boyfriends, I was different from anyone she had yet dated. We got engaged two weeks after we met and were married the next year.

Back when Jim and I were still bachelors, our at-home dining arrangements were primitive at best. Nobody in our circle knew how to cook. Thankfully, there was a small chain of shops in the city called Pasta and Cheese. They sold packages of pasta and containers of Bolognese, pesto, or tomato sauce that even the most inept cook could mix together to make a serviceable dinner at home for four. When Cynthia and I were still dating, we went over for just such a dinner at Jim's. Cynthia offered to help in the kitchen. She was in there for about two minutes and came out with her hand over her mouth as if she was about to gag. "I have to go home," she said. I told Jim that she wasn't feeling well, apologized, and we left. In the cab, I asked what had happened. She told me that she had watched as Jim, not having a colander, ran the pasta through the sink strainer. I feigned horror at this. What I didn't tell her, and what I kept secret for the next twenty years, was that she shouldn't have faulted Jim. It was me who taught him this trick.

—

Overseeing all of *Time*'s vast expanse of human journalistic energy, social interaction, and expense-account chicanery was Henry Grunwald, the editor in chief of the Time Inc. empire. He was not tall, but in his manner and dress, he was an imposing figure. Henry was the son of a noted librettist. The family lived in Vienna until the Anschluss in 1938, at which point they emigrated via Casablanca and Lisbon to New York. He started off as a copy boy at *Time* and worked his way to the top of the masthead. He was a close friend of Henry Kissinger's. As the story goes, one Friday evening, they came down the elevator, heading out for dinner. The lobby of the Time & Life Building was filled with writers heading back up to close the issue. One of them was Robert Hughes, the celebrated Australian art critic whom Henry Grunwald had hired some years before. Both Henrys were fairly pear-shaped and wore their pants up high on their stomachs, and both had heads of gray, frizzy hair. When the elevator doors opened and they stepped out, Bob said, "Ah, Tweedledum and Tweedledee!"

Henry was overly kind to the young staff and would regularly invite a half dozen of us up to the executive dining room on the thirty-fourth floor to have lunch. He would often command the table for a group discussion of some topic: the situation in the Middle East, what was going on in Washington, and suggestions for "Man of the Year"—as it was then called. Most of my colleagues shined during these sessions. I just sat in abject fear of him asking me my opinion. Honestly, you could have filled libraries with subjects upon which I had no considered opinion. Running into Henry on the *Time* floor was equally terrifying. Beyond a "Good morning, Henry," I had no other small-talk arrows in my quiver. During a period of fitness activity, I decided to ride my old bicycle to work. I was heading down 7th Avenue, about to turn on to 50th Street where the Time & Life Building was, when I was cut off by a cab. I kicked the door and produced some heated, fragrant language. Henry popped his head out of the back seat window. I almost fainted. I got to my desk and quickly typed out an apology and ran it up to his office. A bit later in the day, my note was returned with a handwritten message from Henry saying that he had tried to ride his bike to the office years before and a similar incident had happened to him.

One year Henry organized a gathering aboard the *QE2*, which was then docked at a pier on the West Side. The boat never left its mooring, thank goodness, because most of us were desperate to get off and get on with some semblance of a life that evening. And we did get off, but not before Henry made a speech. There was a quartet on hand, and at Henry's first attempt at humor, the drummer hit a rim shot. Henry looked around at him. And the drummer continued to rim-shot Henry's pauses throughout his prepared remarks, whether they were funny or not.

Henry was married to Louise Melhado, who had worked under Diana Vreeland at *Vogue*. In the late '80s, after he had retired from Time Inc., Henry was appointed ambassador to Austria by President Ronald Reagan, and he and Louise took off for the continent and a great adventure. I adored Louise from the moment I met her. And I wasn't alone there. I don't think I've ever met someone with such a wide and deep circle of friends. Both when Henry was alive and after he died at the beginning of this century, their apartment on Park

Avenue, which had once been owned by Gianni Agnelli, became a central focus of so many people's lives. Louise had mastered the art of being a great hostess and filled the apartment with sensational food and interesting company. It was at her dinner table that I first met Mike Nichols and Diane Sawyer, Nick Pileggi and Nora Ephron, and any number of the greats of New York.

Louise was also a sort of den mother for the young writers who had worked under Henry: Frank, Maureen, Jim, Alessandra, Kurt, Michi, Evan, Steve, and me. I used to spend my mid-July birthday with her at her house on Gin Lane, in Southampton, every year. There are a lot of Carters, and like the Joad family, we'd arrive with our car stuffed with clothes and gear and decant into one of her guest houses. Louise became a part of our family, joining us at Christmas and on holidays. Years later, when I left *Vanity Fair* and after my wife, Anna, and I settled in the South of France with our daughter Izzy, Louise was our first houseguest. My life in New York is book-ended in a way by Grunwalds, with Henry being my first boss and Louise one of my dearest friends.

After about five years of ineffectual activity at *Time*, I realized that, unlike stars such as Jim and Walter, my future there was bleak. It was made pretty evident to me that I wasn't long-term *Time* material, the way so many of my friends and colleagues were. I wasn't Ivy League—a credential the magazine put great store in—and I wasn't as buttoned-down as some of my peers. I was happy, though, and I think that the almost giddy exhilaration I displayed just because I was in New York and had this job left my superiors with the sense that I wasn't a serious person. A smile might be somebody's umbrella, but at a conservative temple like *Time*, it could also limit your opportunities. I was shipped up to Westchester County to help with a new weekly magazine that would compete with *TV Guide*—then either the biggest or second-biggest magazine in the country. I admired the man I worked for, Dick Burgheim, and many of the writers under me. But I was miserable being away from New York. I lasted two months; the magazine lasted five. I was brought back to New York in 1984 and assigned to *Life*, once one of the great flagships of the Time & Life fleet, but now more of a trawler, bringing up the rear.

Chapter 6.

From *Life* to
Glorious Days at *Spy*

A fter the smart set at *Time*, I found myself working with a different crowd, a few floors away, at *Life*. It was like moving high schools—but going from one with a championship football team and cheerleaders to one with a volleyball squad and an AV club. In distance, my new office was a few hundred feet from my old one, but in terms of the energy and intellectual spark that had surrounded me at *Time*, it was a world away. *Life*, once the largest and most influential magazine in the country, had fallen victim to its size and the advent of television. By the late 1960s, national advertisers who wanted to reach a sizable portion of the U.S. audience—and who previously steered their dollars to *Life* and its lesser counterpart *Look*—went to the three television networks, CBS, NBC, and ABC. *Life* was a picture magazine in a video age. Where *Life* once brought black-and-white photographs of World War II into American living rooms, one week at a time, the evening news programs now did this with the Vietnam conflict—nightly, on film, and, as they used to say, in living color.

The magazine was edited by Dick Stolley. He had been the founding editor of *People* and moved with a look and purposeful stride that made underlings scurry for cover. As a *Life* correspondent, he had beaten the world to get the exclusive use of the Zapruder film, the only known footage of the November 1963 assassination of John F. Kennedy. I liked him. He had a group of smart young men and women under him. Among them were David Friend (later to join me at *Vanity Fair*), Steve Robinson (who became a top editor at *Sports Illustrated*), Chris Whipple (a reporter who went on to write a number of best-selling Washington books), and Rinker Buck (who later wrote a series of *Boy's Own*–type adventure books, including *Flight of Passage*, about how he and his brother, both in their teens, got a broken-down 1948 Piper Cub up in the air and flew it from New Jersey to California).

My favorite—and my closest—colleague, though, was Bobbi Baker Burrows, the picture editor. She was the daughter-in-law of Larry Burrows, the Vietnam-era *Life* photographer who had died when his helicopter went down over the Ho Chi Minh Trail in Laos. Bobbi, smart and funny, was my savior at the magazine. There were some grandees who still wrote for *Life*, including Loudon Wainwright, who produced a semi-regular column. He had worked at *Time* as well and he was writing a memoir about his career in journalism, seesawing between calling it "My Time at *Life*" and "My Life at *Time*."

The photographers who had made the magazine the greatest photo magazine ever were still milling around the office. Ralph Morse was a regular presence. After returning from World War II, he had photographed NASA's Mercury and Apollo missions that sent Americans into space and then to the moon. John Bryson, a big, rangy Texan, would make regular appearances. He was held in due respect by many of us because he happened to be a good friend of Katharine Hepburn's. Also there was David Douglas Duncan, a man with movie-star good looks who spent much of his time in the South of France and had become a close friend of Picasso's. Alfred Eisenstaedt, then perhaps the most celebrated news photographer in the world, made the occasional guest appearance. Eisie, as he was known around the office, shot the iconic image of an American GI kissing a nurse during the VJ celebrations in Times Square marking the end of the war in the Pacific. Once, when Jim Kelly and I were going to lunch, a couple of tourists were looking for someone to take their picture beside the statue in front of the Time & Life Building. They looked at me and Jim. And then looked at the small man beside us. They handed their camera to Jim. The small man was Eisie. Somewhere I have a contact sheet of portraits he shot of me in the office.

Yes, many of the figures that had made the weekly *Life* great were still there, but that was about it. *Life* had become a zombie monthly, close to dead but moving as if it were alive. Nobody I knew read it and circulation was on the decline. Everyone at the magazine, however, still operated as if it were 1956. They had their beats, their missions, their zeal. They were all specialists, and I was a generalist. They walked with urgency. They talked with urgency. I wrote stories, rewrote stories, and edited the occasional story, but I was desperately adrift and bored. Most days I stayed in my office and read Wodehouse, hidden by a handful of manuscripts. The week's work—which I could do in a few hours—had to be stretched out to a five-day job in order for me to appear busy. One of my duties was editing the Letters to the Editor section. Weeks would go by without a single reader's comment, aside from the occasional screed from a federal correctional facility—*Life* still had its captive fans. I had to fill at least a page, so in a panic I would overnight copies of articles to people at the center or even the periphery of one of the stories in the hope they would write in with praise or a complaint. Anything. I would come home and just flop onto the bed for an hour.

I had nobody I could talk to about my general despair. I didn't want to burden Cynthia. Our son, Ash, was a year old, and Cynthia had enough on her hands. I couldn't unburden my thoughts on my colleagues at *Time*—they were overachieving and racing ahead with vibrant careers. My parents were hopeless. Even without word of my situation, they wanted me to give it all up, come back to Ottawa, and get a proper job. And I couldn't alert my friends in Canada to the state of play. I worried that it would just confirm their hunches— that New York would chew me up and spit me back across that cold and unforgiving Canadian border.

⟶

In late 1985, out of that sense of desperation, I rekindled an idea that I had been kicking around for a few years—a satirical monthly about New York. By this time, I believed that I had a fair grounding in the ways the city operated. I was attuned to the social and business circus acts that made regular appearances in the local gossip and business columns. And alone among my friends, I had actually edited a magazine before. *The Canadian Review* was a failure, but out of it I had learned a valuable lesson. Whatever you do, whatever you build, it has to have a point. *The Canadian Review* was neither right nor left. It was neither highbrow nor lowbrow. It was neither super smart nor super entertaining. It was just a magazine. And it was one edited by people who had never even worked at a magazine before, a fact that was no doubt evident to its readers.

This new magazine would have a point. It would be called *Spy*, and it would be a smart, funny, fact-based monthly about New York. Rigorous in its reporting and fact-checking. And fearless. The name came both from the illustrator Leslie Ward, who signed the caricatures he did for the old British *Vanity Fair* as "Spy," as well as from the magazine Jimmy Stewart worked for in *The Philadelphia Story*. In the film, *Spy* was part of a publishing empire called Dime and Spy, a take-off on Henry Luce's Time & Life.

Looking back, I honestly don't know what I was thinking. Who was I to start a magazine that poked holes in the bloated egos of the city's grandees? I had only been in New York for seven years. I had stumbled through five years at *Time* and then two years at *Life*. I do think that sheer ignorance of the trials ahead is often a blessing. What I didn't know couldn't derail me. I didn't want to do it on my own, though. I needed a partner, someone with a similar outlook and with complementary skills. I approached Jim at one point, but he passed on the idea. I think he just knew what lay ahead of him: the editorship of *Time*. I brought up the magazine idea to Kurt over lunch. We had discussed it before, but only in the most casual way. By the end of our meal, he said he was in.

In the beginning, when we weren't discussing the magazine over lunch or playing the video game *Gravitar* at the Playland arcade off Times Square, Kurt would come up in the late morning to my office at *Life* and we'd try to figure out our editorial vision. Neither of us had a head for business, and we figured we needed someone who did. As it turned out, Kurt's wife, Anne, who had gone to Radcliffe, knew a fellow who had gone to Harvard at the same time and who was at the Rothschild bank and looking to get out. This was Tom Phillips, and he was the beau ideal of a young publisher: tall, good-looking, and athletic. He still is. He loved the idea of the magazine. He was bored with his job and said he'd come in with us.

By this time, Kurt and I had all but set up a *Spy* home base in my office at *Life*. I have no idea if anyone on the magazine's staff cottoned on to what I was up to. If they did, they never said a word about a *Time* writer spending a couple of hours each day in my office. Tom left the bank shortly thereafter and joined us, doing research on his early Macintosh computer and assembling a business plan. (In those days, Macs were the computers favored by business types and IBMs were the computers of the creative class. A decade later, those two allegiances switched completely.) At one point, Tom suggested that we come up with a hundred story ideas for the business plan. Kurt and I went down to the Time Inc. cafeteria with pads and pencils. And we just sat there for what must have been an hour. Finally, Kurt said, "Things Found in the East River." *Hmmm.* And then I came up with "The Ten Most Annoying New Yorkers." *Hmmm.* And then Kurt came up with another one. And so on. In a week we had our hundred potential story ideas.

We worked on the proposal for months. At one point, Kurt and Anne and Cynthia and I decamped to a beautiful old house in Tyringham, in the Berkshires. It was part of a privately owned Shaker village that belonged to George and Betty Kramer, longtime friends of Cynthia's parents. George had been an original investor in *New York* magazine. And Betty's father-in-law, Hawley Truax, from her previous marriage, had been a chum of Harold Ross and his circle. Hawley invested in *The New Yorker* when it first launched in 1925, and then served on its board of directors for almost half a century. Kurt and I worked in their library in Tyringham filled with signed copies of the output of the greats of early- and mid-twentieth-century American literature and criticism. In addition to lending us their house, George and Betty would come to invest in *Spy*, which, given their family history with upstart, New York–focused magazines, we took not only as an act of supreme generosity but as a good omen.

But before that, we had no money and no properly printed prospectus. We had an outline of what *Spy* would be, the most rudimentary of business plans, and those hundred story ideas, all of which we cheekily had printed at the Time Inc. facility in the building. We put together a couple of dummy covers. I had recently written a profile of the supermodel Paulina Porizkova for *GQ* magazine, and so when we needed a cover subject for a story on how "anyone can be a fashion designer," I asked her if she would pose, and she said yes. The other person in the photo was Matt Nelson, acting as the designer to Paulina's mannequin. He was Ash's babysitter from across the street. And so we began courting money. In all our lunches, if the potential investor said yes, they picked up the tab in celebration. If they passed, they paid as a sort of consolation prize.

There was no shortage of hiccups along the way. Martin Peretz, the owner of *The New Republic*, was going to come in with an investment, but backed out because his wife, a Singer sewing machine company heiress, thought we weren't going to be predictably liberal enough. Which was interesting, because his *New Republic* was anything but predictable or rote liberal. His partner in this investment was going to be Ivan Boesky, who was married to the daughter of the man who owned the Beverly Hills Hotel. He was also a Wall Street arbitrageur who was later tried and convicted for insider trading. At the time of our investment talks, as we later learned, he had, at the request of the federal government, begun wearing a wire. The year we launched, a talk he delivered at the Haas School of Business at UC Berkeley reportedly became the basis for the "Greed Is Good" speech Gordon Gekko delivers in Oliver Stone's *Wall Street*. Boesky became a living symbol of the rapacious financial figures of the mid-1980s. A decade after Marty backed out of his investment, his daughter Evgenia came to work at *Vanity Fair*, first as an intern, then as an assistant, and later as a gifted and highly valued writer.

Henry Beard, a *Harvard Lampoon* alum, introduced us to John Goelet. John's family, originally French Huguenots, had been figures in New York going back to the middle of the seventeenth century. It was said that at one point, they owned most of the land on the east side of Manhattan from Union Square to 48th Street. John agreed to put in $500,000—which would make him our largest investor. The others were remarkably blue chip given the scrappy nature of the enterprise, not to mention the outsider status of its founders: Kurt (Nebraska) and me (Canada). We had a *Washington Post* heir. An E.F. Hutton heir, who also happened to be an heir to the Safeway supermarket chain. The CEO of ConAgra, the giant food processor, became an investor. We had a member of the Frelinghuysen family as an investor. Tom's father was CEO of Raytheon, the giant defense contractor. He came in. So did Kurt's parents. Nancy Peretsman, at Salomon Brothers, invested. Bob Montgomery, a partner at the white-shoe law firm Paul, Weiss—and the lawyer for a string of notables including Marilyn Monroe, Andy Warhol, and Cole Porter—served as our counsel. And he invested, along with two of his partners, Jay Topkis and Ernie Rubenstein.

The original plan was to raise $750,000. We went to George Green, the former president of *The New Yorker,* for advice. He looked at our business plan and said, "Double it." Then, after a pause, he added, "And then double it again." We did manage to double the amount we raised before we launched.

About two weeks before closing, John Goelet completely disappeared on us. This was in the days before email and cell phones. To disappear was to disappear. This was not good. And finding $500,000 in half a month was a daunting thought. That week I happened to have lunch with Gary Fisketjon, the editorial director of the Atlantic Monthly Press. Gary was a rising star as an editor of new American fiction, having brought in, among other books, his pal Jay McInerney's *Bright Lights, Big City.* In passing I mentioned the case of the missing Goelet. Gary thought for a moment and then suggested that we should meet Carl Navarre, a champion shot, the owner of Atlantic Monthly Press, and, not incidentally, a Coca-Cola bottling heir. We went to see him, and Carl stepped in and replaced Goelet's half-million-dollar investment just days before we were due to close.

With no grand plan to do so, we launched in the fall of 1986 at what seemed like a perfect moment in the never-ending trajectory of New York. The city had recovered from its near bankruptcy in the 1970s. Financiers and the life-forms that had grown around them—investment bankers and lawyers—were awash with money. The downtown art world was booming. Yuppies, in all their young, upwardly mobile professionalness, were cornering the market on BMWs, yellow ties, and high-tech kitchen appliances. Hip-hop culture was exploding around us. New York had become a city of big hair and egos and long stretch limousines. It was the time of the "ladies who lunch" while their husbands were off draining the bank accounts of widows and orphans. At the same time, AIDS was on its long, deadly march through the gay community. Kurt and Tom and I believed that we knew enough to gin up the perfect magazine for ourselves and our friends. And we were foolish enough to think that all this rampaging and bridge burning wouldn't have an effect later.

In *Spy*, we wanted a magazine of wit, satire, and what Kurt called literate sensationalism. We wanted humor combined with hard reporting. We wanted the voice to be a mixture of *Time*-ese from the 1940s, with its dense, fact-filled writing, and the saucy manner of London's *Private Eye*. To the best of our knowledge, this hadn't been done before in the U.S.—a combination of shoe-leather journalism and bracing satire. There were great journalists. And there were great humorists. But we had to find journalists who could get the story and then write it with a dash of distance and irony.

There were writers out there who were both good reporters and funny. The Style section of *The Washington Post* in those days was particularly fertile ground for writers with a keen, observational eye and a wicked voice. Sally Quinn, Marjorie Williams, and Lloyd Grove were standouts. At *The New York Times*, Maureen Dowd, William E. Geist, and Alessandra Stanley accomplished the near impossible: getting funny, contemporary writing into the paper's gray, bloodless pages. We couldn't afford them, though. Besides, nobody was going to leave a job at one of the nation's celebrated broadsheets for a risky magazine start-up. We needed to develop our own farm team of Dowds and Quinns.

Mad magazine was a huge influence on us. Both Kurt and I read it all through adolescence. Aside from the jokes and the parodies, it did something that we attempted to do at *Spy*. It explained things—how things in the adult world worked. It's where I learned about Madison Avenue, cocktail parties, sororities, movies, TV shows, and all manner of other aspects of American life and industry. Strangely enough, another influence was Looney Tunes, the Warner Bros. cartoon unit. Where Disney animated characters were wholesome and generally uplifting, there was something about Bugs Bunny, Daffy Duck, Marvin the Martian, Foghorn Leghorn, and the rest of the Looney Tunes lot that was darker, more sophisticated, and vaguely anarchic—catnip to young boys of the time. The first images I had ever seen of movie stars like Humphrey Bogart, Clark Gable, and Charlie Chaplin were in caricature form in Looney Tunes cartoons when I was a preteen. Bugs was downright inspirational—cool, collected, and funny in the face of adversity. We wanted to be outsiders on the ramparts picking off the big shots. We wanted to champion the underdog and bite the ankle of the overdog.

Our first issue had the DNA for much of what would come later. We had a feature on the ten most embarrassing New Yorkers, including the thunderous Yankees owner George Steinbrenner and a certain "short-fingered vulgarian"—a slick developer making his debut in the magazine, Donald Trump. A photo essay on what nightclubs looked like in the morning was shot by Sylvia Plachy, the mother of the then thirteen-year-old future Oscar-winner Adrien Brody. Another story attempted to sort out things that back then got mixed up a lot, like Sakharov and Shcharansky, Euripides and Sophocles, and bathos and pathos. A map of gangland New York pinpointed mob landmarks. We ran unflattering stories on John Lydon (Johnny Rotten), Keith Haring, and the writer Tama Janowitz. And we outlined the dietary requirements in a Beach Boys concert contract.

We held the first of several *Spy* "balls" in the vast ballroom of the Puck Building at Houston and Lafayette in SoHo and hired the Kit McClure Band, an all-women swing orchestra. We had them kick off the night with "Sing, Sing, Sing (with a Swing)," the 1936 jazz standard composed by Louis Prima. It became the opening song for every *Spy* event thereafter. Since we had no money for decorations, we made the evening black tie, thinking that the dressed-up guests would be the decor. The turnout was something of a hit with the art, literary, and downtown worlds. A number of bold-faced names, like Andy Warhol and Malcolm Forbes, came to the event, sniffing around to see what all the fuss was about.

We had leased office space on the top floor of the Puck Building. It seemed fitting to us: a century before, the building once housed *Puck*, America's first humor magazine. The space had huge windows and arched, brick ceilings. The offices hadn't been finished when we moved in, and for the first four months construction raged around us. There was no air-conditioning that first summer, and at the end of a day of noise and construction dust we returned home drenched in sweat and looking like we had been working in a chalk mine. We borrowed old desks and chairs from our landlord. A lovely old Austrian man in a military-like uniform operated the cage elevator.

SoHo wasn't quite SoHo then. The name itself was a recent real estate portmanteau for the area South of Houston. The cast-iron architecture provided the neighborhood with proper bones that in years to come would attract the great fashion houses of Paris and Milan. But before that, the cobblestone streets were quiet and shops were mostly one-off affairs, a lot of them selling vintage clothing and furniture. The Gaseteria, an all-night service station, was across the street. *Details* and *Paper* magazines were close by. Mob hangouts were around the corner on Mulberry Street. Clubs like Milk Bar, Area, and Danceteria were nearby and became hangouts as we settled in. Robert Mapplethorpe was a regular at the NoHo Star, the restaurant we went to for lunch most days—which gave it high marks in our books.

SoHo was also rife with the criminal element. One snowy afternoon before Christmas, I bumped into a fellow in the alley at the side of the Puck Building. He asked if I wanted to buy a Sony camcorder. I did. I most certainly did. My second son, Max, had been born, and I desperately wanted to take home movies. But I didn't have the $300 that camcorders cost. The fellow showed me the box, and it looked like it hadn't been opened. He said he'd sell it for $125. I went to a nearby ATM and met him back at the appointed time. We made our exchange, and I raced up to the office with my new purchase. The others gathered around as I opened it. As I got further through the unwrapping, my heart began to sink. I pulled away at the paper, and soon all that was left was a small piece of concrete with some wires wrapped around it. Kurt picked up one of the wires and said, "So this would go where?" The dear ones at the office took up a collection and the next day presented me with a certificate that I could redeem for a real camcorder. I was incredibly touched by this gesture. I thanked them, returned the check, and decided to buy my electronics through more traditional channels going forward.

Kurt and I spent a lot of time in those early months working on the house voice for *Spy*. We wanted a bemused detachment but witheringly judgmental. As I said, we borrowed heavily from *Private Eye* and the *Time*-ese writing of the newsweekly's earlier days. *Time* labeled people with unflattering epithets along the lines of "jug-eared lefty" and was famous for its inverted sentences. Wolcott Gibbs published a profile of its founder, Henry Luce, in *The New Yorker* in the mid-'30s, and wrote the whole thing in an over-egged version of *Time*'s style back then. "Backward ran sentences till reeled the mind. . . . Where it all will end, knows God." We figured that once we got the voice down, the other writers would essentially parody it and then just write like it. Which is precisely what happened.

We made fun of a cast of regular subjects, thinking that the more they were mentioned, the more readers outside the city would care about what we said about them. We also gave them adjective-heavy epithets. Donald Trump was already our "short-fingered vulgarian." Abe Rosenthal, the successful former executive editor of *The New York Times* and later a less successful columnist, became "Abe 'I'm writing as bad as I can' Rosenthal." His wife, Shirley Lord, was always the "bosomy dirty book writer Shirley Lord" in the pages of *Spy*. The poor couple detested us. And with good reason.

One day one of our interns mentioned that he had been at the video store and Abe was in front of him at the cash register. "You didn't happen to see what he rented, did you?" I asked. He had indeed. And the films were a lot bluer than the sort of fare you'd expect from an esteemed *Time*sman. A day or two later, I was having lunch with a friend who worked at *Vogue,* where Shirley was beauty director. In a story meeting the subject of sleep had come up and Shirley described the five-pillow formation—including one between his legs—that Abe assembled prior to nodding off. I combined the video rentals and the intimate details of his sleep choreography and gave the information to our *Times* columnist, the pseudonymous

J. J. Hunsecker, named for the lethal gossip columnist played by Burt Lancaster in *Sweet Smell of Success*. Hunsecker duly put all of this in the next issue. I can only imagine the paranoia this level of domestic intrusion must have set off in the Rosenthal-Lord household.

When Larry Tisch, of the New York Tisch real estate family, bought CBS and began firing hundreds, we ran a column on him and gave Tisch the epithet "churlish dwarf billionaire." My pal John Scanlon called the day the issue hit the newsstands in something of a rage. "Graydon, you've gone too far this time!" he bellowed into the phone. John was working for Tisch, and in the course of our call, he pointed out that, first of all, Larry "is not, technically, *medically*, a dwarf." I wrote this down and in the next issue we reported on the call, quoting a CBS factotum as having given us that correction in those very words. I received an even more furious call from John afterward.

The thing is, by and large, we didn't really know any of the people we were writing about. There was an element of safety in that. It meant that we wouldn't be bumping into our subjects at night. Editing *Spy* was like carpet-bombing at twenty-five thousand feet—as opposed to hand-to-hand combat. That's not to say the subjects didn't bite back. One month we ran an article called "Gore Vidal's 8 Bonus Tips on How to Feud." Tip number eight was "When all else fails, sue." A few days after the issue hit the newsstands, I got a call from Gore. He said that if we didn't print a retraction, he'd sue. Years later when we were working together at *Vanity Fair*, I asked him if he saw the contradiction, or at least the irony, in him threatening to sue over being called litigious, and he said that he didn't. I left it at that. In the Party Poop section another month we ran a photograph of Jill Krementz, the wife of Kurt Vonnegut, identifying her as "champion namedropper and celebrity photographer." Vonnegut called me in a fury. He said that his wife did not name-drop—she simply had a lot of famous friends and liked to talk about them. "Let me leave you with this," Vonnegut said, ending the call, "if you don't already have cancer, I hope you get it."

The core group of editors would meet in our conference room for a lunch-cum-editorial-meeting once a week. Most of the men wore jackets and ties and the women wore tailored pants or skirts. Our tacit bond was the idea that revolutionary writing would have more weight if you didn't look like a ruffian. Kurt sat at one end of the long table, and I sat at the other. We had all carved our initials into it.

There was *SM* for Susan Morrison, who had worked on one of Lorne Michaels's shows and had done a stint at *Vanity Fair.* She was the only one with a proper Rolodex and was our outreach to established writers. She was funny and quick and edited or wrote much of the copy that Kurt and I didn't get around to. We thought of Susan as a true sophisticate, an impression that was ever so slightly tarnished one day when she told me excitedly that a herd of elephants had just come through one of the tunnels into New York.

"They do it every year," I told her.

"What do you mean?"

"It's for the circus," I said. "They even have a name for it: 'Elephant Walk.'"

Forever after, I'd torture her with the expression any time she suggested something that was painfully obvious or well-known.

There was *BH* for Bruce Handy, a lanky, good-looking Californian who had gone to Stanford and had the slyest of wits. *GK* stood for George Kalogerakis, the only native New Yorker, who had come from a dead-end job at *The Times.* His application arrived on Drones Club stationery—something he had had printed up based on the club frequented by Bertie Wooster and Gussie Fink-Nottle in the P. G. Wodehouse novels. He had a wry signature style that we called on when we later published a history-cum-anthology of *Spy. JM* was Jamie Malanowski, a cheerful veteran from the political world whom

Scanlon had sent our way. He was there from the beginning too. Jamie's chief asset, he said when we interviewed him, was that he had "a lead ass"—the inference being that he was a worker. And he was. Joining us later were *TF*—Tad Friend, just out of Harvard, who looked like an extra from one of those old MGM Andy Hardy movies—and *JC* for Jim Collins, a tall, funny Harvard alum who had more talent than ambition. *PS*, Paul Simms, yet another Harvard grad and later a hugely successful showrunner, joined us as well.

The outside world thought of the *Spy* creators as miserable misfits. In fact, they were incredibly sociable, well-dressed, and balanced. They knew their Negronis from their stingers. They knew Wodehouse and Perelman and Waugh. And they were as versed in funny stories from the old *National Lampoon* as they were in high-minded criticism in *The New York Review of Books*. It was positively Hellenic. What set them all apart were their brains and wit. A whole generation of gifted writers flew through our offices, some staying for years, before heading off for the more lucrative playing fields, writing for *The Simpsons* or *Late Night with David Letterman*. It's rare for me to watch an episode of *The Simpsons* and not see a name in the credits that had once been on the *Spy* masthead. They all wrote beautifully, but Kurt was the best of the lot. He composed the funny, lyrical essays that opened each issue. He was able to thread two or three storylines of the previous month's news into a seamless, exquisitely written piece of journalism that just bowled me over.

⌐

Life at *Spy* was by and large a collegial, convivial affair. There wasn't drinking during office hours. But alcohol did lubricate things once the whistle blew. We assumed that many of the younger members of the staff, who would gather at bars in the neighborhood after work, were seeing each other in a manner that can only be described as nonprofessional. One such couple, Aimée Bell and David Kamp, who both started as interns at the magazine, got married and are still happily together. (I am godfather to their son Henry.) Word of the sheer fun we were all having spread quickly, and in no time, I was getting calls from people at Condé Nast and Hearst desperate to come over. Our pay rates dimmed their appetite for working at a scrappy downtown magazine considerably, and all pretty much stayed at their stations. Other magazine editors, desperate to get "edgier" writing, whatever that meant, into their pages, sent emissaries looking to lure our writers for freelance assignments. We had a rotating cast of receptionists, many of them actors and performance artists and all of them more colorful than the people they were answering the phones for.

We strong-armed a number of friends who were proper writers to contribute—Roy Blount Jr., Walter Kirn, Andrew Sullivan, Holly Brubach, Bruce Feirstein, David Owen, Ellis Weiner, Paul Rudnick, and John Heilpern, among others. I approached both Christopher Hitchens and the illustrator Bruce McCall to contribute, but both turned me down. They loved the idea of *Spy*; not so much our pay rates. Young writers like David Kamp, Ted Heller, Nell Scovell, and Henry Alford, all of whom went on to illustrious careers, got their start scribbling away on *Spy* stories.

At one point, the staff writers announced that they were going on strike. They were all getting about $100 a week and wanted something in the region of $125. Kurt and I both hated the idea of an organized protest in the office. Eric Kaplan, yet another brilliant young Harvard grad who went on to a celebrated career writing for television, was working as an intern at $50 a week. He joined the writers in protest. One day he was listlessly sweeping the floor outside Kurt's and my offices, and I started humming "The Internationale." He picked up his pace a bit. Rather than confront the writers as a group—there were only five—we met with them individually. In each case, I would push a piece of paper across the desk with a single name on it: McLean Stevenson. In each instance, the writer asked who that was. And in each case, I said, "Exactly." I told them that he was a cast member who left the hit television show *M*A*S*H* after the early seasons and was never heard from again. In the end, we raised their salaries commensurate with their worth and talents. And so ended the period of labor unrest at *Spy*.

Spy's art direction received almost as much attention as its writing. We had a series of art directors, including Stephen Doyle, B.W. Honeycutt, Alex Isley, and Christiaan Kuypers, all of whom added their own embellishments to the look of the magazine. We wanted elegance in our typefaces, not the goofy fonts so often associated with humor magazines. Our editorial and photo budgets were minimal. We developed a look that included floating heads. These came from public relations photos—which were free to use. We then silhouetted them by hand and used them on a regular basis. They helped give the magazine its distinctive look—a look that has been copied by more established publications for years.

Its sheer shock value made *Spy* an early hit. We wrote about and lampooned everybody who was part of New York's social and professional life, and circulation soared. There had been nothing really like it before, and it caught the city by surprise. In truth, Kurt and I just wanted to come up with story ideas that would make the other one laugh. Tad Friend and Paul Simms spent almost half a year working on *Spy Notes*, our parody of *CliffsNotes*, the collegiate study guides for great literature, with plot summary, major characters, and themes. We applied them to Jay McInerney and Bret Easton Ellis and the rest of the literary brat pack of the '80s and their books *Bright Lights, Big City*; *Less Than Zero*; *Slaves of New York*; and *The Rules of Attraction*. "Even funnier than the originals," we said on the cover. *CliffsNotes* sued our book publisher for trademark infringement. The case went to court and we won, resulting in a landmark verdict. A feature on mob restaurants and residences in the city was either daring or foolhardy, given the fact that many of them were located perilously close to our offices in the Puck Building, which was on the edge of what could still legitimately be called Little Italy. The Gambino family's Ravenite Social Club was only a couple of blocks away, on Mulberry Street, and John Gotti, the head of the Gambino family before he was sent to prison, where he died, was a common sight in the neighborhood. Lisa Lampugnale, one of our fact-checkers, who went on to a successful career in stand-up comedy, remembered, "I'm walking near the offices and John Gotti walks by and I think it's because of the mob address map and Gotti is mad and I'm going to get killed."

Instead of trying to cover the entire media landscape in our magazine, Jann Wenner gave me the idea of just concentrating on *The New York Times*—then a Kremlin-like fortress of inscrutability and intrigue. To write about *The Times* in anything other than groveling praise was to court certain career death. Our monthly column by J.J. Hunsecker regularly poked fun at the editors of the paper. The day the column came out, work would all but shut down at *The Times* while the reporter-level hands photocopied and passed it around. We did a similar column on the then most powerful talent agency in Hollywood, Creative Artists Agency. This one was also written under a pseudonym—Celia Brady, a bastardization of the name of the narrator in Fitzgerald's *The Last Tycoon*.

We had so much inside information on the goings-on at the agency that its head, Mike Ovitz, reportedly hired a private eye to track down the identity of the writer posing as Ms. Brady. The detective failed in his mission. Celia Brady's identity, along with Hunsecker's, remains a secret to this day. Years later, when I was editing *Vanity Fair*, Si Newhouse and I happened to be in London at the same time and we were both staying at the Connaught. We had dinner with some friends of his at the hotel's grill, and at one point Si whispered to me, "You know what I always wish you'd done when you were at *Spy*?" "No," I replied. "What?" He said, "I wish you'd had a column similar to the *Times* column, but about Condé Nast." "Really?" I said. "Why?" He smiled and said, "So I would have known what was going on!"

We had a superb and very diligent lawyer, David Korzenik. I remember once we were arguing a point and I wouldn't back down from something he wanted removed. I felt he was being overly cautious.

Finally, I said, "What are you going to do if I don't take this out?"

And he said, "I don't know, Graydon. I think I might call your parents."

I thought that was funny, so I made the change.

Our notable scoops often took months to assemble—a whole year in the case of creating the complete client list of Ovitz's pathologically secretive CAA. Not even the agents knew all the stars, directors, and writers the company represented. The full list encompassed pretty much all the above-the-line talent in Hollywood at that time. Agents were suddenly busy mollifying stars who weren't getting the scripts they thought they should be after seeing their rivals on the list.

We published a positively groveling letter that Tina Brown had written to Ovitz asking for an interview. Tina had been the editor of *Tatler*, and then had been brought in to edit *Vanity Fair*. Bruce Handy provided a spirited annotation to the letter. Among her entreaties, Tina had written: "Right now, the most hackneyed prevailing perception of you is as a 'packager.' . . . It seems to me that a better term for your role in the life of Hollywood would be a *catalyst*: activating creativity by a gifted sense of talent, material, timing and taste, plus, of course, extraordinary business acumen in putting it all together. Probably no one since [Irving] Thalberg has seeded so many creative partnerships or brought so many movies to the screen." She closed off by saying that, just in the last two months, the following people had written to tell her they read *Vanity Fair* cover to cover: Henry Kissinger, Calvin Klein, John le Carré, Louis Malle, Brooke Astor, and the U.S. ambassador to the Philippines.

The letter, which we had gotten through somewhat nefarious means, had been kept (I was later to learn) in the offices of Jane Sarkin, the magazine's emissary to Hollywood. Jane was on her honeymoon with her husband, Martin O'Connor, at the Coral Beach Club in Bermuda when the issue of *Spy* with the annotated letter was published in the summer of 1990. A call from New York was patched through to her room. Picking up the phone, Jane endured a blistering tirade from Tina. Calls like this persisted for the rest of her honeymoon. I can only imagine Jane's horror when, two years later, I was appointed to be the editor of *Vanity Fair*. She was worried that she'd be fired. I, not really having any appreciative juice with Hollywood, worried that she'd quit. In the end, we spent twenty-five incredible years working together. The topic of the letter and dear Jane's botched honeymoon only came up two or three times a year. It was something we could both, quote-unquote, laugh about.

We didn't set out for *Spy* to be mean, but, like *Mad* magazine, we did want to present what we thought were unvarnished truths about how things worked. What it was like inside the highly secretive Bohemian Grove, for example. It was and is the old-school version of the Allen & Co. Sun Valley Conference. At Sun Valley, large corporations are traded and fortunes made. At Bohemian Grove, a 2,700-acre campground a couple of hours north of San Francisco, former presidents and establishment elders, who already had their corporations and fortunes, traded nations and engaged in naughty-boy juvenilia, like telling off-color jokes and peeing in the redwood forest. It's where the Manhattan Project, established to design and build the first atomic bomb, was launched in 1942. The rules held that no talk of business was permitted, but aside from that, some highly strange and puerile rituals took place.

My brother-in-law Todd Williamson was then working at a restaurant in San Francisco. He told me that the managers at Bohemian Grove were looking for waiters to help out with that year's reunion. And so with a good deal of advance work and planning, we managed to smuggle the writer Phil Weiss into the Bohemian Grove, posing as a waiter. He got the most extraordinary copy, including overhearing Henry Kissinger (an esteemed foreign policy expert in the pages of *Vanity Fair*; a "socialite war criminal" in the pages of *Spy*) telling not particularly funny CIA-KGB jokes. It was seriously good reporting and good writing. And it caused a furor. Three decades later, a member of Bohemian Grove invited me to join him there. I told him that I would dearly like to come, but there was the matter of the story we published way back when. After I recounted some of the details of the report, he thought better of the invitation. "They have long memories," he said.

It was never great to find yourself in the pages of *Spy*. But it was worse never to be mentioned. Nora Ephron told me that when *Spy* came out, she'd rush to the newsstand and leaf through a copy and be relieved when she didn't see her name in it. And then she'd be slightly miffed. There were enough proper nouns in an issue that not having any purchase in *Spy* meant you didn't really matter that much.

⌐

I thought it would be good to have a few advisers for the magazine. So I reached out to Jann, Lorne Michaels, and Clay Felker—all at the top of their various games in the creative-industrial complex.

Jann had founded *Rolling Stone* twenty years before and was still its operating force. Lorne was running *Saturday Night Live*, the show he had created a decade earlier. And Clay had made a name for himself publishing writers like Tom Wolfe, Gloria Steinem, Pete Hamill, and Jimmy Breslin in the weekend magazine of the old *Herald Tribune*. The newspaper folded in 1966, and out of the ashes, two years later, he created *New York* magazine. Clay was in a professional limbo at the time, but still a formidable figure in the magazine world.

I had gone to Lorne during our fundraising period. He turned me down in the nicest possible way. His rationale was that creative people don't invest—others invest in them. To celebrate *Spy*'s impending launch, he took me to a Yankees game. It was my first trip in a stretch limousine. Also in the car was Keith McNally, a restaurateur and the brother of one of my closest friends, Brian. And Chevy Chase, whose career Lorne had launched on *Saturday Night Live*. Chevy had just made *Fletch* and *National Lampoon's European Vacation* and at the time was in some ways the biggest male movie star in the world. He was the host of the Academy Awards the next year and the year after that. That day at Yankee Stadium I watched as a line of dozens of fans snaked up the aisle to get Chevy's autograph.

A quarter of a century later I ran into him at the Chateau Marmont. His career had suffered following far too many confrontations with colleagues and a number of box-office misfires. I was having dinner in the hotel's lobby with friends. There was a piano beside us, and Chevy came over and asked if we minded if he played. We said not at all. For the next three hours, this former movie star and former host of the most important night in Hollywood played the piano—beautifully, I should add—and not a single person came over to ask for an autograph or say hello. Los Angeles, one of the sunniest of American cities, is also, hands down, the coldest.

When it came to *Spy*, Clay's early advice was to run party photos up front so that advertisers had an indication of the sorts of people who were reading the magazine. We did run party photos, but not in the way he suggested. Ours caught the subjects off guard and in their cups, with funny captions written by Susan Morrison. Clay was a complicated figure. A *Time* magazine story about him in 1977 had this to say: "He is variously described by associates and acquaintances as autocratic, devious, dishonest, rapacious, egotistical, power mad, paranoid, a bully, and a boor." He had been close to the *Spectator* columnist Taki and his wife, Alexandra, but after Taki was arrested in 1984 for possession of cocaine and shipped off to Pentonville prison, which once hosted Oscar Wilde, they didn't hear a thing from Clay. A few weeks after Taki had been jailed, Clay finally called Alexandra—but not to wish Taki well or find out how he was faring. He called to get the name of the chintz they used for their living room curtains.

Still, to me, he was a big, successful editor, and I wanted to get his read on our prospects. About nine months after we launched, I went over to see him at the apartment on East 57th Street that he shared with his wife, Gail Sheehy. The apartment had a double-height ceiling and a Juliet balcony at one end of the living room. I couldn't believe editors could live on such a level. He told me that he had been studying *Spy* carefully.

"What do you think we should do?" I asked.

"Fold it," he said. "It's not going to work. You're not going to get the readers you want. It's just not going to work."

Fold it? I thought he was kidding at first. But he wasn't. I was completely numb.

Just then he got a phone call. Clay said, "Hi, Herb." Now the only Herb I knew of was Herb Lipson, who owned a number of city magazines. He had founded *Manhattan, inc.*, a smart monthly edited by the truly gifted Jane Amsterdam that studied New York through its various industries. We were big fans of it at *Spy* and considered it high-level competition. Based on my hearing only one end of the conversation, I could tell that Clay and this Herb were agreeing to something—I just wasn't sure what. That evening, I went with some friends to Elaine's, the Upper East–side canteen for the literary and show business set. We were sitting at one of the round tables along the right wall that Elaine set aside for writers and friends.

Clay and Gail came in. As they made their way through the restaurant, I could see that he was being congratulated for something. We said hello and he continued on, shaking hands and basking in the glow of the attention. I turned to the Vienna-born historian (and later *Vanity Fair* colleague) Frederic Morton, who was sitting at the next table: "Hey, Fred, what's this all about?" Fred just looked at me and said, "You haven't heard? Clay was just made editor of *Manhattan, inc.*!" I was dumbfounded. He'd taken a job at one of our competitors on the same day that he'd told me to fold our magazine. I never spoke to him again.

Clay's warning notwithstanding, *Spy* was a local hit, then a national hit, and then an international one. Not a week went by when a print reporter or a news crew didn't shimmy into the office for a story on this cheeky New York monthly. To some degree, it gave news organizations cover to repeat some of the outrageous things we wrote about our subjects without having any ownership themselves. One time I was on *MTV News* with Kurt Loder, which was very much the voice of the new generation. DJ Jazzy Jeff and Fresh Prince (Will Smith, as he is now called) were also on the show that day. As we were leaving the studio after the taping, they came up to me and asked where I got my overcoat—a Chesterfield in fawn-colored whipcord with a muddy-green velvet collar.

"At Anderson & Sheppard," I said.

They asked who to contact there. I said, "Ask for Mr. Halsey."

Now, Mr. Halsey was, as noted, Norman Halsey, one of the chief tailors at the firm and a throwback to the Edwardian era, both in dress and demeanor. I was more than prepared to hear from him with a query along the lines of *Mr. Carter, we have a Mr. DJ Jazzy Jeff and a Mr. Fresh Prince here and they are inquiring about that Chesterfield coat we made for you a few years ago.* I shuddered with happiness.

At *Spy*, we wrote and produced a number of half-hour comedy shows for NBC, one hosted by Jerry Seinfeld and the other by Julia Louis-Dreyfus, and these were done *before* they started working on *Seinfeld*. At one point we thought it might be good to get a professional agent. Nancy Josephson, who would one day run ICM, suggested Sam Cohn. Now, Sam was truly a legend in the business. He handled much of the big-name New York talent of the time, including Woody Allen, Mike Nichols, Paul Newman, and Meryl Streep. He was famous for his regular booth at the Russian Tea Room, for his habit of eating paper to ease his nerves, and for not returning phone calls. He took us on. After a year or more of complete inaction on his part, we decided to look for another agent. We thought it polite to tell him this before we made any change. The problem was, we couldn't get him on the phone. After months of trying, we just threw up our hands. He stayed our agent, and we never produced another TV show again.

⌐

Kurt, Tom, and I paid ourselves $37,500 that first year. I had two sons, Ash and Max, by the time we launched, and Cynthia stayed home to take care of them. We were blessed by having a rent-stabilized apartment. It had high ceilings, a small library, a living room with a fireplace, French pocket doors, a dining room, and a second bedroom. I paid $280 a month for it. A different time. Today, the apartment would probably rent for twenty-five times as much. Even so, I constantly had to figure out ways to earn extra money. I began drawing a monthly caricature for Emma Soames when she became the editor of *Tatler* in London. They were nothing to write home about—and indeed few subjects or readers did. Emma was a spirited and lively editor. But her magazine was considered too astringent for the Sloane Square set *Tatler* aspired to. That Emma was the granddaughter of Winston Churchill only made the class betrayal sting more.

Emma was let go a few years after taking over and her replacement was a woman named Jane Procter. She wasn't a popular figure in the office, and one of her first directives upon taking over—and a wise one at that—was to rid herself of my wretched drawings. Which she did by fax.

I also wrote a semi-regular column on the comings and goings in New York for the *Evening Standard*, London's then widely read afternoon paper. The column was on a par with my *Tatler* caricatures, and once the paper was taken over by Paul Dacre—a legend for his furies and rudely picturesque language—he got rid of me too. Again, by fax. I then wrote occasional columns for the *Daily Mail*, which Dacre himself had graduated to. Fortunately for him they were rarities, so no need for him to get rid of me in any sort of formal manner.

Though the *Spy* staff itself was paid a pittance (half of them were $50-a-week interns), we arranged for a series of barter deals to help compensate them. One was with a dental office, Lowenberg and Lituchy. They got advertising pages, and the staff got free dental care. They are still my dentists. A number of barter arrangements were with restaurants—most of them in Greenwich Village or farther downtown. They got advertising pages, and we got credit for the amount of the contract at the restaurants. At the end of every issue, we used our barter money to take over one of the spots and have what we called "Closing Dinners." They were raucous, liquid affairs that left most of us straggling late into the night. I don't know of another magazine that did this. Those nights were important. They brought the staff together on a regular basis, and like so much of a journalist's life in those days, they were just plain fun. At Christmas, I would put on a Santa costume and hand out Secret Santa gifts to the staff, who would come up one by one and sit on my lap. Kurt and Tom included. I stole a sort of guttural wolf-growl, faux-licentious style from the old Bob Hope movies. It was the kind of thing that would give HR departments conniptions today.

—

Editorially, we had a hoot. Henry Alford compared Elvis's weights on other planets. *The New Yorker* didn't accept letters to the editor, so we reached out and ran them ourselves. *The New Yorker* didn't have a masthead either, so we spent six months assembling one. We ran a story on Anne Bass, Mercedes Kellogg, Nan Kempner, and the sleek chatelaines then running the salons of the Upper East Side. The story, written by Nell Scovell, then married to one of the lower-ranking members of the Tisch family, was called "Too Rich and Too Thin." This was her first sentence: "In New York there is an inverse relationship between a woman's dress size and the size of her apartment. A size 2 gets a 14-room apartment. A size 14 gets a two-room apartment."

Back in the day, when books mattered more than they do now, certain books could make a certain segment of the city stop. People just sat down and read them—in part so they wouldn't be left out of the conversation. William Styron's *Sophie's Choice* was like that. So were David Halberstam's *The Powers That Be,* Bryan Burrough and John Helyar's *Barbarians at the Gate,* Tom Wolfe's *The Bonfire of the Vanities,* and David McClintick's *Indecent Exposure.* In 1989, *The Andy Warhol Diaries* was published. The book didn't have a narrative beyond the detailing of what Warhol had done every night over the past few decades, including the people he ran into. He had plenty of catty comments. It was a doorstop of a book, coming in at just under nine hundred pages. Everybody was reading it. But it didn't have an index. This was driving both subjects and readers slightly batty. So we decided to produce one. For the next three weeks, a dozen or so interns pored over the book, creating an index that was true both to the diaries and to the voice of *Spy.* We bound it into the next issue. A sample entry:

> Taylor, Elizabeth, mysterious trips to the bathroom with Halston, 49
> resemblance to "fat little Kewpie doll," 115
> "Very fat, but very beautiful," 177
> "John Warner wasn't fucking her," given cocaine by Halston, 178

We devoted an inordinate amount of time creating a "Celebrity Pro-Am Ironman Nightlife Decathlon." This involved sending two interns, John Brodie and Bob Mack, into the night to track and record the activities of British journalist Anthony Haden-Guest, Carl Bernstein, and publisher Morgan Entrekin. Brodie and Mack followed each of the contestants as they made their ways through the pleasures of New York's evening demimonde. An important note: the contestants were blissfully unaware that they were participants in the Ironman Nightlife Decathlon. Our reporters produced detailed accounts of their activities in ten categories, including "hours spent out, number of celebrities seen, number of drinks drunk, and so forth."

And then, of course, there was Donald Trump. In 1983, Art Cooper, the editor of *GQ,* had asked me if I was interested in writing a story on him for the magazine. I wasn't, but I needed the money, so I agreed to do it. Trump was at the beginning of his florid tabloid residency, and since this was going to be his first major bit of national exposure, he let me hang around with him for three weeks. He hated the story when it came out. The piece portrayed him as an outer-borough sharpie with taste that veered toward the showy and the vulgar. And worse, I made the observation that his hands were a bit too small for his body. He was on the cover, and as I later discovered, wanted to keep that issue of *GQ* away from as many of his fellow New Yorkers as possible, so he had his staff go out and buy up copies on the newsstands. (Years later, Si told me that it was the brisk sales of the Trump *GQ* cover that led him to urge Random House to pub-lish Trump's ghostwritten *The Art of the Deal*, which led to the reality TV show *The Apprentice*, which led to where we are now. As they say, a butterfly's wings.)

Trump was not a successful real estate developer and bestselling "author" to us at *Spy*, though. He was a joke. He threatened to sue us and regularly fed rumors of our demise to gossip columnists. At one point we got fed up, and after consulting an actuary—giving him Trump's physical details, age, eating habits, and whatnot—we began a monthly countdown to his own demise, under the headline "Death Be Not Short-Fingered."

I regularly called my old friend from Ottawa, Steve Probyn. Steve was by then working in Whitehall on energy policy for Mar-garet Thatcher, and despite being a serious academic and political savant, he had a wonderful and mischievous sense of humor. One day he said he had a story idea for me. "Why don't you try to get rich people to endorse really small checks?" I liked it. Kurt did too. And so began a yearlong project of seeing whether we could get rich New Yorkers to go to the trouble of signing and then depositing checks in increasingly insignificant amounts. We set up an account for a company called National Refund Clearinghouse. We had a letterhead made up. And the checkbooks arrived from the bank. We sent checks for $1.11 to the home addresses of fifty-eight well-heeled subjects including Si, Leonard Bernstein, Michael Douglas, Salomon Brothers head John Gutfreund, CBS chairman William S. Paley, and Arthur Ochs Sulzberger, the publisher of *The New York Times*. In those days, you had to endorse checks on the back and then someone—presumably an underling—would go to the bank and physically deposit them. Within two months, twenty-six, or almost half, of our subjects had endorsed and deposited the $1.11 checks.

We wanted to see if we could entice the thirty-two people who didn't sign those checks by upping the ante. We sent them refund checks for $2. Six of them went to the trouble of endorsing and depositing them. This list included Carly Simon, Candice Bergen, and Richard Gere. At the same time, we wanted to see what the threshold was for the ones who had signed the $1.11 checks, so we sent them refunds of $0.64. Over the next few months, thirteen signed and deposited the $0.64 checks. This list included Si, Rupert Murdoch, Henry Kravis, Cher, Adnan Khashoggi, and Donald Trump. We decided to push our luck further, by sending this last group checks in the amount of $0.13.

Now remember, this project had taken almost a year of mailing, waiting, remailing, and so forth. The checks for $0.13 went out, and we continued about our business. Within a few months we had our finalists—two men of wealth who took the time and trouble to endorse and deposit checks for $0.13. One was Khashoggi, at that time the most notorious arms dealer in the world. And the other one was a certain short-fingered vulgarian. One of the few wealthy New Yorkers we didn't send checks to was Leonard Stern, the owner of the Hartz Mountain pet-food empire. That's because his son Eddie was the one who did the story—under the pen name Julius Lowenthal.

On the editorial side of things, Kurt and I ran the show, with Susan, George, Tad, Bruce, Jamie, Jim, and Paul as our deputies. Kurt and I ate lunch together, worked a few feet apart, had regular dinners, and even socialized with each other. It was about as close to a marriage as you can get without the touching or taking out the garbage. I wish I could remember a serious disagreement—just for dramatics' sake—but I can't. Well, there was a heated discussion with Joanne Gruber, our gifted managing editor, who also handled copy-editing duties, over the words *careered* and *careened*. But that was about it. And in Tom, we had the most simpatico of business partners. He wasn't the greatest ad salesman. But he was a clever strategist. And his chief love in the whole enterprise was the writing in *Spy*.

—

My schedule was fairly routine in those days. I got into the office around 7:00 and left at 5:30 so I could be home for a family dinner. Once the kids were off to bed, I would edit manuscripts and plan the next day at a small desk in the living room. During the off-school months, I was what was known in New York in the old days as a "summer bachelor." I would stay in the city during the weekdays while Cynthia, Ash, Max, and our third son, Spike, spent the summer in Washington, Connecticut. We had a two-hundred-year-old colonial on the town green that was always badly in need of something—paint? repair? demolition? I found it a haven and imagined myself living there well into old age.

Our apartment building had an ancient wiring system that caused fuses to break with the addition of any sort of extra electrical device. We had an air conditioner in the bedroom that I could only turn on in the summer months if I unplugged the refrigerator. So, from the end of Memorial Day through Labor Day, I had cool air at night, but absolutely no refrigeration. Our landlord, Sol Haselnuss, was justifiably furious that we had this huge, rent-stabilized apartment in his building. If I was even an hour late in paying the rent, an eviction sign would go up on the door.

We couldn't afford to send the kids to camp, and besides, we all loved being with each other. So I came up with "Camp Carter"—a loose assembly of activities that included a version of our own Olympics. I even had medals made up for them. I loved fishing, and after an early dinner I would head over to the Shepaug River near our house for an hour with my fly rod before it got dark. Birthday parties in New York were extravaganzas with clowns and magicians and ponies and whatnot. All things that we couldn't afford. I can juggle and manage a few magic tricks, and so one year I bought a clown costume, figuring that I could use it at my own kids' birthday parties and amortize it over a few years. The first time I tried it with a few tricks like pouring a pitcher of milk into a rolled-up newspaper or poking a large needle through a balloon or juggling four tennis balls, the five-year-olds were either catcalling me or just bored. I retired the getup after that first performance and stored it at our house in Connecticut.

Brian McNally and his wife, Anne, lived near us. Their son James was with us one year on his birthday. Anne was in Paris and Brian was tied up in New York with a problem at one of his restaurants. We got a cake for James, and Cynthia suggested I do some magic tricks to keep him occupied until Brian arrived. I put on the costume, with its bald head and tufts of hair, big floppy shoes, and a wire around the waist that made me look enormous. I had just entered our kitchen prepared to do my tragic assortment of tricks when Brian walked in. He had a camera in his bag and quickly took a snapshot—a photograph he continues to haunt me with to this day. I look like one of those demented serial killers who chases children through corn fields in horror films. Brian gave the photograph to our friend Mitch Glazer, and when I stayed with him and his wife, Kelly, at the house they rented in Martha's Vineyard, they had dozens upon dozens of copies of the photograph made up and taped to every conceivable surface, including under the toilet seat. I wish there was a happy ending to this story, but there isn't. Two of my best friends steadfastly refuse to give up this photo.

—

I phoned my parents in Canada every week. They were happy that I was happy, but I don't think they ever completely understood what I was doing. They certainly never commented on anything in *Spy*. My mother once said that she couldn't understand the magazine at all. Her only compliment during those years came after I was named by *Maclean's* magazine, the Canadian version of *Time*, as one of the "10 Sexiest Canadians." She saw the story and called me to tell me how incredibly proud she was.

In 1989, three years after our launch, *Vanity Fair* commissioned Annie Leibovitz to take a group photograph celebrating the new magazines on the newsstands: publications with names like *Sassy, Wigwag, Taxi, Spin, Model, Egg,* and *Fame*. The '80s were an explosive time for magazine start-ups in New York, and there were some gifted editors in the picture, including Adam Moss (*7 Days*), Betsy Carter (*New York Woman*), Terry McDonell (*Smart*), Annie Flanders (*Details*), and Susan Lyne (*Premiere*). Kurt and I were in the photo, holding copies of *Spy*. Those titles are all pretty much gone now. Publishing a magazine is a brute when it comes to the finances. You have your staff and rent and electricity, all of which must be paid on a regular schedule. You have to pay the writers, photographers, and illustrators. The magazines are then sent all over the country to wholesalers and then individual retailers. The magazines go on the newsstands for a month. And maybe ninety days later, you get paid for the copies sold. Similarly, advertisers—even the flush ones—only paid after sixty to ninety days. The less-flush ones often didn't pay at all. This is all to say, the more successful we got, the more strained our cash flow got.

About two years in from our 1986 launch, Si Newhouse had asked to meet with us, expressing interest in buying *Spy* and bringing it into the Condé Nast fold. In those days, Si ruled over a significant tranche of the city's creative engine. It would not be unreasonable to say that his sway over the minds of America's highbrow and upper-middle-brow readers was without precedent, before or since. On the books side of things, he controlled Alfred A. Knopf and Random House and all their various imprints. With Condé Nast he oversaw *Vogue*, *Vanity Fair*, *The New Yorker*, *Gourmet*, *GQ*, and *Architectural Digest*, among other titles. Writers, photographers, editors, stylists, social-ites, and Hollywood stars—they all wanted to get before his eyes. I think Si was fully aware of his influence over the upper reaches of American print culture, but he wore it all lightly. He might well have been the least boastful powerful person I have ever met.

Kurt and Tom and I put on jackets and ties and headed to the Upper East Side apartment of John Veronis, then the publishing in-dustry's major banker. After the meeting, which lasted an hour, Si gave us a lift back to the office. His car was something uncharacter-istic for him: a stretch limousine. They were in favor in the 1980s, but by the '90s had been replaced by more discreet-looking town cars. Along the way, trying to make pleasant chitchat, one of us asked him what magazines he found interesting. He mentioned *October*, an obscure journal published by MIT that focused on contemporary art. It was a choice we found both mystifying, in that we had never heard of it, and impressive, in that, again, we had never heard of it.

The car dropped Si off at the old Condé Nast offices, at 350 Madison Avenue, tucked into the west side of the block between the Paul Stuart store and the flagship Brooks Brothers store. It then took us down to the Puck Building. We discussed his offer on the ride and then back at the office. As much as we would have loved to work with Si—he was Si Newhouse, after all—we all felt that it was important for a magazine, especially one like *Spy*, to stay independent in its early years. Also, and this is important, we were having too much fun doing it on our own. The next day, Tom called Veronis and said that we would be declining a sale, at least for now. This was a decision made perhaps rashly and foolishly.

By 1990, the magazine was in trouble financially. Our business plan and fundraising were premised on *Spy* being a largely New York magazine with a circulation around 25,000. By the time the *Vanity Fair* photograph of all the editors ran, our circulation was international, and we were selling upward of 150,000 copies a month. It looked good on the outside. But the math just didn't hold up. The gap between when we had to spend the money and when we would get paid for advertising and copies sold was still uncomfortably wide. The initial outflow—on staff, rent, writers, and paper and printing—had grown dramatically, and it dwarfed our initial predictions. We had spurned Si's advances to buy the magazine, and that was the last time anyone came knocking. After a long and wrenching conversation in our conference room, Kurt, Tom, and I decided that we had to sell *Spy*.

We sold the magazine to Charles Saatchi, the British adman, and Johnny Pigozzi, an investor, heir to the Simca car company, and, like Charles, a noted art collector. Shortly after finalizing the sale, Kurt and I were invited to come see Charles and Johnny in London. We were sent tickets for the Concorde. This was about a zillion steps up from the economy seats at the back of the plane that we had become accustomed to. New York to London on the Concorde was supposed to take three hours, but somewhere off the coast of Ireland one of the engines blew. The plane went from 1,400 miles an hour to under 700 miles an hour in a few seconds. It was like hitting a brick wall. We made an emergency landing at Shannon and waited for another British Airways plane to be rounded up. In all, the trip took us about eight hours, just slightly longer than it would have taken aboard a 747.

We had dinner with Charles and Johnny at Charles's house in London. There was a Magritte in the foyer. And a Carl Andre installation of loose bricks on the floor near the door. Charles and Johnny said that they wanted *Spy* to compete with *Vanity Fair.* Which to us was a tall order, in that for the past five years we had been essentially the anti–*Vanity Fair.* And we were operating on a shoestring. It was difficult not to like them both, but for me, the change in ownership and the requested redirection of the editorial mission was unsettling—a bit like the flight over from New York. Kurt was more sanguine about the new order in the *Spy* offices. Faxes would come in from Johnny telling us to do this and that story and put this or that celebrity on the cover. In those days, I used to bristle easily. I felt that it's one thing to coedit a magazine you've started. It's a completely different matter to do the same job under the thumb of someone else. Charles and Johnny didn't ask us to sign employment contracts. Which was somewhat hurtful. But also liberating. For reasons that escape me now, I had a relatively positive attitude about the future.

Chapter 7.

Interlude at *The Observer*

I n the evenings I had started to tinker with something I'd been mulling for a long time—a twice-weekly Berliner-size newspaper that would come out on Tuesdays for shopping ads and on Thursdays for entertainment ads. But I was not going to do it like a regular paper. It was going to be based largely on the major industries that drove New York and the people who steered them: fashion, television, media, advertising, law, theater, government, and art. My idea was to focus on half the professions on Tuesday and the other half on Thursday—but with enough overlap in the two editions that most readers would want to buy both. So, television would be in the Tuesday edition, say, and theater in the Thursday one. Each issue would be anchored by a feature on each of the professions for that day, as well as an attendant industry gossip column.

At lunch with Harry Evans, the former editor of *The Sunday Times* of London, I laid out my plan in some detail, to get his thoughts on the project. And then a few weeks after that, I was invited to a dinner at the East Side apartment that he and his wife, Tina Brown, shared. I was no sooner over the threshold than Tina grabbed me and said, "Harry has the most brilliant idea for a new New York newspaper!"

I was still doing a lot of freelance writing well into the night to make ends meet, including writing for *Vogue* under a year-to-year contract. In addition to *Vogue*, there were any number of pieces I did for other magazines, including *Rolling Stone* and *Esquire*. I measured out my assignments in units of tuition. At a lunch with Anna Wintour, who was editing *Vogue*, I mentioned the newspaper idea. She said that I should talk to Si about it. This was about three years after our discussion with him about buying *Spy*. I called Si's office and was given an appointment to meet with him at 6:00 a.m. a few days later. Si, I knew from chatter around town, was a very early riser. I got dressed carefully, thinking this might be one of life's turning points. I pulled out my now well-worn nail-head gray Anderson & Sheppard suit and, it being winter, the Chesterfield overcoat that DJ Jazzy Jeff and Fresh Prince had so admired.

I got to the Condé Nast Building a little early and walked up and down the block in front of Paul Stuart, rehearsing what I was going to say. It was bitterly cold. Finally, at about 5:55, I took the elevator up to Si's office. I don't know what I expected, but I found it to be unlike any professional space I had ever seen before or since. The walls were covered in original art—all of it from George Herriman's *Krazy Kat* comic strip, a popular newspaper feature between the wars. Si's desk was white, modern, and expansive, with legs that tapered up from the floor the way they do on Saarinen tables. They were covered in the same white carpeting as the office. The effect was of a massive double-tower cat scratcher. On the desk were perhaps a dozen copies of his magazines, along with clipboards, yellow legal pads, black Sharpies, and one of those rubber fingers bank tellers used to use for counting bills.

Si got up to greet me and asked if I would like some coffee and I said, yes, that would be lovely. We sat down and his assistant brought in iced coffee in tall, thin glasses. I was too nervous to drink mine. I explained the paper idea to him. He said it sounded like a good idea but that it was not a great time to launch something like this—this was early 1991. Si thought the country was going to go into a recession. I said, yes, of course, I get it, you're probably right. The meeting drew to a close. I'd put my overcoat over the chair, and as I got up and was thanking him and wrestling with getting my arm into the sleeve, the tail of the coat hit the glass. Like at no other point in my life, time just slowed down as I watched the coffee and the ice fly out in an arc and onto the white carpet that now looked like the hide of a pinto. I kept saying over and over again how sorry I was. Si smiled and put his hand on my shoulder. I will love him forever for his next words. "Oh, don't worry about it," he said. "I do it all the time." Knowing now how Condé Nast operated in those days, orders to have that carpet cleaned or replaced would have been put into effect by the time my feet hit the pavement.

In the end, I never did start that paper. On my rounds to drum up financing, I met with Arthur Carter, a former Wall Street banker who had a house near ours in Connecticut. He was the owner of *The New York Observer*, a desperately sleepy Upper East Side weekly broadsheet that was printed on salmon-colored paper, similar to that of the *Financial Times*. It had a classical look that borrowed heavily from *The New York Times* and *The Wall Street Journal*. *The Observer* was painfully, almost weepingly, dull. It seemed to go out of its way to parade its dullness. On page 2, a valuable piece of real estate in any newspaper, the previous editor had run a map of New York. Not a detailed map or one highlighting the various business areas of the city, like "the flower district" or "the button district," but just a map with the avenues and major side streets. It ran every single week. *The Observer* was that dull. Arthur said he didn't want to invest in my newspaper idea. Instead he offered me a job, editing his own newspaper.

I didn't tell Kurt or Tom about *The Observer* until I had accepted Carter's offer. My feeling was, I suppose, that either they would have tried to talk me out of it or they would have ridiculed me for taking on such a lame paper. That is something I wish I could do over. The news caught them by surprise and I couldn't blame them for being upset. And so, in the summer of 1991, I left *Spy* and Kurt and Tom and the glorious staff, and took over *The Observer.* I had worked out a six-month, nine-month, and twelve-month plan of what I would do to change the paper. Most of my friends thought I had lost my mind.

Arthur's former lawyer, John Sicher, had been running *The Observer,* and whatever gene is part of the makeup of a decent editor, John was missing it. My assistant at *Spy,* Aimée Bell, whom I had hired out of graduate school and who would go on to be my deputy for the next quarter of a century, came to the paper with me. Aimée was perhaps the most efficient, most organizationally practical person I had ever met up to that point. Her father had been a GE executive, and she grew up in a large, accomplished Irish family—light on the Catholicism—in Scranton, Pennsylvania.

The Observer's editorial offices, in a once-grand town house on 64th Street, near Park Avenue, were pleasantly Dickensian. There was worn-oak wainscotting in the public areas and there were fireplaces on each floor. Once I had settled in and gotten to know the staff, I went to work on my plan to make *The Observer* at first readable and then, hopefully, a must read. My overarching thought was to treat the Upper East Side like a small town and make this the newspaper for that town. Every Monday morning, I would come into the office at 5:30 and put Post-it notes on the computer terminals of the half dozen reporters I had inherited. Each Post-it had the story I wanted them to cover for the next issue. By lunchtime we had hashed out the basic outlines of each piece and the reporters went to work.

I would also read the international papers over the weekend and would come in with clippings of stories I thought we could buy the foreign rights to. Aimée would contact the papers, talk down our already low circulation figures, and work out remarkable deals for us to run the pieces. Sometimes we got them for $5 or $10. On Monday afternoon, I would fax all the story ideas to Barry Blitt, the Canadian illustrator and future Pulitzer Prize winner, who was just beginning to make a name for himself in New York. He had done drawings for us at *Spy*, then continued with me not only at *The Observer* but at *Vanity Fair* and *Air Mail*. On Wednesday, we'd pick up Barry's drawings, which would be used to illustrate the stories on the front page.

I brought in John Heilpern, who had left *Vanity Fair* in a snit over something, and I hired John Lahr, who had been a theater critic in London, to write about theater for *The Observer*. I also hired Dafydd Jones, the Boswell of England's Eton-Oxbridge set, to be our house photographer. He had been working at *Vanity Fair* shooting party pictures, but he had a growing family and wanted a professional life that didn't include endless rounds of people drinking to excess. He set up a darkroom in *The Observer*'s basement.

I wanted the staff to be up on the doings of the characters who made up the city's business and nightlife. The city's tabloids ran a number of gossip columns then, and rather than buy multiple copies of each, an intern would scoop them up every morning, copy the columns, and assemble them in something we called the "Gossip Pack." (It was something we had started as an economy measure at

Spy and I continued this at *The Observer* and *Vanity Fair.* After 9/11, we still had an assistant prepare a morning dossier for the staff, but in addition to idle gossip and Wall Street tittle-tattle it included news about the attacks and, later, the wars in Afghanistan and Iraq. We called this addition the "War Pack.")

At a lunch with John Scanlon, he said, "You need to get behind a cause."

I asked him what he meant.

"A cause, a cause. Find something that you can bang on about week after week. It will help get you noticed."

I used to ride my bike in Central Park a lot on the weekends, and I grew to love the open-avenue Mall near the East Seventies. At one end of the Mall was the Naumburg Bandshell, a neoclassical half-domed wedding cake of a structure. It was more than sixty years old, and it looked like it needed a bit of love. I couldn't remember a time when an actual concert was last performed there. For the past three years, there had been a move afoot in the mayor's office to tear it down. The bandshell was admittedly a bit of an architectural eyesore, but I loved it. It seemed more in place in a European park than a New York one, and I guess that was half its charm. My hunch was that something more hideous would go up in its place. So, taking up Scanlon's advice, every week I ran—on the front page no less—a feature about the highlights of the bandshell's storied history and how the city was set to tear it down.

At one point, Betsy Gotbaum, who was the city's parks commissioner, announced an actual date for the demolition. It was a few months out and so I put a weekly demolition countdown clock at the top of the *Observer*'s front page. Betsy started to get calls about it and finally she telephoned me in a fit of frustration and asked if I would meet her at the bandshell. Late in the afternoon of the next day, we met in the park. She showed me the decay, and then the mess left behind by homeless people who had spent the night in the bandshell. Even though I adored and admired Betsy, I was really quite thrilled that I had gotten under her skin on this issue. My argument was that just because it had become a locus for the occasional vagrant—the central thrust of her argument for demolition—this was no reason to tear it down. *The homeless were everywhere*, I said. *If you used that rule of thumb, you'd have to raze half the city.* A few weeks later, Betsy reconsidered her decision. In time, the privately funded Central Park Conservancy took on the job of bringing the bandshell back to its former glory. Every time I walk or drive by it, I say a little prayer for Scanlon.

—

At about the six-month mark, I detected that people were actually reading the paper and it was becoming a thing. That's unfortunately when Arthur began showing an interest in the operation and started offering me story ideas, most of which were dreadful. He had a fiery temper that I tried my best to stay well away from. And I kept him away from my staff as best I could. One day he screamed at Aimée over some perceived misdeed, and I told him he could never talk to anyone on the *Observer* staff like that ever again—and that if he did, we'd all walk out in protest.

I had to have lunch with Arthur every week after the issue shipped to the printers. The lunches were always at Lutèce, on East 50th Street. The restaurant, now long gone, was one of the bastions of old-world French cooking, alongside La Caravelle, Quo Vadis, La Côte Basque, and La Grenouille. It was overseen by its celebrated chef and owner, André Soltner, who would make a performative cameo at lunch hour. I met former president Richard Nixon there one day. He was living in the East Sixties then, and I think he had a lot of time on his hands. He worked his way through the dining room, and when he got to our table, he pressed his business card into Arthur's and my hands. As the months wore on, I grew to despair of those Lutèce lunches. You want the owner to be invested in the success of the enterprise. But you don't want him *too* invested, if you know what I mean. I just wanted to be left alone—which is the overarching goal of all editors.

The paper was getting noticed, though, and so I started sending a couple dozen complimentary copies to friends, many of them editors in Britain and on the continent. I didn't know this at the time, but Si would take a twice-yearly tour of all his international properties, with stops in Milan, Paris, and London. He was on one of these trips in early 1992, and as he told me later, everywhere he stopped, he would see copies of *The New York Observer* in his editors' in-baskets. Si returned to New York under the misguided impression that the paper was a huge international hit—that *everybody* was reading it. About three months later he called me and asked if I would like to get together for a coffee after work. I said of course. This was a Thursday. The meeting was set for Monday.

By this time, I had settled into my life at *The Observer*. I liked the staff. I liked the frequency. And the charms of the rambling old town house had had their effect. Aside from Arthur's meddling and his temper, I liked all of it. And I was relieved by its success—even if it was not the runaway international must read of Si's imagination. On our drive up to Connecticut that Friday, Cynthia and I discussed the meeting with Si. "What if he offers me something like *GQ* or *Details?*" I said. "I don't know if I could do either one. And besides, I'm happy where I am." But I was making $150,000 at *The Observer* and my tuition bills at that point were about $75,000 a year, so there wasn't a lot of money left over. I fretted all weekend about how I was going to handle whatever he was going to say or offer. I was dying to be a part of Si's glittery literary empire. And God knows, we could have used the extra money. On the other hand, I didn't want to take a job that I didn't think I'd be very good at.

On Monday, I hopped in a cab and headed over to Si's apartment at UN Plaza. We settled in a long window seat that overlooked the East River.

Si got right down to it.

He said, "I have two magazines and I wonder if you'd be interested in either one of them."

I braced myself.

"*Vanity Fair* and *The New Yorker.*"

My heart skipped a beat, and I could feel the dryness on my lips. I swallowed. At *Spy*, we'd made an industry out of making fun of *Vanity Fair*, relentlessly—the writers, the editor, the content, everything. It was constant and withering. But I had read *The New Yorker* since I was a kid. I explained my very awkward history with *Vanity Fair* and its staff and contributors.

Si just said, "Well, I guess it's *The New Yorker* then." I felt weak and had trouble speaking.

I was about to leave when he mentioned that we should probably talk about salary. "I was thinking about $300,000," he said. Normal Graydon would have jumped at this. But some rare showing of nerve that had never previously presented itself to me formed words in my mouth that were so outside my general character that I blush about it to this day.

I said, "Oh, that is so wonderful, Si, but the thing is, I'm making that now." A complete and utter bald-faced lie, as you know.

Si thought for a moment. "Well, how much do you want?" he said.

I drew a breath and replied, "Well, I'd love to double that."

Si thought for another moment, then just shrugged and said, "Okay."

Chapter 8.

My *Vanity Fair* Education

I now had the dream job of every magazine person in the world. But I had to keep it all completely secret because the then editor, Bob Gottlieb, was in Japan with, as it turned out, a future colleague, Ingrid Sischy. At home, we came up with a code word for *The New Yorker*. We called it "the Pencil." This was so that Cynthia and I and the kids could discuss it in public places, like restaurants. Outside of that little circle, I told my agent, Andrew Wylie, and Jim, who by then had become one of the top editors at *Time*. They were hugely helpful in figuring out my path forward. Every night after dinner and the kids had gone to bed, I worked in the kitchen, mapping out, as I had done before taking over *The Observer*, a six-month, nine-month and eighteen-month plan. I wanted to change this most revered, if now slightly ossified, magazine into something that would please me as a reader and, with luck and in time, please others. I made lists upon lists of the writers and editors I would bring in. I'm in no way a disruptor for the sake of disruption. My changes would be incremental rather than radical. I believed that I would be at best a caretaker at *The New Yorker*. I certainly didn't feel worthy of filling the shoes of the three people who had gone before me, the magazine's founder, Harold Ross; his successor, William Shawn; and Gottlieb. I figured that, once the news got out about my new job, I would not be alone in that opinion.

About two weeks after the fateful meeting with Si, one of his assistants called me and said that they were going to be announcing the change in two days' time.

The morning of the announcement, Anna Wintour called me and said simply, "Graydon, it's going to be the other one."

I said, "What do you mean?"

She said, "It's going to be *Vanity Fair*. Act surprised when he tells you."

I thought, *Oh fuck*. And I had no choice, I felt, but to accept the news. By this time, in our simple little minds, Cynthia and I were already living on my new salary. We talked about fixing up the kitchen in our apartment a bit and replacing the leaky roof on our house in Connecticut. When Si called, an hour or so later, he said there was a change of plans: "It's going to be *Vanity Fair*. Are you okay with that?" I said yes, of course, absolutely. I put the phone down and began to worry. Behind the scenes, what had happened, clearly, was that Tina, then at *Vanity Fair*, had at the last moment insisted on moving to *The New Yorker*, and Si had agreed. I couldn't really fault either of them in this decision.

But I would be starting without a chance to make the sort of plan I had mapped out for *The Observer* and *The New Yorker*. The clever conscript, caught in this position, would have asked for a little time. *Let the current staff put out the next couple of issues, and I'll take over two months down the road.* That way I would have been able to develop a road map, a plan for what I was going to do with the magazine and who I was going to bring in. And knowing Si, as I came to, he would have been fine with this course of action. But I didn't know that then. I figured that I wouldn't get paid unless I was actually at the wheel. We were a one-income, three-child family. Our third son, Spike, was by then four years old. Money was always scarce. It was never a contentious issue, but frequently a topic of conversation. I felt I had to start immediately in order to stay above water, but without the month or so of preparation I had devoted to what I thought would be a different job. It was an error I would come to regret.

Because of the veil of secrecy that Si had draped over the whole transition, I hadn't been allowed to inform Arthur Carter that I was going to leave *The Observer*. At one point, word began to dribble out. The evening it did, I got home and Cynthia told me that Arthur had already called the apartment. She said that when she picked up the phone, he barked, "Where is he?" Arthur was never one for tact or niceties. I called him back. He was furious. I was to finish off that week's issue and then clear out. I went in the next day to work on my final issue. At the end of the day, I went to Harry and Tina's apartment in the East Fifties. This was where we were to draft the press release announcing the changes. When I knocked on their door, Harry opened it and said, "You idiot. You leaked!" I hadn't at all. I was terrified that if word got out, the whole deal would be off. I hated him for saying that. In addition to Harry and Tina, also there were Steve Florio, the publisher of *The New Yorker*, and Ron Galotti, the publisher of *Vanity Fair*. Harry went to the computer and began banging out a press release. He produced paragraph after paragraph on the accomplishments of his wife, and at the end a few sad sentences about the poor fellow who would be taking her place.

In those days, I tried to live by the old newspaperman's motto of always edit with your hat on—that is, be prepared to leave at any moment. So I didn't have a lot of possessions to take away from the

Observer offices. After we closed that final issue, I delivered a teary farewell to the staff. Arthur's lawyer came to say goodbye. He was embarrassed, I could tell, when he added, "Mr. Carter hopes you won't take anything that doesn't belong to you." I looked around at the threadbare decor and aging equipment and burst out laughing. *The Observer* went on to greater heights after I left, under the steady hand of Peter Kaplan. One of the minor ironies, if you can call it that, is that both *The Observer* and the Puck Building, *Spy*'s old home, were later taken over by the family of Donald Trump's son-in-law Jared Kushner.

—

V*anity Fair* was truly a child of the modern age. Condé Nast— the man, not the company—hired Frank Crowninshield, a sophisticated aesthete-about-town, to edit a publication he had cobbled together from two titles, *Dress* and *Vanity Fair.* It was an inspired choice. Crowninshield had not only been a part of the group that assembled the fabled Armory Show in 1913, which introduced modern art to America, he was also one of the founding creators of the Museum of Modern Art. Crowninshield put out four issues of *Dress and Vanity Fair* in 1913. Then wiser heads decided to drop the *Dress* part.

The name *Vanity Fair* came from the Thackeray novel, which itself was based on a place with the same name in John Bunyan's *The Pilgrim's Progress.* Nast had purchased the title from the British company that owned both *Vanity Fair* and a pleasingly anachronistic weekly called *The Lady,* which offered household tips and ran advertisements for maids and housekeeper jobs. In Crowninshield's hands, over the next twenty-two years, *Vanity Fair* became *the* chronicle of the Jazz Age, with a staff that included Dorothy Parker, Robert

Benchley, P. G. Wodehouse, and Clare Boothe—later Clare Boothe Luce. It attracted some of the great writers of the early part of the century, including F. Scott Fitzgerald, Gertrude Stein, Djuna Barnes, T. S. Eliot, A. A. Milne, and Aldous Huxley. Covarrubias did many of the caricatures that went on the cover. Edward Steichen was the magazine's house photographer. With its emphasis on Jazz Age fizz, it fell out of fashion with the onset of the Depression and the rise of Nazism, and in 1936 Condé Nast folded it into *Vogue*.

In 1981, Si Newhouse announced that he was reviving the title and installed Richard Locke, who had been at *The New York Times Book Review*, as the editor. Si's instructions to Locke were to produce a *New Yorker*—which he did not yet own—but with pictures. Although Locke did just that, somehow the magazine never measured up to the epic promotion campaign prior to its launch, and he was replaced by Leo Lerman and then by Tina Brown. It grew in stature, and by the time I got there, the editorship was considered one of the plum jobs in journalism.

Two weeks after leaving *The Observer*, Aimée and I turned up at the Condé Nast Building for our first day of work. Tina hadn't yet vacated her office on *Vanity Fair*'s floor so we were assigned to a sort of holding pen on the executive floor that had been vacated by Dick Shortway, the departing publisher of *Vogue*. In the afternoon of that first day, I met with the senior staff in the magazine's conference room, where Si introduced me. To say that the collective mood was funereal would be putting a rosy tint on it. New editors generally mean changes, and changes can mean unemployment. When the new editor had spent the past half decade ridiculing the magazine, its senior staff, its contributors, and its house style of over-oxygenated writing, well, that did nothing to lighten the mood. I would have hated me if I was in their place.

I was already getting word that the staff was in revolt. As were the advertisers. The publisher, Ron Galotti, made no secret of his feeling that he had drawn a weak hand. Almost immediately there were rumors—in print and out of it—that I was going to be fired. And I hadn't even put out an issue. Also, at that point I wasn't an American citizen. I was a Canadian with a green card—a work visa that was strictly tied to employment. If I lost this job, I could be sent home. And in disgrace.

Shortway's office was not large, and meetings with outside writers and editors on staff at *Vanity Fair* often resembled the stateroom scene in the Marx Brothers' *A Night at the Opera*. When we at last moved down to the editorial offices on the *Vanity Fair* floor, we encountered what I recall was a riot of burgundy and teal. On the walls outside, where the assistants sat—the job came with two!—Tina had hung framed newspaper and magazine articles that had been written about her. All had been carted off to her new digs at *The New Yorker*, save for one. I didn't want to be seen removing it. This would be a Page Six item waiting to happen. Aimée had an idea. "Let's ask to have the wall painted." The next day, painters arrived and removed the last remnant of Tina Brown's wall of fame.

I would get to the office at 5:00 or 5:30 in the morning to read and edit. I was under terrible pressure. *Vanity Fair* was an exponentially bigger operation than *Spy*, and unlike *Spy*, I hadn't created the magazine, and I was by myself without Kurt. Talent-wise, going from *The Observer* to *Vanity Fair* was like going from managing a boy band like One Direction to managing the Metropolitan Opera. The industry was ridiculing me. The New York establishment, so long coddled by *Vanity Fair*, was in something of a panic.

One day I got a call from Mort Janklow, then one of the leading literary agents. He said, "Well, you've got the job. I just want to make sure you're careful with certain people."

I asked him what he meant by that.

He said, "I just think, you know, you've got this job now, you're going to have to play politics a little more."

In the back of my mind, I recalled that Mort had done time in the pages of *Spy*. One story involved two women meeting at the returns counter of a prominent jeweler in New York. Both were returning necklaces that had been given to them. Both necklaces were identical. And then they discovered that both had been given to them by the same man, Mort Janklow. This may have had something to do with his call. His message to me was *You're not playing on the sandlot anymore. You're in Yankee Stadium, and you have to tiptoe around the people who run it.* I thanked him for his advice.

The first two years at *Vanity Fair* were pretty dreadful. The atmosphere was so poisonous I wouldn't even bring my family into the office. The Tina Brown allies who had been left behind were deeply hostile and subversive. Readers were horrified by my editorial decisions—or so I was told by the holdover staff. Aimée remembers the time as the most hurtful in her life. ("And I went to an all-girls Catholic school with daughters of Mafiosi.") The advertisers—many of whom had also been subjects of interest in *Spy*—were livid. My predecessor had done flattering cover stories on both Ralph Lauren and Calvin Klein—two of *Vanity Fair*'s more prominent advertisers. I wasn't about to continue that trend. But I did have to get them on side. Ralph Lauren, who like most men is sensitive to comments about his size, had been, in fact, a regular *Spy* branch of study. Often we'd run a photo of him with the words "Not actual size" accompanying the caption. Ralph was one of the first people Si thought I should have lunch with. He was guarded at first—how could he not be?—but over time we came to a truce of sorts, and later became friends.

But in those early days and months, pretty much everything went wrong. With a big magazine, you have to constantly feed the beast. For *Vanity Fair*, with anywhere between 120 and 150 editorial pages to fill each month, you have to assign a properly significant story (three thousand to fifteen thousand words) every three days in order to survive. Stories often took months to report and write. Then a month to edit, fact-check, and lay out. Then weeks to print and distribute. Figuring out stories that were both topical and would be of interest months down the line was the key to success. When I arrived at *Vanity Fair*, there was almost nothing lying around that I thought was worth publishing. There was a wonderful dispatch—about Russia, as I recall—by David Remnick, which mysteriously had not run, but by that point it was out of date. I cobbled together the fall 1992 issues as best I could. It would take me the better part of a year to get to the point where issues were able to be built around stories that I wanted rather than ones I could lay my hands on. But first there were some assignments that I had to address that were already in train.

Norman Mailer had been assigned to cover the 1992 Democratic National Convention before I got to the magazine. One night after dinner, as I was editing manuscripts in the kitchen with the convention on television in the background, the cameras panned to the expensive seats in Madison Square Garden, where the famous and important were sitting. And there was Norman, talking to people sitting around him rather than being on the floor where I assumed news was being made. He was up there the next night, and the night after that. When he turned his article in, I read it and thought, *I can't believe I'm doing this, but I simply can't publish it.* There was almost no reporting in what Mailer filed. Much of it was simple observation of what had transpired and it would feel mighty dated by the time it reached readers' hands. It lacked any detail from the back rooms or the floor of the convention. He might as well have watched it on the kitchen television with me. This wasn't brilliant *Armies of the Night* Mailer. This was coaster Mailer, phoning it in for a $50,000 assignment fee. We arranged for a meeting. I was only a few weeks into the job and here I was about to tick off a two-time Pulitzer Prize winner and one of the singular figures of American letters.

When we met at the *Vanity Fair* offices, I said over and over how much I admired him and his writing. Which went down well. But then I had to come to the hard part, the part where I had to tell him that I wouldn't be publishing his piece. Norman was incredulous. In the flurry of words aimed in my direction, he pretty much covered all my own insecurities about being in the job. And he added a few shortcomings that up to that point I hadn't yet considered. After he stormed out, I sat there thinking that this was perhaps the bravest, stupidest thing I had ever done professionally. *What was I thinking?* I said over and over to myself. I should have probably just run the damn article. Later that summer, I doubled down on my steadfast idiocy. Mailer had also been assigned to cover the Republican National Convention in Houston. Not wanting to repeat the drama, I killed that assignment before he even left for Texas. He was paid in full for both assignments. It says much more about Norman than about me that both he and his wife, Norris, were always civil to me afterward. And he never mentioned the whole sorry episode. I certainly wasn't going to bring it up.

The day of the Mailer encounter was traumatic in other respects. Later in the afternoon, Cynthia called to say that our middle son, Max, who was six at the time, had suffered a terrible fall while riding. The horse had stumbled trying to navigate a small jump. Max fell to the ground, and the horse had stepped on his helmet, crushing it. I left the office immediately and drove up to Connecticut. At the hospital in New Milford, Max's head and the upper part of his face were so swollen that he was almost unrecognizable. I stayed with them for the next two days as the swelling began to reduce and the doctors told us that the danger period appeared to be over. I returned to the office for a day and then went back up to Connecticut Friday afternoon. We stayed by his bedside for the weekend.

⟶

I was constantly worried that I was going to lose my job. The only encouragement I got was from Si. An editor is only as good as the support of his or her proprietor. And here, Si had no peers. If he ever wobbled over his decision to hire me, he never showed it. There was a newsstand in the lobby of 350 Madison run by a slightly quirky husband-and-wife pairing, Margit and Helmut. She was on the large side and he was tall and thin. A Jack Sprat couple, as Aimée used to call them. They were from the old country, though I was never sure which old country. Germany seemed to be the consensus. Margit and Helmut ruled their domain like the Ceauşescus had Romania. Merely reaching for a magazine would result in a booming "Are you going to buy dat?" Most important, they knew everything that went on at Condé Nast long before anyone else did. Their newsstand was on the right just before you turned the corner to go to the elevators. It was impossible to miss.

Just before you got to them, there was one of those old-fashioned black address boards with horizontal seams and white plastic capital letters spelling out executives' names and their floor numbers. Si's was at the top. And farther down came the publishers and the editors. Every morning during those first couple of years, I would glance discreetly to my right to make sure that my name was still on the board. Then I'd say hello to Margit and Helmut. I figured they would know first if I was on my way out. I'd be able to gauge my fortunes just by the look on their faces. That's how tenuous I felt my residency at *Vanity Fair* was.

Matt Tyrnauer, who had been a young staff member at *Spy*, and who had written for me at *The Observer*, came over as an editor and shared an office with Aimée. They were inseparable. I inherited a managing editor in Pam McCarthy, who took to looking at me as one would a dog who had just chewed a favorite shoe. And she had good reason. At *Spy*, we reported on an incident that took place during the Brown-era *Vanity Fair* in which two staff members had papered the walls of the office of one of the editors with pictures of naked men. An investigation, led by Pam, was launched to find the culprits. A private eye was reportedly brought in. Suspects were questioned. In the pages of *Spy*, we referred to it as "the McCarthy Era" at *Vanity Fair*. Our days together were not to last. A few weeks in, Pam departed for *The New Yorker* and Chris Garrett arrived as my new managing editor.

Chris had been at *Condé Nast Traveler* and before that at *Tatler*. She was and is an incomparable presence, an English rose with the grace and look of Audrey Hepburn and the wisdom of Plato. She had worked for one of my idols, Mark Boxer, the editor of *Tatler*. Marc, as he signed his pictures, was also a master caricaturist—he had illustrated, among other things, the covers for the paperback edition of Anthony Powell's *A Dance to the Music of Time*. Michael Thomas, the writer, gave me the originals to those covers and then thought better of the gesture. He asked for them back. And I gave them back. But first I made color scans of them, which I have framed in the master bedroom of our house in Connecticut. Anyway, Chris and I have been together, tethered to the editorial masthead, for more than thirty years now.

She is a master of diplomacy, tact, and empathy. The managing editor's job is to run the operation, calm the staff, and look after a zillion tiny details in order to get an issue out the door once a month. All of which Chris did without breaking a sweat. We used to call her "the Velvet Hammer," so gifted was she in delivering bad news. We believed that she could fire somebody and receive flowers from them the next day. From that first day on, we spoke pretty much every morning for the next quarter century. Chris would shimmer into the office like Jeeves. You wouldn't hear any footsteps, she would just be there, looking incredibly composed. Arms at her side was a good sign. Arms folded meant that there was some horrendous issue at the magazine that we needed to sort out. She was quite Sir Humphrey-ish in her mastery of rhetoric and could get me to think her way by some circuitous route that I'd lost the road map for long before. She generally got her way, and in the most pleasant manner possible.

I then brought in Beth Kseniak to handle "communications"—masthead-speak for public relations. Beth was stylish and beautiful, and moved through the hallways like a thoroughbred racehorse. She was also a no-nonsense veteran of the Time Inc. publicity machine. She never sugarcoated bad news but also never lied to reporters when they called about some slipup of ours. Which in the early days were many. She might have pleaded. But she never lied. At the sight of both her and Chris walking my way with their arms folded, my pulse would quicken. It only meant bad news. One holdover I warmed to almost immediately was Wayne Lawson, a peerless editor with a calming manner. I came to rely on Chris, Aimée, Beth, and Wayne—and then Jane Sarkin—not only for giving me advice I probably didn't want to hear but for words of encouragement that I did.

—

I got encouragement from others, including Diane von Fürsten-berg and Barry Diller. In 1986, Jann Wenner threw himself a birthday party at Canal Bar, Brian McNally's bustling new restau-rant in SoHo. Jann took over the whole place, covered the ceiling in balloons, and summoned his crowd of bold-faced contemporaries—

Barry and Diane, Calvin and Kelly Klein, Billy Joel, Malcolm Forbes, Ahmet and Mica Ertegun, Andy Warhol, Fred Hughes, Lorne Michaels, David Geffen, Paul Simon—and me. Jann put me beside Diane. The trail of desecrated reputations and egos at the hands of *Spy*—which was about to launch—would soon make me a difficult dinner person to seat. But for now, I was a pleasant guest with a nice suit and a willing smile. Diane was a great dinner mate, and from that evening on, we saw a lot of each other and became very much entwined in each other's lives.

We live near each other in Connecticut, and back when our house didn't have a pool, we would take the kids over to Diane's for a swim. Her place was more of a compound than a house, really, with a number of outbuildings, including something I had never seen before: a screening room. Hers doubled as a library. On one side it was floor-to-ceiling with books. Back when movies were still released on giant film reels, she would hire the projectionist from the local theater and have him screen films that had just come out or were about to come out. Her longtime boyfriend was Barry Diller, one of the more charismatic figures in Hollywood and New York. And it was Barry who would arrange for the films to be sent on loan.

Barry had been named the head of Paramount Pictures when he was just thirty-two and ran it for the next decade. He then took over 20th Century Fox and during his time there launched the Fox network. By the time I was made head of *Vanity Fair*, Barry had left Fox and was thinking about his next move. Diane suggested I go to see him to get his advice. He invited me to have lunch at his house in the hills above Sunset Boulevard. When I arrived, I found him working outside using another thing I had never seen before: a laptop computer. I was nervous about the meeting. Everyone knew that Barry didn't suffer fools, and I worried that I was precisely the sort of fool he'd find not worth suffering. Also, we had written about him in

Spy. I didn't remember any of the details, but it being *Spy* and all, my guess is that at times it had not been favorably. He greeted me with generosity as well as a simmering layer of mistrust. I so appreciated the first part of that last sentence. And completely understood the reasoning behind the second part.

In so many circles, Barry and Diane's friendship validated me. I had asked Diane to come on as a contributing editor when I got the *Vanity Fair* job and she said yes, and she stayed on the masthead until my final issue.

—

Not long into my new job I was surprised to learn that attending fashion shows would be part of my remit as editor of *Vanity Fair*. I had never been to one before. Fashion shows serve two major purposes: to generate press and to get store buyers to order the things they see on the runway. They rarely start on time. The seating is tight and the benches positively monastic. Editors went to shows out of respect for the designers—or at least the ones who put advertising pages into their magazines. My early days at *Vanity Fair* happened to coincide with the era of the supermodels. So at the very least, what you were witnessing, clothes aside, was a certified moment in the annals of supermodelry.

My first outing was a Calvin Klein fashion show. It took place in a spare gray space downtown that looked a lot like the clothes on the models. David Geffen was seated beside me. I knew who he was. I knew the music he had championed and the films he had made. He asked me how I was doing, and we started talking, and that developed into what I can only describe as a wonderful, if lopsided, friendship—much like mine with Barry—with him way up on top and me several steps below on the food chain. The thing is, like

Barry, David was kind to me when I really needed a friend with wide influence in those early, fragile days at *Vanity Fair*. And their acceptance gave me a huge boost in confidence.

A fashion event also brought me together with a couple who would become a huge part of my life. I met them in Paris at a summer dinner at Karl Lagerfeld's vast hôtel particulier during the couture shows. I was there to wave the *Vanity Fair* flag and indicate to the big Paris fashion houses that we cared about their business. At the Chanel show, I noticed a very attractive couple sitting opposite me—Kelly Lynch, an actress in the ascendant, and her husband, Mitch Glazer, a screenwriter. The designers regularly flew out stars from Hollywood to liven up front rows that were otherwise populated by fashion editors in their black-on-black working kit and New York matrons and the wives of Middle Eastern potentates who could afford the vast expense of a couture gown.

That evening, at Karl's, I made my way around the tables looking for my place card. I began on the perimeter, figuring I would be seated with the wretched refuse of the fashion business. As I worked my way forward, I finally found my seat. And it was between two of the reigning supermodels of the time, Claudia Schiffer and Cindy Crawford. I don't know about you, but in the presence of such epic beauty, I absolutely freeze. I was completely at a loss for words. I mean, what exactly do you say to a supermodel? I did my best, and was discussing something that seemed to completely bore Claudia when there was a commotion across the room.

Richard Gere and Brian McNally were standing face-to-face, and it looked like one of them might hit the other. Piecing the evidence together the next morning, I found out the reason. Brian had recently closed one of his restaurants, 150 Wooster Street. It had run hot for about two years and then just sort of drifted, as hot restaurants so often do. Richard's former girlfriend, Sylvia Martins, a

Brazilian-born abstract painter, had invested in the restaurant and lost her money, and Richard was after Brian for the loss. (She later married a Niarchos, so presumably this is no longer an issue.) It looked as if Richard was going to slug Brian. Which would have been a strange way for a Buddhist to handle such a situation. It would also, I believe, have left him the worse for wear. Brian grew up on the mean streets of Bethnal Green, in East London, and knows a thing or two about handling himself in a fistfight.

Security personnel separated the two men. Brows were mopped. Seating arrangements were hurriedly changed. I almost wept as Cindy Crawford, then married to Gere, was whisked away from my table, and then Claudia Schiffer. In their place glided the attractive actress and screenwriter from across the runway earlier in the day. Mitch had grown up in Miami and moved to New York to become a journalist and later a screenwriter. He wrote with Michael O'Donoghue and had been close friends with John Belushi. Kelly had made a name for herself with *Cocktail*, *Drugstore Cowboy*, and *Road House*.

We wound up having a wonderful evening, the three of us. But I didn't see them after that night until the next spring, outside Mortons late on Oscar night. I was getting some fresh air, and they sidled up beside me while they waited for their car. We resumed whatever we had been talking about at Karl's that night—Brian probably. And we have never really stopped talking. We've gone on family vacations together and our children are as close as siblings. Near our house in Connecticut we had a small fishing camp on Lake Waramaug. Like the cottage we had when I was growing up, it provided cheery family summers filled with Evinrude-motor smells, canoeing, and fishing off the dock with the kids using worms or lures. The camp had a bunkhouse with six berths. Mitch, who is not what anyone would call a seeker of wilderness activity, bravely volunteered to stay in the bunkhouse with the kids one night. I had an old bearskin rug in one of the other rooms. Later in the night, I tied the bear's feet to my hands and with rope strapped the bear's head over mine. I tiptoed up to the screen window closest to Mitch and began growling and scratching. He turned on the flashlight and rocketed out of bed with a shriek.

Mitch is godfather to our youngest daughter, Isabella—Izzy to us. Her christening was to take place at the church where Anna and I got married near our house in Connecticut. Mitch, who is Jewish, asked what he was supposed to wear to a christening. I told him that the traditional dress at an Episcopalian service was a cassock. He numbed at the thought but asked if I could help get one for him for the ceremony. I called the *Vanity Fair* fashion department and they said they could get one from a movie prop house. I asked that it be a few sizes too large. On the day of the christening, Mitch came down wearing the cassock. The sleeves fell over his hands and the hem puddled on the floor the way Mickey Mouse's sorcerer's had in *Fantasia*. He was so despondent that a half hour before we were to head over to the church, Anna broke down and told him that I was playing with him and that a suit and tie would do.

Chapter 9.

My Advanced
Vanity Fair Education

Going from *Spy* and *The Observer* to *Vanity Fair* was like moving from a youth hostel to a five-star hotel. We had a receptionist in the elevator area who handled calls and directed guests to the correct offices. Her name was Bernice, but everyone called her Bunny. She might have been the most popular person on the floor. A lovely woman in an English maid's uniform came to make fresh coffee every few hours. My office had an adjoining private bathroom so luxurious that when a colleague from *Spy* came up to visit one day, she said it looked like Mitzi Gaynor's. At *Vanity Fair*, as I mentioned, I had not one but two assistants.

When traveling on business, I stayed at the Connaught in London, the Ritz in Paris, the Hotel du Cap in the South of France, and the Beverly Hills Hotel or the Bel-Air in Los Angeles. Suites, room service, drivers in each city. For European trips, I flew the Concorde. I took round-trip flights on it at least three times a year for almost a decade. That's something like sixty flights. My passport picture was taken by Annie Leibovitz! The top editors were given a car and driver in the city. My own driver, a charming man named Sergei Boulii, was with me for almost my entire time at Condé Nast. He had grown up in Siberia and spent time in the Russian army—and it showed. He had huge forearms and a tree trunk for a neck. With short-cropped thick blond hair—almost white—he looked a bit like Robert Shaw in *From Russia with Love*. He may have seemed like someone you didn't want to mess around with—but once you got to know him, it was impossible not to be warmed by his lovely smile and gentlemanly manner.

Staff members could expense their breakfasts—not a working breakfast with a writer or photographer. Just breakfast. Large dinners at home were catered. Flowers went out to contributors at an astounding rate, sometimes just for turning a story in on time. One staff member who was a holdover from the old regime would get so depressed at the mere thought of my being there that she would send flowers to herself just to perk up her spirits. On the company account, of course.

There was much in the way of financial secrecy. I was mystified at first about my pay arrangement. Half my salary came in a check from Condé Nast. The other half came from the *Staten Island Advance*—the original pillar of the Newhouse empire. On matters involving money, I was instructed to see Paul Scherer. Paul's accounting firm was in Midtown. The main floor of the operation was the size of a small ballfield, with row upon row of desks stretching out into the distance, like they did in Billy Wilder's film *The Apartment*. There were hundreds of workers grinding away at adding machines. The firm had one client: the Newhouse family.

I had lunch twice a year with Paul, either at the Four Seasons or at Da Silvano. He was a three-martini man from the old school. And experience taught me to make any sort of request at the end of the meal rather than the beginning. His wife, Janice, was a formidable creature who worked in the city's public school system. She was walking into the Condé Nast Building on Madison one day when a group of activists from People for the Ethical Treatment of Animals were outside protesting *Vogue*'s slavish affection for fur. Janice was wearing her mink.

"Do you know how many animals had to *die* for you to wear that coat?" one of the protesters yelled at her.

She stopped, turned, planted her feet on the pavement, and shouted, "Shut up! Do you know how many animals I had to *fuck* to get this coat?"

It was hard not to admire this woman.

Everybody at *Vanity Fair* had an assistant. All the deputy and senior editors. The photo editor. The art director. The fashion editor. At Condé Nast, there were interest-free loans to buy houses or apartments. Even the moving costs were covered by the company. Cynthia and I desperately needed a bigger place for our growing family—in a short time, with the addition of our daughter, Bronwen, there were now four kids—and so we bought an apartment in the Dakota. Like so many New Yorkers, I had always been entranced by the building. It loomed large in both old New York history and the city's contemporary culture. Much of the fascination was due to the people who had lived there—not just John Lennon and Yoko Ono, but also Leonard Bernstein, Lauren Bacall, Jack Lemmon, and, in the 1950s, Boris Karloff. Can you imagine being a kid there on Halloween and knocking on *his* door? It was, and is, a fortresslike anchor at the corner of 72nd Street and Central Park West that had been designed by Henry Hardenbergh, who was also the architect of the Waldorf Hotel and the Astoria Hotel, which were at one point combined to form the Waldorf Astoria and then torn down in the 1920s to make way for the Empire State Building.

The architect Basil Walter came in to design the millwork and oversee the renovation. We filled it with old pieces from our parents and French flea market finds. At Thanksgiving, we'd take the kids up to the roof to watch the Macy's Thanksgiving Parade. And for the first time, I had an office at home. It was small and windowless, but it was mine, all mine—away from the hectic, glorious antics of four children. I papered the walls with 1940s ordnance survey maps and hung from the ceiling a huge model of a DC-3 that I had bought at a flea market in Connecticut. It's where I could think and edit and plot out the next issues.

—

It took a while to adjust to the job. I remember, early on, the first Annie Leibovitz cover shoot I went to. There might have been about thirty people milling around the studio. There was a stretch of folding tables end to end, groaning with food. I thought, *Who eats this sort of food before getting their picture taken?* I discovered that it was for the crew. I went back and saw that the food budget was more money than we'd spent on all the editorial content for an entire issue of *Spy.* There was one issue of the magazine when we were running low on money and Kurt and I wrote about half the issue under pseudonyms. (P. G. Wodehouse had done the same thing at the old *Vanity Fair.* He'd written so many articles for one issue that Crowninshield said he couldn't have three Wodehouse bylines and asked him to come up with another name. Wodehouse came up with C. P. West, which came from Central Park West, where his apartment was.) After witnessing the catering extravaganza of Annie's shoot, I returned to the office and said to Chris, "Look, they can live like us at the office, they can order in, they can order pizzas like we do on late nights."

About halfway through my tenure at *Vanity Fair,* I bumped into

Susan Morrison on our floor. Susan had gone from being our stalwart deputy editor at *Spy* to a brief stint following me as the editor of *The Observer* and had then landed as an editor at *The New Yorker*, a floor below. I asked her if she was visiting Bruce Handy, an editor at *Vanity Fair* and a colleague from our days together at *Spy*.

"No," she said, "I've come for the eyebrow lady."

"What do you mean, the eyebrow lady?"

"The eyebrow lady. The one who comes every month to do everyone's eyebrows. She's the best in the city. I'll show you."

We walked through the office down to the photo department. The eyebrow lady, Maribeth Madron, had set up base camp in one of the offices, with the tools of her trade neatly organized on a desk. And there was a line of about a half dozen staff members chatting and waiting their turn. I walked away dumbfounded.

I went to see Chris.

"Chris, do you know there's an eyebrow lady on the floor? And apparently she comes every month or so."

Chris gave me the sort of look you'd give someone who just noticed that the bathrooms had running water.

"Maribeth's the best in the city."

"Yes, yes, so I've heard. But how long has this been going on?"

Chris thought for a moment and said, "Oh, I don't know. Twenty years?"

This, in its essence, was *Vanity Fair*. Younger people would never understand the expense-account stories of the time, because that all disappeared with the Great Recession, in 2008. But at *Vanity Fair* in those early days, anyone on the editorial floor could take out pretty much any amount of reasonable cash just by signing a chit. Aimée had perfected the expense-account system. She figured out early that the accountants budgeted your expenses based on what you spent the previous year. This meant that what you needed to do was set a high bar early and build on a large amount of expenses. And I was fine with this. I wanted my editors out in the field, meeting with writers and bringing in ideas. The last thing I wanted was to have editors eating at their desks.

⌐

As flush as the operation was, I knew I had to change the culture at *Vanity Fair* if I was to survive and perhaps thrive. Both socially and journalistically. I edited every single word that went into the magazine—and continued to do so for the next quarter century. At the beginning, I wanted to change the voice, which mostly meant cleansing the florid baroqueness of the language. In the *Vanity Fair* I inherited, a restaurant wasn't a restaurant, it was a "boîte." A book wasn't a book, it was a "tome." A party wasn't a party, it was a "fete." People didn't say something funny, they "chortled" or "quipped." I issued a list of words henceforth banned from *Vanity Fair* copy. Out went words like *abode, opine, plethora,* and *passed away* (for died). Out went *glitzy, wannabe,* and even *celebrity.* Out went *chops* (for acting abilities), *donned* (as in put on), *A-list, boasted* (as in had or featured), *coiffed, eatery* (for restaurant), *flat* (for apartment), *flick* (for movie), *fuck* (okay in a quote, but not with regard to the actual sex act), *honcho, hooker, schlep* (as in to lug something somewhere), *scribe* (as in writer), and *Tinseltown.* All found their way into the copyedit boneyard.

I also had to make the culture less poisonous—because poisonous it most surely was. You could feel the venom in the corridors. Changing this certainly wasn't easy, but gradually, Chris and Aimée and I tried to soften the office atmosphere. I wanted to take it from the viperish nest it had been and make it a warmer, more collaborative place. About two years in, I came to the somewhat belated conclusion that the animus came from four offices—all of which were filled with leftovers from the ancien régime.

There was Marina Schiano, the style director or, as her masthead title had it, creative style director, which I always found funny. Surely style director should have implied a certain amount of creativity. She had been a muse for Yves Saint Laurent in her younger days. The men in the art department found her exotic. I had trouble getting over her bitter attitude toward just about anyone in her orbit. She once said to me that Franca Sozzani, then the editor of Italian *Vogue* and one of the more gentle, welcoming members of the Newhouse tribe, was "one of my best friends. *But she is a pig!*" Marina couldn't stand me, and try as I might, I couldn't get her around to my way of thinking. She was paid upward of $350,000 to do the styling for eight magazine covers per year. I was told by somebody on the staff that one of her duties during Tina Brown's reign was apparently to show up at her apartment and help style her clothes for the day. I wasn't sure whether that was true or not, but I had been dressing myself in the mornings since I moved out of shorts and had no real need for this service.

Then there was Sarah Giles, an import from London and someone the new *Vanity Fair* hands like Aimée and Matt believed was a plant, left behind to shower dinner-party mates with tales of our incompetence. Her parents were Lady Kitty Giles and Frank Giles, of "Hitler Diaries" infamy. Sarah didn't really have a function at *Vanity Fair*, as far as we could tell. She had had the reputation of being an effective story fixer—although I think it might have been Sarah who told me this. To everyone's amusement, she did have a pet rat, named Ratty. What her purpose was at that point, aside from delivering dispatches about my inadequacies around town and protecting her friends in the magazine's pages, escaped me.

Michael Caruso was a senior editor who bristled at every edit I made to his copy. There were a number of stories in Page Six during this period pitting him against me, and in all of them he came out as the white-hat savior of journalism and me as something far less than that. He once said to me that he'd never had a meal at a restaurant in the past ten years that he didn't order off the menu. My back started getting itchy when I heard that.

And finally there was Charles Churchward, the art director. He was certainly talented. But in the end, he struck me as the sort of person who worked better with a stiletto pinned to his neck. My brand of attempted collegiality, for lack of a better word, just never gelled with Charles. He left of his own volition and decamped to the *Vogue* floor, where he worked for the next decade or more.

The first three—Schiano, Giles, and Caruso—I let go all the same week. It was more people than I had fired in my life up to that point. I simply told them that this wasn't working for me and that I thought it was time for them to spread their wings elsewhere.

I said to each of them, "The trouble is, you've confused politeness for weakness." Caruso was in a state of disbelief. He said, "You've got to be joking."

I said, "No, not joking at all."

I was surprised by the result of the purge. Rather than have the rest of the office in an uproar, the staff was quietly thrilled with what I had done. And despite the fact that I am, at heart, a beta male, this moved me, at least in some eyes, closer into the alpha category.

As far as the office environment went, it was like pulling open the curtains at Miss Havisham's. Everything seemed sunnier. I may have actually developed a spring in my step. People started working with each other in a noncombative manner. Interoffice memos were being signed off with an unheard-of "Thank you." I began to bring Cynthia and the kids into the office. Things had changed. Even rumors of my imminent sacking began to die down, helped very much by a piece the columnist Liz Smith wrote after a lunch with Si New-house, saying, in effect, Graydon's not going anywhere.

At Condé Nast, the top editors of the various publications called themselves "editor in chief" on their mastheads. My feeling was that this was a faintly ridiculous title. I went with "editor"—aside from David Remnick when he took over *The New Yorker*, the only one in the company to do so.

One major advantage in these rocky early days was that there was no budget at all—that is to say, the budget had no ceiling. I could send anybody anywhere for as long as I wanted. The cost and the expenses involved were sometimes enormous. One article, about the near collapse of Lloyd's, the London insurance market, on which there will be more later, may have been the most expensive per word magazine story ever written. And we never published it. I had the excitement, as an editor, of being able to commission the best working writers and photographers anywhere, and to offer them exclusive contracts.

———

The first person I reached out to with my new checkbook was Christopher Hitchens—who had so politely turned me down when we were launching *Spy*. I first met him in the 1980s at a party in Greenwich Village, when he was writing for *The Nation* and was then known mostly to the tribal Left. Christopher was among the last great liberal public intellectuals, but he was one with wit and charm—which made him much more palatable to people in the middle and even to conservatives. By the time I got to *Vanity Fair*, he was writing for Lewis Lapham at *Harper's*. I called Christopher, and with Si's checkbook in hand, got him to sign on. Christopher and I went to Elaine's that night to celebrate and, God, if we didn't bump into Lewis—the same Lewis who had treated me so generously when I first came to New York. Christopher told him that he was going to be leaving *Harper's* to work at *Vanity Fair.* Lewis handled the news with supreme elegance. I think he realized that it would be better for Christopher to be introduced to the much wider audience *Vanity Fair* would offer. We sat down and had a drink. Well, many drinks.

Christopher was to write a column each month as well as articles and profiles. His well-calibrated but unflagging intake of alcohol and nicotine produced nothing but swift and faultless prose, even after lunches or dinners where others would be *hors de combat.* Dinner was a bacchanal of anecdote and erudition, recitations from *Flashman* and Wodehouse giving way to declamations from Gibbon and Homer. He was infinitely funny, better company than just about anyone. As for the writing and drinking, I remember going to lunch at La Goulue when Aimée and I were at *The Observer.* Christopher had a couple of scotches before the starter, a couple glasses of wine with the main course, and then a brandy to wash things down afterward. Back at the *Observer* offices, we plunked him down in front of a typewriter and he banged out a review of a thousand words of near perfection in less than an hour.

I never saw Christopher drunk but occasionally I witnessed the physical effects of such attrition on his system, a pointer to his early death. He wrote about the subject during his book tour for *God Is Not Great.* Hitchens even smoked in the shower, arm extended beyond the curtain, and claimed that this was where he'd come up with the book's title. "Fueled with scotch and above all with nicotine—an Irish newspaper described me in this period as taking 'rare oxygen breaks'—I managed a series of epic eight-day weeks on the road, and the grand memory of it will always linger. Except that I became abruptly and horribly convinced that there would be no fond memory upon which to dwell. A voice began to speak insistently inside my skull: 'You aren't going to live to spend a dime of these royalties.'"

One year we invited Christopher to an annual *Vanity Fair* gathering for the advertising sales staff at the PGA National Resort in Palm Beach. The off-site get-together was ostensibly to get the business side charged up for the sales season ahead. Editors had to attend and would bring along a few of the writers to liven things up. The editor's job was to give a rough road map of the year ahead, editorially. I'm sure there were editors at some Condé Nast titles who knew exactly what was coming up from month to month. I was not so blessed. Given that *Vanity Fair* reacted to the news, and that news in the future hadn't yet happened, it was almost impossible to explain in detail what we had in store for the next year. I would nevertheless stumble my way through an exciting but largely fictitious plan for the year and then turn the podium over to one of my colleagues.

There was a lot of drinking in the evening. Christopher came, and as the night poured on, someone at the hotel put on calypso music and brought out a limbo pole. It all went downhill from there. The next morning, as we were checking out, a lovely young woman from the hotel came to me and asked if Mr. Hitchens was part of our party. I told her that indeed he was. She brought me over to a window that looked out on the first tee. Young, fit men were walking around in their golf finery, waiting to tee off, and there, leaning on the ball washer, was Christopher, still in the wrinkled off-white linen suit from the night before, heaving up everything he had consumed at dinner. I went over and gingerly escorted him off the course.

The great cause of Christopher's life as a writer, he said, was "to oppose manmade delusions, the 'mind-forged manacles,' as Blake calls them, of superstition and religious totalitarianism." He originated "Hitchens's razor"—a proposition to go along with Occam's: "That which can be asserted without evidence can also be dismissed without evidence." When Christopher arrived at *Vanity Fair,* he had to be looked after, as did all the writers. My philosophy has always been that if you take care of the talent, so to speak—the writers, the photographers, the illustrators—you'll get better work out of them than if you threaten or browbeat them. So I set Christopher up with Aimée. She became his editor and then one of his closest friends up until the day he died.

Writing is a tough business—especially the sort of detailed, rigorous, long-form narrative journalism that *Vanity Fair* came to be known for. And this sort of reportage has its own unique set of demands. *Vanity Fair* writers were sent to the far corners of the earth to report. They would leave their families for weeks or months at a time and return home and on deadline had to assemble all the reporting and write a good tale—almost like a condensed book. Every one of their facts then had to be backed up by the researcher—or researchers—checking the article. And then the story had to be reviewed by the legal editor. Sometimes this process, from idea to final copy, would take three or four months. Stories that ran as long as seventeen thousand or twenty thousand words might take even longer.

If there is a scoop in a newspaper story, it's often in the first sentence. If there is a scoop in a weekly magazine story, it's generally in the first paragraph. But in a long-form magazine piece, the scoop could be in the seventeenth paragraph. This is because the newsbreak has to take its place within the thread of the narrative. I believe that all great magazine stories must have a combination of the following elements: narrative (that is to say, a beginning, a middle, and an end), access (to the principals, or those on the immediate periphery of the principals), conflict (always a welcome addition), and disclosure (moving the scholarship on the topic at hand along—in other words, new information). You can get by with three of these necessities. But with four, you have a great chance at producing a memorable work of journalism. A perfect *Vanity Fair* piece would slip in somewhere between the news reports on a particular story and the inevitable book on it. Our articles were bolstered by on-the-spot reporting—we flew correspondents to wherever they needed to be—and by narrative skill and length. By the time we got to a story, there would often not only be a beginning and a middle but also, blessedly, an end. The arc of the tale was set.

An article could be killed for various reasons. Perhaps it didn't meet expectations—although that was a rare occurrence given the caliber of writer I worked with. Perhaps in the course of closing our story another magazine published one on the same subject that was just as good—this was another reason to kill it. For writers not on contract, I had a rule that I wouldn't break, even when the fortunes of magazines everywhere began their slide: I never paid a kill fee—a staple of the business. A kill fee meant the writer generally got about a quarter of the amount the story was assigned for if it didn't run for one reason or another. I had been a writer in my recent, previous life, and I knew just how brutal the whole ordeal was and how most in the trade lived from assignment fee to assignment fee. Whether we ran the story or not, the writer got paid in full.

The editor's job can also be likened to that of a choirmaster. You have all these disparate voices. It's the editor who must somehow join the gifted soloists together in an issue to form a sort of choral harmony. Some writers—especially the ones who had been editors in the past—were terrific at coming up with their own story ideas. Others relied on me and the other editors to come up with the ideas. Marie Brenner, one of my favorites, and a master at the long-form journalism we practiced, had a habit of coming in with ideas that I thought were less than inspired. On a couple of occasions, I got her off her notion by telling her that she was a home-run hitter and that even if she did a brilliant job on the story she was suggesting, it could never be more than a double. *You should never step up to the plate unless a home run is a possibility,* I would tell her. Marie would leave the office saying how right I was and a day or two later we'd come up with an idea that would allow her to hit another home run. Marie's body of *Vanity Fair* work was extraordinary. She produced one explosive story after another, many of which were turned into films, including Michael Mann's 1999 film *The Insider,* and Clint Eastwood's 2019 film *Richard Jewell.* Writers like Marie, Sebastian Junger, Michael Lewis, Maureen Orth, and Bryan Burrough, all of whom crafted journalism like novelists, became vital parts of the *Vanity Fair* stable. They wrote their stories like mini novels.

Bryan was a perfect practitioner of this form of journalism. He was also the second writer I hired after Christopher. Bryan had spent almost a third of his life—he was then just thirty-one—at *The Wall Street Journal,* where he was a star investigative reporter. He was a straight-shooting Texan and, along with his *Journal* colleague James B. Stewart, was one of the most acclaimed business reporters of his generation. Out of a series he produced for the paper on the $25 billion takeover of Nabisco—one of the ultimate spectacles of Wall Street avariciousness in the 1980s—came *Barbarians at the Gate,* a huge bestseller, which he wrote with fellow *Journal* reporter John Helyar. Bryan had just written, when I hired him, *Vendetta,* about James Robinson III, then the head of American Express, and the irrational lengths the company went to in order to discredit the financier Edmond Safra.

Bryan didn't really see himself as a business writer, though. He saw himself as a general nonfiction narrative writer. You could get a version of the narrative from public documents and research, but to really get into the characters, you need somebody on the inside to guide you along. Some writers love to check in every few days or every week, but Bryan was like a short-order cook. You gave him the assignment. If he accepted it, he just disappeared for six weeks and then a manuscript would land on your desk. We rarely talked between the time of assignment and delivery. He just went off and did it.

The masthead grew and grew. Very few people left the magazine whom we didn't want to leave. In my early days, the roster included Bob Colacello, a wonderful writer, social observer, and reporter, and Maureen Orth, based in Washington, who wrote an investigation, soon after I arrived, that broke the story of Michael Jackson's serial sexual abuse. Michael Lewis joined *Vanity Fair* after the turn of the century and produced some of the most inventive magazine writing of the time.

Over the years we corralled some of the best writers, photographers, and illustrators in the magazine business at the time. Among the essayists or specialists were Christopher, A. A. Gill, James Wolcott, Fran Lebowitz, Michael Kinsley, Amy Fine Collins, Gore Vidal, Paul Goldberger, and Laura Jacobs. The battering ram of reporters included Robert Sam Anson, Judy Bachrach, Peter Biskind, Kara Swisher, Buzz Bissinger, Howard Blum, Patricia Bosworth, David Halberstam, Frederic Morton, Nina Munk, Mark Seal, Ingrid Sischy, Evgenia Peretz, Emily Jane Fox, Leslie Bennetts, Andrew and Leslie Cockburn, William Langewiesche, Mark Bowden, Kevin Sessums, Sally Bedell Smith, Nick Tosches, Carl Bernstein, Evan Wright, Nancy Jo Sales, Lili Anolik, Jim Windolf, the partnership of Donald Barlett and James B. Steele, William D. Cohan, Bethany

McLean, Michael Wolff, Sarah Ellison, Kurt Eichenwald, David Margolick, William Prochnau, and Suzanna Andrews. I was especially pleased that so many *Spy* and *Observer* hands wrote for *Vanity Fair*, including not only Kurt but also Walter Kirn, John Heilpern, Ned Zeman, George Kalogerakis, Elissa Schappell, Henry Alford, Matt Tyrnauer, Bruce Feirstein, Bruce Handy, and David Kamp.

The photographers on the masthead were the best you could find anywhere in the world: Annie Leibovitz, Jonathan Becker, Bruce Weber, Helmut Newton, Herb Ritts, Mario Testino, Mark Seliger, Snowdon, Todd Eberle, Larry Fink, Patrick Demarchelier, Harry Benson, Timothy Greenfield-Sanders, Jonas Karlsson, Mary Ellen Mark, Brigitte Lacombe, Michael O'Neill, and Dafydd Jones. For illustrators we had Bruce McCall, Ed Sorel, Hilary Knight, Tim Sheaffer, and Robert Risko. Great word rates certainly didn't hurt the assembly of this formidable roster. If Si wanted a writer or a photographer (or an editor, for that matter), he went after what he wanted. And more often than not, he got it. Once, in an annual contract negotiation with Annie, *Vanity Fair*'s principal photographer, it came down to a $250,000 difference between what her agent demanded and what we were willing to pay. "Oh, give it to her," Si told me finally. "We don't want to nickel-and-dime them."

⟶

D ominick Dunne was a significant element of the franchise that I inherited and was, for a long time, a huge asset to the magazine. He could be prickly—especially to the younger staff, which I was not fine with. But we needed him, and, to a great extent, he needed *Vanity Fair*. The magazine's readers devoured his monthly dispatches from the 1993 trial of the Menendez brothers—two rich kids from Southern California who shot their parents as they watched TV and ate ice cream—and he would soon become perhaps the most famous print journalist in the world for his monthly and ongoing and knowing coverage of the O.J. Simpson courtroom circus.

One thing Nick brought to these murder stories was a defined moral stance. He wasn't objective, like most crime and courtroom reporters. He was there to defend the rights of victims. This impulse went back to the tragedy of his daughter Dominique, who was murdered by her boyfriend, John Thomas Sweeney. Sweeney was convicted of the murder and served a total of three and a half years in prison. Writing about the case—Nick's first story for *Vanity Fair*—had brought him back from a failed career as a film producer. The narrative arc was one that Hollywood would appreciate, as he went from alcoholism, a breakdown, and the death of his daughter to a new career as a reporter and television star.

Vanity Fair writers like Nick were paid like no other writers. He was well on his way to earning half a million dollars a year, plus generous expenses and months of free and continuous accommodation at the Chateau Marmont or the Beverly Hills Hotel during the Menendez and O.J. Simpson trials he covered for us and later the trial of the music impresario Phil Spector, who shot a young actress, Lana Clarkson. We treated our stable of writers like the stars they were. This meant assigning them to diligent, talented editors and dispatching flowers or bottles of scotch at regular intervals. I bought Nick the same Christmas gift every year: a dozen square dark blue Smythson notebooks with his name embossed on the covers. Each one had about two hundred light blue pages. These books became a hallmark of his during the O.J. trial, as he made his copious notes. Nick had filled them all by the end of the trial, and I had to give him his next Christmas batch early that year.

—

Newsstand sales were a monthly measure of a magazine's success in those days. When the numbers were good, they kept Si's lieutenants off my back. I cared about the quality more than the sales, and above all, I wanted readers to read. It was the covers, though, that sold the magazine. For the subjects of those covers, movie stars were for the most part the lingua franca of the global newsstand. And *Vanity Fair* was sold all over the world. Each country had its own music stars, political stars, and literary and artistic lights. But movies, at least back then, were the element of the culture that were universally acknowledged. Tom Hanks was not just an American film icon; he was an international film icon.

The covers and their fraught celebrity shoots were the tasks I found to be the most taxing and dreary part of my job. Some people will tell you that there's a "science" to creating a cover that will sell— that there are colors you should use, words you should use, numbers you should use. I thought this was all nonsense. The company at one point plied us with consultants. We met with them. It was a forced march, certainly, and most of their suggestions were painfully obvious. Long lists of celebrities would be passed around, ranked by the degree to which the public "loves" or "hates" them—as if that was some sort of surefire guide. At the end of the day, we thanked them and resumed trusting our instincts. I've always felt that one of the reasons there are editors is because the public doesn't actually know what it wants. Nobody knew they needed a smartphone before Steve Jobs introduced it. With magazines, the editor's job is to be consistent but not predictable in covers and to regularly deliver surprises. Sometimes a cover you expect to be a big hit turns out to be a dud, and vice versa.

Jane Sarkin, *Vanity Fair*'s features editor, was our Hollywood and show-business conduit. She booked—wrangled, as they say—pretty much every cover. She also, along with Krista Smith, our West Coast editor, organized the photo portfolios embedded in all of our Hollywood issues. Jane cultivated and dined with agents and publicists. She described herself—when she ended up on TV for one of her covers—as a very ordinary girl from New Jersey. But Jane wasn't ordinary; she was exceptional. She had started as a receptionist at Andy Warhol's *Interview* magazine and rose, she would say, because while she was working, most of the rest of the staff was in the basement doing coke and having sex. Jane loved the world of movie stars and celebrities, and they trusted her.

Jane had exceptional stamina as a celebrity handler and ego tamer—skills that came in useful when keeping agents, publicists, and overbearing managers at bay. She also kept them away from me, for which I will be eternally grateful. In addition to all of this, Jane served as Annie Leibovitz's full-time in-house connection, which was not the easiest of tasks. Annie was as tough on those around her as she was on herself. What I appreciated about Jane was that, despite the operatic drama surrounding her job, she never ever came to me with a problem, only with a solution.

Among her gets was the first picture, taken by Annie, of Tom Cruise and Katie Holmes's baby, Suri. It's hard to imagine now that this was a great national obsession. But in the spring of 2006, it was. Because the couple hadn't wanted publicity for their newborn child, rumors and conspiracy theories built to a fevered pitch: they hadn't actually had a baby; they had, but it had been taken away by the Scientologists; or, alternatively, there was a baby, but it wasn't Katie's. Or Tom's. In 2006, he was the biggest star in Hollywood, and the search for Suri was Jane's big truffle hunt. She had worked on many covers with Tom and, after a while, she got the exclusive. He invited Jane and Annie to Telluride, where they spent a week doing the story on Suri in great secrecy. Jane wrote the cover article herself. We were so concerned about a leak that we sent Annie's pictures to the printers chained to the wrist of a security guard. The pictures were stolen anyway by someone at the plant who tried to peddle them to the papers. We found the person and shut that operation down. With a fair amount of padding, we managed to somehow spread the Cruise "family album" over twenty-two pages. Looking back at it now, I honestly find it difficult to understand what all the fuss was about.

I would regularly get Christmas gifts from Tom. One year he sent me a document in plexiglass with a base that allowed it to stand upright on a surface. Printed on the document were some twenty tenets of Scientology, including "To increase the numbers and strength of Scientology over the world" and "To make this world a saner, better place." We had an L-shaped dining banquette in the kitchen of our house in the Village, where we had moved after the Dakota, and as a sort of joke, I put the tenets alongside the books that sat on the shelf that ran along the perimeter of the banquette. We had any number of people over for lunch or dinner over the next two years, and not once did anyone mention the Scientology edicts. Anna and I realized later that friends must have left our place suspecting that we were under Scientology's control. One year, for a charity event, Tom invited us to sit at his table. We said yes and arrived at the venue and discovered that we were seated not only with Tom but also with David Miscavige, the head of Scientology, and Anne Archer's son, Tommy Davis, who had something to do with Scientology's Celebrity Centre in Hollywood. This weirded us out a bit. But they were all very pleasant, and blessedly, dinner was not followed by anything in the way of recruitment attempts.

Chapter 10.

The Great
Billionaire Proprietor

Si Newhouse knew what he was doing. He spent what had to be spent and he wanted to make it show. He was also a gambler. After Si bought *The New Yorker* in 1985, he hung in there for decades taking huge losses before finally, under David Remnick, sometime in this century, it resumed profitability. His biggest wager was the relaunch, in 1983, of *Vanity Fair*, which had been dormant since 1936. The magazine lost close to $100 million before it slipped into profit under Tina Brown. It was just on that turn to profitability when I washed up on its doorstep. Si didn't want to lose money; he wanted Condé Nast to be profitable. But his slice of the Newhouse empire, Random House and Condé Nast, were like two small skiffs in a sea of tankers. The major moneymakers in the Newhouse stable were the newspapers and the cable businesses. Those were run by Si's younger brother Donald. The two were incredibly close and would have dinner most Sunday nights at Sette

Mezzo, on Lexington between 70th and 71st, where they discussed aspects of the family's sprawling businesses.

Donald's portion of the empire may have brought in the big money, but Si's Condé Nast was the glamorous part that kept members of the family on the lists for the fashion houses of Paris and Milan and got them good tables at the better restaurants in New York and beyond. Condé Nast and its collection of carriage-trade magazines was the beautiful jewel that Si both inherited and built. And what he loved about Condé Nast were the magazines themselves, particularly *Vanity Fair*, *Vogue*, and *The New Yorker*. I do believe that great companies are built around owners or leaders who truly appreciate what they make and sell. In Si's case, he loved magazines, their heft, their look, their quality. In Si, I had stumbled on the greatest billionaire magazine proprietor of all time.

When I arrived in New York in the late 1970s, Condé Nast was a third-tier publisher. Time Inc., with *Time*, *Sports Illustrated*, *Fortune*, *People*, and *Life*, was the top of the heap. Then came Hearst, with *Esquire*, *Town & Country*, and *Harper's Bazaar* among its titles. And then way down below, there was Condé Nast, with *Vogue*, *Mademoiselle*, and *Glamour*. The Condé Nast magazines were beautiful, but nobody took them or the company seriously. Si changed all that. Beginning in the early 1980s, he launched or acquired *Self*, *GQ*, *Wired*, *Details*, *W*, *Architectural Digest*, *Gourmet*, and *Bon Appetit*. His relaunch of *Vanity Fair* was, at the time, the biggest, most electrifying magazine start-up in ages. I wrote an application letter to Leo Lerman, the Condé Nast veteran who was made editor when Richard Locke, the magazine's first one, had been shown the door after just four issues. Leo, who only lasted a few issues himself, wrote back, saying he would have loved to have met with me, but he, too, was headed for the door.

Si brought Tina Brown over from London to run the ship. By

the time Si bought *The New Yorker* in 1985, he had turned Condé Nast into the dominant magazine company in the country—and with his cousin Jonathan's expansion of the business throughout Europe and Asia, the dominant magazine company in the world. The week I started, Si asked me if I would like his bound volumes of the Crowninshield-era *Vanity Fairs*. They had belonged to Crowninshield himself. Si had sold his place in Palm Beach and these were part of the family belongings that would be coming north. Si was explicit in telling me not to use them as a guideline for my *Vanity Fair*. But he thought it would be instructive to get a grasp of the full history of the magazine. I still have those beautifully bound editions at our place in Connecticut.

Magazines are expensive propositions, and they survive and thrive on the advertising pages their publishers sell. Si kept a close eye on what was coming in. When a new issue of one of his magazines came out, he would go through it with his rubber finger, tallying the advertising pages on yellow legal pads with a thick Sharpie, the way prisoners count days in a cell—four vertical lines and a diagonal slash for the fifth. His father, Samuel Sr., had launched the family business with the *Staten Island Advance*, a daily that covered the sleepy New York borough of Staten Island. That's why the company that owns Condé Nast is called Advance Publications. Sam Sr.'s wife was named Mitzi. She was petite and trim and a beautiful dresser who favored Dior and Chanel. One day in 1959, Sam came home and told Mitzi that he'd just bought her favorite magazine. "Which one?" she asked. "*Vogue*," he replied. She at first thought he meant a copy of the magazine. He corrected her by saying that he had paid $500,000 for all of Condé Nast. Si told me that, in fact, his father had made a mistake. When he got to the office the next morning, he realized that he'd paid $5 million for it. Which still turned out to be one of the great bargains in the history of publishing.

When Sam died, Donald took control of the newspapers and the cable businesses and Si got Condé Nast and then Random House. The Newhouse newspapers had been famous at one point for their lackluster editorial output. Donald, and later with his son Steven, went through his properties paper by paper, making vast improvements in each one. In many cases, they became the dominant newspapers in their states, which meant that in the days before the internet drained off a crippling portion of their ad revenues, they were highly profitable. Si told me that at one point newspaper profit margins were in the neighborhood of 27 percent annually, meaning the Newhouses kept $27 of every $100 their papers brought in.

In addition to Condé Nast, Si also oversaw the publishing group under the Random House umbrella. At his side for most of Si's time at Condé Nast was Alexander Liberman. When Si and his wife, Victoria, moved to the UN Plaza on the far east side of Manhattan, just north of the UN Building, Alex moved there as well, to a sprawling apartment practically devoid of color. He was both an artist and an art director—although more skilled at the latter than the former. Alex was born in what is now Ukraine and arrived in New York with a résumé that had its first foothold in the prewar era of modernism. In his younger years, he turned up in Paris as the art director of *Vu*, a darker, almost Germanic version of *Life* and *Look*, where he worked with Brassaï and André Kertész. Alex was a man of impeccable old-world manners. He had one of those thin mustaches that lined his upper lip—the sort that hotel managers favored in screwball comedies.

Alex's uniform was a dark suit with a white shirt and dark tie. His courtly and deferential manner masked an arsenal of political skills that were said to rival Machiavelli's. I never saw this side of him. In all likelihood this is because I was never a threat, though it might also have had something to do with an exclusive I managed to get for *Vanity Fair*. During my first year at the magazine, the art world began burbling with rumors that hundreds of paintings presumed destroyed during World War II—part of the two million art treasures looted by the Nazis from museums and private owners—were still extant. The word was that they had been grabbed by Stalin's troops and had been hidden in the vast storerooms of Soviet museums for half a century, their existence a state secret.

In 1994, the Hermitage in St. Petersburg announced that it was going to exhibit an extraordinary cache of Impressionist paintings from this hoard. We spent two weeks figuring out who was going to be in charge of this exhibit and then successfully negotiating for the exclusive world rights. The collection included Degas's *Place de la Concorde*, van Gogh's *Landscape with House and Ploughman*, and Renoir's *Party in the Country at Berneval*. There were also works by Gauguin, Pissarro, Picasso, Cézanne, Courbet, Matisse, and Daumier. All were believed to have been destroyed. When the prints of the collection arrived at the office, I called Alex. He came down to our floor, and for the next two hours we pored over those magnificent images. I remember his almost boyish excitement as we sifted through the treasures in the planning room, choosing which ones we wanted and how we wanted to display them. The twenty-one-page feature we did on the pictures was not only a worldwide exclusive but also our own little private accomplishment.

—

Much as Si appreciated the outsize influence of his magazines, he wasn't one to swan around the smart drawing rooms where his magazines wound up. It just wasn't his style. What he really loved were the magazines themselves. As objects. And as businesses. He loved them the way his brother Donald loved the family newspapers. Although modest in aspect and manner, Si ran his fiefdom the way I imagine Louis B. Mayer ran Metro-Goldwyn-Mayer in its heyday. Condé Nast was indeed like an old movie studio, with Si in the center and his constellation of stars surrounding him. Most of what I've read about Si—generally by people who didn't know him—gets him wrong. He is often described as a strange, eccentric fellow. He may have at times been eccentric, but in a way, he was one of the sanest people I've ever met. He was also the least jaded of any person at his income level you could possibly meet.

Si had his passions: for his wife, Victoria; for their pugs; for art; for magazines; for books (Random House ones, generally); for architecture; and for films—two of his favorites being *D.O.A.* (the 1949 one with Edmond O'Brien) and Ernest Schoedsack and Irving Pichel's 1932 classic *The Most Dangerous Game*. He also loved gossip. He may have been born into an incredibly wealthy family, but to my mind he had no real interest in money per se. In his professional life and in his personal life, Si's great focus was never on cost—it was always on quality. He had a singular appetite for art, and with a superior eye and a healthy bank balance, he acquired one of the great private collections of postwar art in America.

He was an early riser, getting to work before the sun came up— and before the day's traffic could clog the streets. He ate lunch at noon—I don't mean noon-ish, I mean 12:00 sharp. He ate simply and quickly. Nothing to drink, not even water. He said he was allergic to garlic, so there was none of that in the company cafeteria. Bernie Leser, a veteran hand from the London and Australian wing of the empire, told me that in the days when Si smoked, he often puffed between bites. He generally left the office around 3:30. Si was religious about his fitness routine. I was once having a drink with Warren Beatty at the bar of the Hotel Bel-Air, in Los Angeles. Si came in with Victoria and Donald and Donald's wife, Sue. We went over to their table and Warren made a point of saying that he and Si had been working out in the same gym in New York a few weeks back, and that he could never have kept up with Si's fitness routines. It was one of the many times I saw Si positively beam.

If they didn't go out, Si and Victoria would watch movies at home. They had a laser disc player, a technology of epically high quality, and they'd watch that night's film in a little alcove in their living room. On one side of the alcove was a full-size Lucian Freud naked self-portrait; on the other side was a painting of a nude woman with her legs spread apart. His art collection was constantly being refreshed. Every time I'd go up to their apartment, the walls would be hung with different works. Some came from storage. But others came after he had flipped a picture that no longer interested him.

I remember a rare lapse in Si's legendary eye when we were out in Los Angeles for the Oscars. Si and Barry Diller had had a mild falling-out, and David Geffen had planned a sort of make-up dinner at his new house in Beverly Hills. It had been owned by Jack Warner, and David had bought the house and everything in it, film scripts and Oscars included. He'd had it redone by Rose Tarlow, and walking through the rooms was like being at MoMA but without the crowds. Included in the collection were a number of paintings that David had bought from Si. While the rest of us were having cocktails, David took Si on a tour of his former treasures. Si suddenly noticed a horizontal Jackson Pollock on the wall.

"David," Si said, pointing to the picture. "Where did you get that one?"

David looked at it and then turned back and said, "You're kidding, right?"

"No," Si said.

And then David said, "I bought it from you!"

"Ooooh," said Si. He looked at it again. "I hung it this way," indicating with his hands that he had hung it vertically.

In the office, Si wore car shoes—those Italian moccasins with the little rubber buttons on the soles—navy blue chinos, a tan sweatshirt, and a polo shirt. That was his standard uniform. He kept a suit and tie in his office, Superman-style, in case he had to go to the Four Seasons. That's where the Newhouses would hold their regular publishing lunches. It would be Si; Donald; Steve Newhouse; Sonny Mehta, who ran Knopf; and Alberto Vitale, Sonny's boss and the head of Random House.

—

I had lunch with Si every couple of weeks. Like others before me, I learned to prep for the meetings, because he rarely wanted to talk about business. He was much more interested in art and film, and gossip from Washington, Europe, and the West Coast. Having lunch with Si was to be peppered with a lot of questions. When there was a problem, he used his own, occasionally awkward, Socratic method of asking questions on the way toward finding a solution. He took his time when speaking. If you asked him a question, he would formulate his answer slowly, waiting for the right thought and the right words to form in his mind. Newcomers to a conversation with Si would rush to fill the void as he fermented his replies. Veterans knew to wait. The result was that all his responses and opinions were measured and well considered. I had hundreds of lunches and dinners with him, and I can't recall Si ever saying anything rash or ill-informed.

When we were still at 350 Madison, we used to eat in one of the booths along the back wall at 44, the restaurant in the lobby of the Royalton on 44th Street. This is when Brian McNally owned the restaurant. It was a two-block walk from the office. One day I wore an off-white linen summer suit, one of the few I owned, along with a pair of seasoned but well-cared-for brown lace-up shoes. As we came out that day from lunch, the heavens opened. I've never seen rain like this in my life.

My first thought: these are my favorite shoes, and they will be ruined. My second thought: How do I get Si the two blocks back to the office? Like in a movie, a Checker pulled up and somebody got out.

I said, "Si—a cab!"

We hustled into the car. Even the few steps from the door of the Royalton to the taxi left us soaked.

"350 Madison, please," I said, apologizing to the driver for the short trip. Then I realized that I didn't have any cash. We had put our lunch on Si's house account.

I whispered, "Si, do you have any money?"

He whispered back, "No, do you?"

I shook my head. As we got close to the office, I said to the driver, "Sir, I'm going to have to go in and get some money."

The fare was going to be around $2.50. I said, "I'll give you twenty dollars if you'll just wait while I get it and bring it back."

We pulled up to 350, and I said to the driver, "So are we good? I'll go in and get the money and bring it to you."

He turned around, looked at us, thought for a moment, and finally said, "Okay, but the little guy's got to stay in the car."

The people who worked for Si, by and large, worshipped him. He was a compassionate, curious person in a job where you don't often find such types. And despite his habit of firing editors who weren't performing, he was loyal. As a result, there were a good many grandees still on the payroll at Condé Nast when I took the job. I would go and have lunch with Leo Lerman every few weeks. We'd sit at his desk and I would pepper him with questions. Aside from his short stint as editor of *Vanity Fair*, he had worked for *Vogue* during the Diana Vreeland era.

At dinners at Leo's vast apartment at the Osborne, on 57th Street, you would encounter all the great figures in the art and fashion worlds from the previous half century. He had wielded considerable, if quiet, authority at Condé Nast across the decades, and Si treated him with great courtesy. Leo used to wear Turkish smoking hats to the office along with elaborate, flowing outfits that covered his weight gain. He used a cane after an accident in a cab left him walking with difficulty. With his unruly white beard, he resembled Kris Kringle, the German version of Santa Claus. Leo had, with Alex, initiated Si into the company when he came in as a young man. After Leo's stint at *Vanity Fair*, Si moved him upstairs and gave him the important-sounding but fairly meaningless title of "editorial advisor."

I was a pretty wobbly steward of *Vanity Fair* during my early years at the magazine. But if Si had doubts about my abilities—and he had ample reason to worry—he never showed them. He instinctively knew that there is no guidebook to being an editor. It's one of the few big jobs in the world for which there is no course instruction. It's all about instinct, confidence, a willingness to try and fail, and having a vision that hopefully forms over time. Most important, as I've said, for an editor to thrive, he or she has to be blessed with a comforting and supportive proprietor. In this respect, Si had no equal. Not once in twenty-five years did Si ever tell me to stay away from somebody he knew. Not once, despite all the family's various social and business interests and possible conflicts. Si was clever in making his policy of noninterference quietly known to a wider circle. Very few people called him up to ask a favor or to exert pressure on an editor, and if they did, he could honestly say, "I have nothing to do with that." He never suggested stories, and he never suggested we not do stories. He gave an editor all the tools to be successful. If you weren't, it wasn't Si's fault, it was your own.

A rare instance when I found myself inadvertently testing his editorial distance came by chance, and in my first year on the job. A lawyer named Ed Hayes was a friend of Si's, and he and his wife, Susie, invited me to dinner at his house in New York. He said that Si and Victoria would be there. I don't like going out on a Friday night at the best of times. In those early days, I was completely spent by the end of the week and just wanted to be at home with my family. But I had to say yes. As it happened, we had just published an extract from Anthony Summers's big book *Official and Confidential: The Secret Life of J. Edgar Hoover.*

The part of the book that we ran was about parties that took place at the Plaza Hotel, where Hoover, then still head of the FBI, and his friends—including his reputed boyfriend, Clyde Tolson— would all dress in women's clothing. Roy Cohn, counsel to the notorious Red-baiter Joe McCarthy, was part of the crowd. I had met him years earlier when I had been assigned by *Time* to cover his fifty-fifth birthday party at the house of Bob Guccione, the publisher of the softcore men's magazine *Penthouse.* At the time, Cohn was still one of the most feared and powerful lawyers in New York. Like so many right-wing gay men at the time, publicly he was defiantly antigay. He was also the last person you ever wanted to face off with. Among other black marks against him was that he was Donald Trump's lawyer and had schooled him in the dark arts that propelled his long march from the gossip pages to the front pages of the city's tabloids.

Over dinner, Si said, "I read the Tony Summers piece."

I was pleased that he had read it and said, "Amazing, isn't it?"

To which Si replied, "You do know that Roy was my best friend growing up?"

I stumbled for a moment and then said, "What do you mean?"

Si said, "He was my best friend."

I discovered later that when Si was a young fellow on nightclub prowls, Cohn would get him out of scrapes from time to time. The dinner went downhill from there. Ed made a big show of lying down on the sofa and falling asleep. I myself was almost delirious with exhaustion and now with anxiety as I wrestled with the fact that I had included the best friend of my new boss in a story about a ring of closeted men prancing around the corridors of the Plaza Hotel in black shifts and boas. Si never brought Cohn or Hoover and the Plaza up again, and for that I will be forever grateful.

A s much as I grew to admire and adore Si, I was nevertheless constantly terrified of being fired. At a certain point, it was no doubt an irrational fear. Or perhaps it was a holdover from my perilous first two years at the magazine. Whatever the reason, I was always alert to potential discord between us. And we did have a few disagreements. Once the magazine was roaring and hefty with ads, Si would talk constantly about making it a weekly. I thought this was a misguided idea. The whole beauty of the magazine was the breadth of the stories in each issue—there was always so much to pick from in the table of contents. A reader might not give a hoot about a long profile of someone from the fashion or social worlds, but in that same issue they might love the story of a literary feud or a big political or business scandal. A weekly, which would have fewer pages, would dilute this catholic spread across areas of interest and diminish it considerably. Also, I had settled into the monthly pace. It agreed with me, and I am at heart a bit lazy.

At one lunch, I mentioned that I was thinking of adding cartoons to the magazine. The most important part of an issue was what we called the "well." This was the big splashy, photo-heavy central section, where the major feature stories opened, each running six or eight or ten pages. Since these articles ran long, they would continue to the "jump" at the back of the magazine—which ran to about twenty or thirty pages of endless type. I thought cartoons on each spread in the jump could liven them up. I had already had a lunch at Da Silvano with a half dozen prominent cartoonists and they were all on board. I told Si about my plan and was thoroughly taken aback by his response. He told me categorically to forget this. Cartoons, he said, were a significant part of *The New Yorker*'s franchise, and I should stay away. It was one of the rare occasions that I told him something I had planned for the magazine, and I took care not to repeat my mistake.

Another disagreement occurred over the International Best-Dressed List, which had been created by Eleanor Lambert, a turbaned, public relations legend in the fashion world who had also helped to create the Costume Institute at the Met. I—along with three of my *Vanity Fair* colleagues, Aimée, Reinaldo Herrera, and Amy Fine Collins—had for a number of years been on the nominating and selection committee of the List. It was all a highly secretive affair, and the results were announced each year to much fanfare—although the hoopla was pretty much confined to the rarefied hothouse of the social and fashion worlds.

When Eleanor was winding down her business, she asked the four of us to take it over. Which we agreed to do. A small item appeared in the papers about the handover, and Si brought it up at lunch.

"This should go to *Vogue*," he said.

"What do you mean?" I asked.

"Anna should be in charge of this," he replied.

I said, "I'm sorry, Si, but Eleanor specifically did not want the List to be managed by a fashion editor."

"Well, we should own it then." I told him that there wasn't anything really to own. I left the lunch a bit shaken and hoped that the matter wouldn't come up again. And it didn't.

Our biggest disagreement came over the U.S. invasion of Iraq in 2003. I, along with my colleagues at *Vanity Fair*, were almost uniformly against the war. This put us at odds with almost every other journalistic outlet in the country—not to mention every other major editor. Si himself was pro-war. We need it for the oil, he would say. I told him that at least two of my children would soon be draft age, and that I was damned if I was going to risk their lives over oil deposits in the Middle East in a war against a nation that had nothing to do with the 9/11 attacks. In the buildup to the invasion, I wrote on the editor's page about the foolhardy and potentially devastating consequences, and continued to write against the war after the invasion, month after month.

One day at lunch, Si told me to knock it off. He said that I was becoming boring on the subject. I was shocked by his vehemence. And a little hurt. I avoided the subject in the editor's page the next issue. But I resumed writing about the invasion the issue after that. And Si never mentioned it again.

A good part of *Vanity Fair*'s punishingly expensive journalistic costs was covered by our advertisers. It was the editor's job to deliver a magazine that advertisers would want to be part of, and it was the publisher's job to get the ads into that magazine. At Condé Nast, and I expect elsewhere, the general feeling was that an editor was only as good as his or her publisher, and conversely, a publisher was only as good as his or her editor. A thick magazine, stuffed with advertising, and with great newsstand sales, was considered a successful one. I had great appreciation for the skills of my publishers. Knowing the importance of *Vanity Fair* to the overall company, Si presented me with the best he could get his hands on: Mitch Fox, Pete Hunsinger, Ed Menicheschi, and Chris Mitchell.

Si took considerable care in putting together the editor-publisher teams that led his magazines. After I had suffered through one who was pleasant enough but had failed at the essential element of the job—that is, selling advertising pages—I asked him if we could consider Ed, a magazine veteran who had worked at *Vogue* and whom I didn't really know except that he was well liked by those around him. I had planned a weekend at Camp David, the compound on Martha's Vineyard owned by Larry David and his wife, Laurie. Si wanted complete secrecy surrounding the switch to Ed and suggested that we get together that weekend. The company chartered Ed a plane and flew him to the Vineyard so he and I could see if we could work together. I had to tell our hosts about the surprise visitor. Ed arrived and we talked for an hour or so and he flew back to New York.

That night at dinner, Larry said I should definitely bring Ed to *Vanity Fair*.

"But you didn't even meet him," I said.

"No," said Larry, "but he looked great in a blazer."

That was good enough for me. Ed came on as my publisher and we had many years of thick, ad-filled magazines together. A page in *Vanity Fair* back then cost advertisers upward of $100,000.

Some editors put the advertiser at the top and the readers below. I took the opposite approach. Everything my staff and I did was in service to a single reader. If that reader came away satisfied with the issue they had just bought, there was a good chance they'd come back the next month. And maybe get a friend to do so as well. I never did studies of who our readers were or how much they made, but after a certain point, I had a pretty decent idea of what they were looking for in an issue of *Vanity Fair*: A tasteful but arresting cover that they could leave on the coffee table without too much embarrassment. An assortment of compelling stories encompassing current history, feuds, scoops, and scandals from the worlds of literature, art, fashion, show business, politics, Wall Street, and Silicon Valley. And, always, a dispatch from trouble spots out there in the world beyond. Si funded all of it and took pride in the vast social and political reach of his magazines.

Chapter 11.

A Monthly Magazine
in a Daily World

I don't think I had a proper editorial meeting the whole time I was at *Vanity Fair*, at least of the kind you see in movies or on *Absolutely Fabulous*—of the "What's new, what's hot?" variety. I met one-on-one with the editors, a stable of gifted journalists that included, during my time at the magazine, Aimée, Wayne, Cullen Murphy, Doug Stumpf, Dana Brown, George Hodgman, Elise O'Shaughnessy, Mark Rozzo, David Friend, Jon Kelly, Bruce Handy, Katherine Stirling, Anne Fulenwider, Peter Newcomb, and Mike Hogan. We'd review what their writers were working on and what stories we thought we should cover. I had a "planning board" in my office. It stretched from floor to ceiling and was about fifteen feet wide. It looked like something from Churchill's War Rooms. The board had been hand-lettered in Johnston Underground type by Michael Imlay, a New York eccentric who navigated the city—rain, sleet, or snow—by bicycle. One year I asked him if he could paint the house number above the front door of our place in the Village.

He told me he couldn't because he was booked for the afternoon do-ing the colored circles on one of Damien Hirst's multimillion-dollar "dot paintings."

In Michael's hand-painted type, the months ran along the top and the section headings ran along the left margin: Politics, World Affairs, Literary, Style, Arts, Social, Crime and Scandal, Business, and so forth. Each story would get an index card, printed out with the name of the story, the author, the editor, and, in small type, whatever the peg, or reason to run it on a certain month, was. Each month, the cards were moved along the top axis as old issues were cycled into history and new issues were being assembled. The cards were pinned to the board by an assistant standing on a stool. The planning board was where the real combat happened, where the bat-tles for space were fought, and where stories I'd commissioned lived or died. It was a stand-up process.

It could be tense for the editors: two or three stories may have been prepared for the same slot. Stories could have been worked on for a year or more. And if you weren't there, your story's fortunes could suffer. Some stories never ran. Some just stayed on. There were a million reasons why stories didn't run—and they made up about 20 percent of all the stories commissioned, quite a sizable part of the budget. Stories that didn't run for a year were generally re-moved from the board.

I can think of one notable exception. I had commissioned a story about Oskar Speck, a twenty-five-year-old German who escaped his bankrupt country in 1932 as the Nazis were coming to power and, without much in the way of money or a plan, set off in a foldable kayak on a journey that took him halfway around the world for more than seven years. It was an epic, thirty-thousand-mile paddle, packed with near-death escapes, all the way to Australia. As he battled sharks, hostile locals, and malaria, Hitler rose to power and WWII began. The story was written by William Prochnau and Laura Parker. We all loved it when it came in. On the planning board, it carried the name "Nazi Canoe Trip." Whenever some story suddenly fell out of an issue and we were casting around for a replacement, someone in the planning-board meeting would always shout "Nazi Canoe Trip!" But for one reason or another, it just never ran. Month in and month out, it moved its weary way along the planning board. Its index card had so many pinpricks it was beginning to look like a colander. Prochnau did other stories for us in the meantime. But for almost sixteen years, "Nazi Canoe Trip" was a fixture on the planning board. Bill was sixty-four when he wrote the story. After I announced my retirement in 2017, I was determined not to leave the magazine without publishing his piece, and it ran in my final issue. Bill was eighty when it finally ran, and he was thrilled. He died shortly thereafter.

—

Putting together a monthly magazine in those days was a tricky proposition. A daily newspaper, by and large, reflected the day that preceded it. A weekly magazine that came out on a Monday, say, generally reflected the week that preceded it. With a monthly magazine, it can't be about the month that preceded it, because it takes a month or two to put the issue together, then it's got to be printed and distributed all over the country. We regularly would have more than four hundred pages in an issue, and the assembly seemed to take forever. A monthly magazine had to carve out its corner of the culture. And *Vanity Fair*, like *Esquire* and *The New Yorker*, was a general-interest magazine, and so, unlike the case with special-interest titles like *Field & Stream* or *Car and Driver*, everything was, in a way, a potential subject.

Within two or three years I knew exactly the kind of story I wanted. When I assigned a writer, I could imagine what the opening pages of the piece they turned in would look like, and I knew roughly where it would be in the magazine. In time, we had our own slice of the culture. It was sophisticated, knowing, and international. This may have had something to do with being an outsider—from Canada, no less. When I was growing up, half of our imported culture came from the giant to the south, and the other half came from Britain and Europe to the east.

I'd come into the office every Monday with five or ten ideas in the full knowledge that once I'd let everything ferment a bit, maybe one or two would end up being ideas actually worth pursuing. The difficult part was assigning stories that were not only newsworthy but would have relevance two and a half months—or more—down the line, when they appeared in the magazine.

We were almost never the first to report on a particular story, so my feeling was that if we were going to be late, we had to be complete and revelatory. Our stories became the interim version between the newspaper and the weekly reports on the one hand and books on the other. In ten thousand or fifteen thousand words, we could tell the taut, dynamic narrative arc of a story in a condensed version of the book that would inevitably follow.

Assembling an issue of *Vanity Fair* was like producing a movie each month. Behind each piece was a crew of fact-checkers, legal editors, photographers, assistants, photo researchers, art directors, and crucially, the editors who worked so closely with the writers. Then finally, a press rollout that Beth got down to a science. We wanted to make each new issue feel like an event. If we couldn't have the brisk currency of the weeklies, we could try to get each issue noticed and in a big way. Accuracy was a major part of our proposition. We had about two dozen checkers on full-time staff and then we'd bring in more for a big issue—no small expenditure.

Sometimes we'd assign four or five fact-checkers to a big story in order to close it quickly. One key step once the fact-checking was nearing its end was a line-by-line review directed with infinite patience and skill by Robert Walsh, our legal editor. Si and the Newhouses were seen as having very deep pockets, and *Vanity Fair,* given the sorts of stories we published, was a frequent target for libel threats. Hardly a month went by when we did not receive a "Singer letter," an ominous communication from Hollywood lawyer Marty Singer expressing disappointment with what the magazine had said about one of his clients and hinting at dark consequences in the future.

I was always petrified about plagiarism or a writer just making something up. Every time a big case of either one surfaced at another publication, I would call in Chris, Robert, and John Banta, the head of fact-checking, to ask if we had enough safeguards. I remember being somewhat jealous of *The New Republic* for the wildly colorful stories they published by Stephen Glass. When it turned out that he had fabricated almost all of them, we had another one of our editorial-safeguard summits. Christopher Hitchens happened to be in the office that day, and after the meeting told me that I shouldn't worry so much.

"Why?" I said.

"Because unlike *The New Republic,*" he said, "you run photographs of your subjects."

Having such photographs was protection, up to a point. That's not to say we didn't make mistakes. One small but memorable error came in a story on Salvador Dalí. A man in the piece was described as the "late boy toy" of Dalí's wife, Gala. Soon we heard from the man himself, pointing out that he was very much alive. I was glad the fellow was still with us, but this is never a letter you like to get. In another issue, I'd written that the American deficit was approaching "6.84 trillion dollars." At the last moment, and just before the magazine went to press, a fact-checker changed my figure to "6.84

quadrillion dollars," a number I'd never heard before. It was at the beginning of the internet, and I was subjected to warranted online ridicule for some time afterward. I implored Chris Garrett to gently ease out the fellow who had written in the error.

"You can't," she said. "It would be getting rid of him for cause."

"Why else do you get rid of anybody?" I replied.

Chris was always on the suitably cautious side, and the fact-checker left a few years later of his own accord. I'm sure he's working for Google or Meta now, making quadrillions a year.

I cared deeply about the look of *Vanity Fair* and would spend hours with the art-direction staff, choosing the photographs we would be using and then going over each layout, moving the pictures around and figuring out where the headlines would go. Magazines are both words and images, and I divided my time at the office pretty evenly between the two. Once we'd chosen the cover image, it was time to write the coverlines. Writing effective ones was essential to the over-all goal of getting someone to pick the magazine up at a newsstand. I was good at this, but probably not great. We spent a considerable amount of time on the interior headlines for each story as well.

I had lunch at the Four Seasons once with Don Hewitt, who had created *60 Minutes* for CBS, and who ran it for the next three and a half decades. He told me our coverlines and headlines were lacking—although I think he used more flavorful language.

"What do you mean?" I said.

He had a copy of the September 2005 issue with him.

"Look at this one," he said, pointing to the opening spread of a story by David Margolick about the 1938 world heavyweight fight between Joe Louis, a Black American, and Max Schmeling, the white German champ. Our headline was "War of the Worlds."

"Not catchy enough," Don said. "What about something like

this: 'How Did a Fistfight in the Bronx Make the Front Pages of Every Newspaper in the World?'"

I confessed that his was indeed "catchier." Not that anyone appeared to notice, but after that lunch, *Vanity Fair* headlines and coverlines had a lot more question marks at the end. Such was my coverline education.

I always imagined the whole effort as a pyramid. At the top is that single reader. Everybody else involved in assembling an issue was a building block toward that pinnacle. The job at hand was to get the person holding that issue to read an individual article, and we'd do anything possible to make them want to do that. I felt that if we could make that one person feel that the cover price and the time spent with the magazine were worth it, she or he would come back the next month. I felt that there had to be umpteen entry points into an article. Perhaps the headline would grab a reader's attention, or the summary-like description that followed, or the pull quotes.

Hours upon hours were spent each month on photography under the direction of Susan White and a photo research team led by Jeannie Rhodes. I read and marked up the stories in pencil whenever they came in. I'm told that, until they got their sea legs, newcomers to the staff had a bit of difficulty interpreting the deeper meaning of some of my comments. "Epic," for instance, could mean either fabulous or too long. A benign "Let's discuss . . ." was indeed a call for actual discussion, but often carried an unspoken ". . . when I'm in a better mood than I was after reading this." I was later told that a deeply edited manuscript with no comment at the top was never a good sign.

Many of the stories were expansive investigations. But they could only run long if they were entertaining. I edited every story that went into *Vanity Fair* with a pencil and a printed manuscript. The pencils were thicker than normal ones (easier on the fingers), and I had the stories printed so that the type was only on the left side of the paper. The right side was for comments and edit changes. Reading the piece on the page was a preliminary exercise in gauging how the reader would come to the story. I felt that if, while I was editing a particular story, I kept putting it aside, that was a bad sign. The best pieces I edited in one sitting. We never did studies, but I always imagined the reader as someone getting on an eight-hour flight somewhere, buying a copy of *Vanity Fair* beforehand, and being absorbed during the waking hours of the trip. My focus always was on that one reader on that one flight, and it was our job to do everything in our power to ease the discomfort of that single journey. The advertisers not only dressed up the magazine with their beautiful images, they funded the journalism, the office, the lights, the heat. But they were our partners—our silent partners—not our customer. Every month, I wrote a thank-you note not just to each advertiser, but to every writer and photographer after the issue was published. These would be clipped to early "First Run" copies of the magazine and hand delivered. In the early days, I wrote these notes out myself. But as the issues got thicker and thicker, the task started taking the better part of a day, which I could not afford, so I started composing them on a computer and then transferring them to my stationery, which I ordered from Benneton Graveur in Paris. The cards were crisp and thick and had a classic look to them. I remember thinking, *this is just the kind of note I would love to receive myself.*

The editors were the absolute key. For one thing, they were generators of ideas. No single top editor can have enough good ideas to fill a big magazine issue after issue. I needed editors to be idea engines as well. Every few months I'd ask all of them to submit a list of stories they thought we should pursue, matching the stories to specific writers. I'd collect all these "ideas memos" and spend several days reading, then return the memos to the editors and meet one-on-one. I wanted the editors to also function as their writers' managers, inasmuch as most of the contributors were on exclusive annual contracts and received healthy monthly stipends. It was our responsibility—both for the finances of *Vanity Fair* and the writers' careers—to keep them working on stories that went on to appear in the magazine. This also involved a certain amount of psychiatry, hand-holding, confidence management, career advice, and, in the end, actual editing.

Vanity Fair editors were deeply involved with their writers. At any one time, there were five or six text editors under me and they would spend hours upon hours upon hours editing copy, both grammatically and in scope—often with the writers sitting alongside them. Each editor had a roster of between six and ten contract writers and perhaps another dozen outside writers who wrote occasional articles. When their contract writers were on assignment, the editors would deal with them almost on a daily basis. And then they would work closing the stories with the fact-checkers and lawyers. An editor's job is not just to be a grammarian; we had copy editors on staff to fix things. An editor's job is to tell a writer that this is the most important thing they will ever do, get the story in, and then a few months later convince them that this next story is the most important thing they'll ever do and reel that story in. It's also about being appreciative of how difficult it is to be a writer. Much more challenging, certainly, than being an editor—editors never have to stare down at a blank piece of paper. At the same time, the glory goes to the writer rather than the editor, which I think is only fair. They were the ones who got their names on the cover of the magazine. Not the editors.

Wayne Lawson was the longest-running editor at *Vanity Fair*, and was not only a dab hand with a pencil but a ferocious booster of the writers he worked with and a legendarily wonderful colleague. He had grown up in the Midwest, made it into Princeton, drifted into books and then to magazines. He was a martini man, in the good, old-fashioned sense. He loved opera and the ballet; being single, he would often conscript one of the younger members of the staff to join him for dinner and a trip to Lincoln Center. He had been hired away from *The New York Times* by Richard Locke before the 1983 relaunch and retired more than thirty years later.

Dominick Dunne's stories worked in large part because of Wayne. Nick brought in the good raw material, and Wayne would work with him to turn it all into compelling magazine narratives. When Maureen Orth was covering the Michael Jackson trial, Wayne flew to Los Angeles to work with Maureen on site, ensuring that the article made it into the next issue. As Maureen, Marie Brenner, Bob Colacello, and many others knew, Wayne could both shape and sharpen. With Hunter S. Thompson, Wayne would use what was usable almost exactly as Hunter wrote it—but a lot of what Hunter sent was diffuse or off topic. "I would come home, in those days, and find long messages from Hunter on my message service," Wayne remembers. "Along with exhortations like 'Hey, Wayne, we've got these bastards on the run.'" Wayne was especially good at handling the art historian John Richardson, who was always at work on his magisterial four-part biography of Picasso. I found John to be prickly on occasion, but in Wayne's hands he would purr. Wayne was also a gifted talent scout. He knew good copy when he saw it. He noticed a Texan writer named Mark Seal who was writing mostly for an airline magazine and a few local publications. He commissioned him to write a piece for us, and Mark went on to become one of the magazine's star contributors. His classic stories included the Rupert Murdoch–Wendi Deng breakup, the Hatton Garden jewel heist, and three news-making dispatches on the Madoff scandal.

I had taken all sorts of part-time jobs when I was growing up in Canada. Parents there didn't give their children any kind of pin money. You had to earn it yourself. There was a graveyard near us called the Beechwood Cemetery and every spring they put out an announcement for high school kids to come and dig graves. Ottawa was so cold that for about six or seven months of the year, the ground was completely frozen. In late May, when the ground had thawed, I signed up. They gave you a shovel, and then you were to spend the day digging graves. It was backbreaking, and that, combined with the whole ghoulish aspect of the endeavor, drew the curtain on my career as a gravedigger. I quit the next day. (When I was named the editor of *Vanity Fair*, I was interviewed by a British reporter and I mentioned this day of digging graves, and the headline was something like "From Gravedigger to the Editor of *Vanity Fair!*")

As much as I hated some of my part-time jobs, the funny thing is, these are all the things I look for in somebody else's résumé. I love seeing the history of a young person who has worked in retail or a restaurant. If you can handle three or four tables of difficult diners, the magazine business is a breeze by comparison. I don't warm to a résumé filled with gold-plated internships and performative volunteer work.

You're only as good as your assistant, and to be an assistant at *Vanity Fair* required specific skills. Aimée Bell had changed my life at *Spy*. She was phenomenal and made me realize what a difference a good one can make. At *Vanity Fair*, my two assistants sat outside my office and processed the stream of visitors, phone calls, letters, and complaints. It was a lot of air traffic control—incoming, outgoing—because there was not much in the way of hierarchy at *Vanity Fair*. We had perhaps 150 employees on the floor, and I dealt with about 60 of them on a regular basis. My door was never closed. I liked to spend an hour and a half in the morning editing and going through my notes. Then I would go into the planning room to see how the magazine was progressing. I'd have a regular daily meeting with Chris, and then I'd see the editors.

The assistants had to set up my office in the morning, which meant going through the mail and organizing it in folders. I can work through any kind of noise or dust, but what I can't work through is chaos on a desk. So I tend to keep things orderly. I told my assistants two important things: don't use my bathroom, and keep my pencils sharp. I'm very particular about sharpened pencils—I have them everywhere. I'm also particular about the type of pencil I use. I buy vintage 5H ones online because old pencils have graphite and keep the point longer. My issue with pencils goes back to my childhood. My father was one of those people who sharpened a pencil with a knife, which left it about as sharp as the end of your finger. When I became an adult, one of the first things I bought was a proper pencil sharpener. I have probably a thousand pencils sprinkled throughout my office, apartment, and house. This is what your upbringing can do to you.

My assistants' survival depended on how well they managed a first line of defense; how adept they were at giving me some time and space and keeping my desk uncluttered; and how skillfully they judged and sifted the phone calls, importunate slips of paper, and general gatekeeping.

The best assistants are calm, anticipatory, discreet, and diplomatic. They're the first people visitors see when they come to the office. Mine were instructed to call people Mr. or Mrs. or Ms. until they were told otherwise. Before hiring them, I would test them on the phone and make sure that they had appropriate phone manners and were respectful. I'd check their handwriting to see if it was legible. At *Spy*, we used to give prospective interns and assistants a quiz to see if they shared cultural references similar to mine and Kurt's. "What was the name of the dog in the *Thin Man* series?" That sort of thing. I instructed all assistants at *Vanity Fair* to not talk about the office when they went out to dinner, because young people eat at restaurants where the tables are about the size of a legal pad and separated by a space that would snag dental floss. Other people can hear you. Use code words. Don't talk shop in the elevator. At Condé Nast, the competition rode up and down with us. Be curious. Ask a million questions. If you're not asking questions, you're not learning. By the end of my time at *Vanity Fair*, three of my assistants had risen through the ranks to become editors at the magazine.

One of my first assistants at *Vanity Fair* was Pat Kinder, a serious, professional executive assistant who had previously worked with CEOs. She was English, and a bit Miss Marple-ish. She had a beady eye and she knew her stuff. But because the office called for two assistants, I needed to find a second one. I was at the Royalton one night and noticed Dana Brown. He was working as a barback—as it sounds, the person who stacks the bottles at the back of the bar. When we'd have dinners at our apartment at the Dakota and Brian McNally catered them, Dana would be there. I liked the way he moved around, the way he addressed people. He had a certain crisp charm to him. I asked Brian if it would be okay if I hired him, and Brian reluctantly, but generously, said yes. Dana had dropped out of school and had never even thought of a career in the magazine world. Anytime I spotted an assistant trudging slowly through the office, I would tell them to watch Dana and walk like him. Eventually he became one of my most valued editors, looking after Buzz Bissinger, A. A. Gill, Rich Cohen, and many others. His writers absolutely adored him. Dana was always a quick study and in time became a fine writer in his own right.

One night at a dinner at the Dakota, Diane von Fürstenberg

dropped out sick. So I told Dana, who was helping set up, "Dana, put your jacket on, you're taking Diane's spot at the table." He was seated beside Georgette Mosbacher. Although her husband had been in the Reagan administration, she had carved a path for herself, and I liked and admired her. She was a cosmetics entrepreneur and a Republican activist, and she later served as American ambassador to Poland. Georgette was also a character. Lee Radziwill happened to be sitting at another table. Dana had no idea who anyone was, but he had brushed up and turned on the charm. At a certain point, Georgette had to fly back to Washington, so she left the dinner a little early. I could hear the phone ringing in the kitchen at the end of the hall. I whispered to Dana if he could answer it. He got up from the table and went to the phone. On the other end was someone from New York Hospital asking for Lee Radziwill. Dana thought Georgette was Lee, so he said, "I'm so sorry, but she's left." As we discovered the next morning, it had been the hospital calling to say that Jackie Kennedy was in the last throes of life and wanted to say goodbye to her sister, Lee. We felt dreadful about the mishap. But as I say, Dana was a sponge for telling detail, and from that day on, he made it his business to know who everyone was, and in all realms of *Vanity Fair*'s prescribed world.

—

For students of masthead cryptology—and, if you are, bless you, you're a dying breed—"contributing editors," at least at *Vanity Fair*, generally fell into a number of camps. There were writers who produced superb work on a consistent basis. There were writers who produced good work on a sporadic basis. There were writers who, for one reason or another, barely produced anything at all. And then there were people we thought of as fixers. These were people in society or in a particular field or city whom we leaned on to provide introductions when writers were dispatched to unfamiliar territory. These contributors could also provide informed background on the subjects the writers were reporting on and make sure they were generally pointed in the right direction and knew who was who.

The first port of call for any writer heading to England or Europe was our London editor, Henry Porter. His role required a number of skills: writer, editor, counselor, as well as fixer. I had hired him almost immediately after I got to *Vanity Fair*; I wanted a London editor I could trust. I had met Henry shortly after we started *Spy*. He came over to do a story on us for the London *Sunday Times* and showed up with his Beethovenish head of hair, a leather jacket, a rakish scarf, and a fountain pen and notebook. The next time he came to New York, just as a visitor, he called me up and we had lunch, and we've been friends ever since. Henry is more robust than a lot of Englishmen. We loved the same things—predominantly fishing, painting, and books. Henry left *The Sunday Times* for a number of top jobs. He edited *The Illustrated London News* for a few years, and I wrote a column about New York for him. Then he edited the *Sunday Correspondent* magazine, and I wrote for him there too. Along the way, he has produced a bookshelf of acclaimed thrillers.

At *Vanity Fair*, most of our writers were New York–based, and when an assignment sent them across the Atlantic, Henry would set up guides to help steer them through the thickets of a story. That he was, aside from being an accomplished journalist, also funny and charming made him immensely popular with the staff. Henry also has what I would politely call a mild temper. He was frequently storming out of jobs and quitting. And about every two years or so, something would happen at *Vanity Fair* that was to his disliking, and

I'd get a phone call. "Ha! Okay, fine, you can do without me!" he'd say and threaten to give his notice. I would just ignore him and pick up the thread a few days later—after he'd forgotten that he'd quit. I think his time at *Vanity Fair*—he left when I did—was the longest at any job he'd ever had.

Because of his somewhat short fuse, it was a particular delight to play mild pranks on him. We had the actor and director Bradley Cooper on the cover one month, and in the photograph, he was playing billiards. We designed it so that the coverlines curved around three balls in the foreground of the photograph. The one at the front and the one behind it were quite large and then there was a small one off to the left, half in, half out of the frame. We had two editions of the magazine, the U.S. one and a British-European one. They were generally identical but with different advertising. Sometimes we'd make tweaks on the British cover. In this case, on the half-in, half-out ball off to the left, I put "nry orter ex ape." Because the left side was out of frame, you couldn't see an *HE*, a *P*, an *S*, or a *T*.

I called Henry a few days after the issue came out and asked him how he liked the issue. He said he liked it very much.

"What about the cover?" I asked.

He said, "Yes, I saw it."

"And have you taken a really close look at it?"

"Hold on a second," Henry said.

I could hear him going to find the magazine. Then he came back to the phone and unleashed some highly creative malediction.

A singular addition to the magazine was the arrival of Cullen Murphy. I had once heard him speak at the publishing program at Sarah Lawrence. He was a rising writer, but what set him apart was not only a flowering head of russet-colored hair, but the fact that he wrote the *Prince Valiant* comic strip that was for years illustrated by his father. That, I thought, was really something. He was the managing editor of *The Atlantic* when, in 2006, the owner, David Bradley, decided to move the magazine from Boston to Washington. Cullen is a northeasterner through and through and decided to stay put. I must have read this in the paper somewhere and called him. We met for lunch at Sant Ambroeus on West 4th Street near my house.

Within minutes I knew that his skills and taste were what I was looking for in my desire to continually elevate the magazine. Cullen called me a few days later. He had compared the contents of *The Atlantic* with those of *Vanity Fair*. And following this thoroughly unscientific study, he thought that about 75 percent of what appeared in *The Atlantic* could have run in *Vanity Fair* and about the same percentage of stories in *Vanity Fair* could have run in *The Atlantic*. The remaining 25 percent resulted in the difference between economy and first-class airfare. He had just finished work on his book *Are We Rome?* and said that he was up for a new adventure. With Cullen I also got William Langewiesche, one of the finest long-form journalists working at the time, and the great Mark Bowden, author of, among other nonfiction classics, *Black Hawk Down*.

Cullen also brought in Joseph Stiglitz, the Nobel Prize–winning economist. He corralled Masha Gessen to do the first major profile of Putin, an article that became the basis for Masha's subsequent authoritative biography *The Man without a Face*. Cullen was the editor for a pair of legendary investigative reporters, Don Barlett and Jim Steele, and for Todd Purdum, who wrote elegant stories from the recent past that were absolute charms. Patti Smith and Anjelica Huston wrote for us, and Cullen edited them as well. He did all this from Boston and came down by train twice a month. He was a revered figure in the office, someone always willing to spend time schooling or bucking up a younger staff member. He returned to *The*

Atlantic after I retired from *Vanity Fair,* where he continues to school and buck up younger staff members.

—

I was ever alert to receiving an email from someone whose last name was Newhouse. I was attuned to the name in the way moths have infrasonic sensors to detect the presence of bats. I could almost anticipate them before they landed in my inbox. I had Si in New York and Si's nephew Jonathan in London. And, occasionally, I'd get a social note from Steven, who was also in New York. One day my stomach fluttered and a few seconds later there was a ping, and, lo, there was an email from Jonathan. It was a note suggesting that I consider bringing Daphne Guinness on board as a contributing editor. Daphne became a singer and songwriter in later years, but at that point my best estimation was that she was a socialite with international reach. I assumed that what Jonathan had in mind was some sort of occasional fixer role in London, or in whatever world capital she happened to be at the moment.

I had met Daphne in the past, but really I didn't know her all that well. I got in touch and we arranged to have lunch at the Monkey Bar, which I was then part owner of. We sat in one of the booths in the front room of the restaurant, the part with old monkey murals, red-checked tablecloths, and a '50s-era television that played episodes of *Sergeant Bilko* on a continuous loop. Daphne entered looking otherworldly. Big head of black-and-white hair: black on one side, white on the other. Like Elsa Lanchester in *The Bride of Frankenstein,* but with vaster dollops of beauty and glamour. She carried herself with an aura of assuredness as she approached me— the way a shark handles itself in the presence of an anxious seal. We engaged in some pleasant chitchat and at one point I mentioned that

Jonathan thought she might be a good candidate for a contributing editor's slot. I thought this would please her.

She shook her head and said she couldn't possibly take on new duties. She had too much on her plate. I was a bit surprised, as I just assumed that Jonathan had broached the subject with her before he wrote to me. *What to do?*

"Really," I said. "What are you working on?"

"Gloves," she replied.

"Really," I said again. I wasn't quite sure where this was going, so I mumbled something to the effect that perhaps we could do a little something on her glove collection in *Vanity Fair.*

"I don't think so," she said.

I *hmm*ed for a moment and then asked, "What sort of gloves?"

At which point she explained that she had made just one.

"As a sort of prototype?" I asked.

"No," she said, "I'm only making one."

Well, this threw me a bit. I could feel my head swimming.

"I'm not sure what you mean," I said.

"It's made of gold and diamonds," Daphne replied.

Lost. Completely lost. Drowning at sea.

"Interesting." I said. Then, trying to advance the conversation, I added, "Well, perhaps we could use it in one of our photo shoots."

"Oh no, that wouldn't be possible," she replied.

Lost. Taking on water.

"Um, why not?"

"Because it only fits one person!" she replied as if explaining an elementary aspect of science to a particularly thick schoolboy.

Completely at sea here. Not enough air in the room. Losing consciousness.

"Oh, well then, perhaps we could photograph *you* wearing the glove?"

I caught the attention of a waiter and made a discreet *Can I have the check?* scribbling motion in the air. Daphne caught me mid-signal and I pulled my hand down.

"That would be a possibility," she said. "But of course, it would have to be a cover."

I regret to report that the *Vanity Fair* masthead was never blessed with Daphne Guinness's name. And the subsequent covers of the magazine went Daphne-free. And glove-free.

Chapter 12.

A Charm Offensive and
the Oscar Party

hen I was working at *Time* in the early 1980s, I was dispatched to Los Angeles to cover the Oscars. The magazine had more seasoned, better-connected people out there to write up the actual ceremony and the results. I was there to vacuum up a bit of color, a job for which I was woefully ill-equipped. After I arrived, I unpacked my things and realized that I hadn't brought a notebook or pen. So I folded and then tore in quarters three or four sheets of the hotel stationery and pocketed the room pencil. Jim Kelly came out as well, and we made plans to meet up with Alessandra Stanley, then one of the correspondents in *Time's* Los Angeles bureau. Alessandra took us to dinner at Musso & Frank, that glorious grill on Hollywood Boulevard that is as much a symbol of the dusty old studio town as you could find outside George Cukor's living room or Tom Mix's cowboy boots.

I had somehow been assigned an enormous suite at the Chateau Marmont, with a vast living room and three sets of French doors leading out onto a long terrace. I learned later that they thought I was the actual editor of *Time*. Jim and Alessandra and I gathered in the room for drinks while I got dressed in a midnight-blue dinner jacket with a thin shawl collar that I had bought for $5 at a second-hand shop in the Village. I went off to the Oscars and Jim and Alessandra stayed in and watched the awards on television—which, based on my limited experience, is much more fun than watching from up in the nosebleed seats of the Dorothy Chandler Pavilion, where they were then held. After the ceremony, Alessandra and Jim and I met up for a drink at Tramp, then a fashionable watering hole. The big after-party for the awards in those days was the one organized by Irving Lazar, one of the first people with the job title of "superagent." He was short, bald, and owlish, with round black oversize glasses. He had been given the nickname "Swifty" by Humphrey Bogart. To my mind, if you're going to be given a nickname, having Humphrey Bogart as the donor would be a badge of honor. Not so for Lazar, who reportedly hated it.

Swifty, as everyone nevertheless called him, essentially invented the idea of a viewing party. The first one was held at the Bistro Garden in 1964, the year *Tom Jones* won the award for Best Picture. The guest list was populated by the cream of old Hollywood. And in the style used by columnists of the day to refer to them, the invited included the Gregory Pecks, the Henry Fondas, the Jimmy Stewarts, the Michael Caines, and the Billy Wilders. The guests watched the ceremony during dinner on televisions placed throughout the room. Once the Oscars were over, the winners from the awards, along with the audience rabble, made dutiful cameo appearances at the Governors Ball—then and now a dreary industry affair. After that, statues in hand, the chosen few hightailed it to the Bistro Garden to kick off their shoes, see Swifty, and preen among their equals and lessers.

Jim and Alessandra and I decided that this was the place we

needed to be. After perhaps one too many drinks at Tramp, we set off to see if we could talk our way into Swifty's party. We all had *Time* press cards and we looked eager, if green—both in the professional sense and, by that time of the evening, around the gills. We made it past the first checkpoint and were about to gain entry to this Valhalla of old Hollywood glamour when a strong arm stopped us at the door, turned us on our heels, and pointed us in the direction of the street.

—

When I got to *Vanity Fair*, I got in touch with Swifty. I asked him to lunch, and he accepted. I don't think he quite knew what to make of me. I was fascinated by his clients and flooded him with questions. At one point or another, Swifty had handled the careers of many of the titans of American letters in the middle part of the last century. The list is long, and it included Tennessee Williams, Irwin Shaw, Vladimir Nabokov, William Saroyan, and Truman Capote. He had also managed the careers of Ira Gershwin, Noël Coward, and Cole Porter—and one of my hero of heroes, the playwright Moss Hart, whom I admired not only for his enchanting memoir, but for the plays he wrote with George S. Kaufman, notably *The Man Who Came to Dinner* and *You Can't Take It with You*. I was a sponge for anything about any of them. Swifty must have looked kindly, if quizzically, upon me, because the next year he invited me to attend his vaunted Oscar party.

Swifty's party had, by this time, moved from the Bistro Garden to Spago, the restaurant on the north side of Sunset owned by Wolfgang Puck. He still held it to about 150 guests for the dinner viewing party. Spago, unfortunately, was divided into two rooms. Clearly there was an A room and a B room. The A room was for Swifty's old guard of Pecks and Fondas and assorted Hollywood aristocrats. The B room was for not-quite headliners, a few industry figures, and people like me. I didn't know anyone at the table I was assigned to, and so while all eyes were on the television screens, I was able to study Swifty as he made his rounds through the two rooms like a prison guard inspecting the exercise yard. He literally shouted at people who wanted to table-hop or get up and take a bathroom break during the telecast. "Sit down!" he would bark. Or sometimes, "Shut up." It was not what you would call a relaxed atmosphere.

After Swifty died, in December 1993, I called in Wendy Stark, our West Coast editor, and Hamilton South, our special projects editor, to float the notion that perhaps we might pick up the slack after Swifty's death. We had the resources and the aesthetic, and, I believed, we appreciated the history of Hollywood more than the people who actually worked and lived there. I was still on a back foot in those days and pretty desperate for anything that might dig me out.

The timing on our part was not auspicious. Nobody, it seemed, cared much about the Academy Awards anymore. Swifty and his party had been fading. Young stars had grown tired of the awards circuit. Grunge was the fashion of the day, and getting dressed up was considered infra dig. Academy members avoided the ceremony in droves, and Hollywood had turned its back on one of its trading assets: glamour. I thought this was a mistake. Glamour, or even the more prevalent ersatz glamour you found in Hollywood then—and now—was a vital part of the industry's allure and currency. I thought if we told the story of Hollywood and its glamour and fabulous history and excess to the current stars and creative engines, we would have perhaps a moderate chance of success.

Growing up in Canada, movies were a window into the world of adult drama, comedy, and sophistication. Westerns, war movies, Dust Bowl dramas, screwball comedies: I loved them all. I had a great love, especially, for the early days of Hollywood. From books and magazines, I knew who everybody was, I just didn't know the people themselves. I figured that I would be a safe host in that, as much as I liked movies, I didn't want to be in the movie business.

It helped that Si also adored movies. Most nights, he and Victoria would be watching a film at home, flanked by the naked Freud and the naked woman with her legs apart. Or they would have an early dinner and see some forgotten classic at the Angelika down on Houston Street. Si also had close friends out in Los Angeles, including David Geffen; Terry Semel, then cohead of Warner Bros., and his wife, Jane; and Disney CEO Michael Eisner and his wife, Jane. I figured that he would appreciate the idea of *Vanity Fair* slipping into Swifty's velvet slippers. At the same time, I didn't want to embarrass him out there with a flop of an evening. We had very little time to prepare. Swifty died in December. The 1994 Oscars would be held the third week of March. We had less than three and a half months to pull together the party for Hollywood's biggest night of the year.

For a venue, I wanted a place with a single room, so there would be no A and B delineation. I wanted it to be relatively tough to get in, but with no gradations of status or power once you were inside. Everybody would be treated the same. And I wanted good food and wine. The reigning power restaurant at that time in Los Angeles was Mortons, owned by Peter Morton, the impresario behind the Hard Rock Cafe. Monday was the big night at the restaurant going back years. Celia Brady, our pseudonymous Hollywood columnist at *Spy*, used to sign off her dispatches with a breezy "See you Monday night at Mortons."

In those days, the Oscars were held on Monday nights, so the location seemed fitting. The restaurant itself was a good-sized single room with green leather banquettes along one wall and a Francis Bacon triptych at the far end. I asked Hamilton South to call Peter to see if we could book it for March 21, the night of the Oscars. He reported back the next day with some bad news. Peter had already promised it to his best friend, Steve Tisch, a producer—and a member of the Tisch real estate family. After the Larry Tisch "dwarf billionaire" episode in *Spy*, the Tisches were certainly not in my corner. But I'd met Steve before, so I called him and suggested we do that first party together. He agreed.

There was immediate competition from Tina Brown, who decided to stage a splashy *New Yorker* lunch a few days before our first Oscar try. We were staying at the Bel-Air, and unfortunately our room looked out over the lawn where *The New Yorker*'s marquee was being erected. Every day I watched as the tent went up, and then after the lunch, I watched as the tent was dismantled. The party had caused such distress to the lawn that the hotel ripped up all the grass to make way for new sod. For two days, it was a brown ugly stretch of dirt—to me, it looked like it might be a worrisome metaphor for our own outing a few days on.

I decided to make that first Oscar dinner intentionally small in scale. My feeling was, and is, that if you are in uncharted waters, as we most certainly were, and there is a chance of failure, you want as few witnesses to the disaster as possible. We invited a hundred guests for dinner to watch the awards on television screens positioned around the room, and another hundred for the party afterward. For the dinner part, we invited the best of old Hollywood and the best of new Hollywood, and a mix of writers, artists, musicians, and other members of the culture complexes of New York, London, and Europe, including Billy and Audrey Wilder, Mick Jagger, David Hockney, Gore Vidal, Gene Hackman, and Nancy Reagan. That year's Oscar attendees came after the ceremonies, including Robert De Niro, Anthony Hopkins, Tom Cruise and Nicole Kidman, Liam Neeson and Natasha Richardson, and Prince.

Sara Marks, who organized the event and indeed handled all events for me over the next quarter of a century, ran the planning and execution like a field marshal. Sara was a master of detail who had spent time working for Mick Jagger as his assistant. She brought in Patrick Woodroffe the Stones' lighting manager, to design the outdoor and indoor lighting, and two English veterans, Pete Barford and Victoria Swift, to handle the build-out. All stayed with *Vanity Fair* throughout my time there. Basil Walter, who had worked on our Dakota apartment and our *Vanity Fair* offices, came in to handle design—as he was to do for every event we did at the magazine from then on.

Another element in our plan was devised by our director of public relations, Beth Kseniak. Space in the parking lot in front of Mortons could accommodate three dozen broadcast television crews—domestic and foreign—on rows of bleacher-like standing areas. We had press photographers roaming the area as well. The result was that it had the intentional kinetic fervor of an old Hollywood premiere—flashing light bulbs, people yelling, lots of high energy. Select members of the press were let inside on a revolving basis. People came out of the party to stand and watch the arrivals and the hoo-ha. By the end of the evening, I realized that we were on the map.

By having no cordoned-off area inside, everybody mixed with everyone else. If you're a successful movie actor, you don't really get to meet other movie actors unless you've been in a movie with them, because you're working all the time. So most actors don't know all that many other people in their industry. I watched as they excitedly navigated the room, meeting fellow actors whose work they admired. They were fascinated by music people, especially. My guess is that it's because music people don't just perform, they actually create what they perform. I don't think an environment like this had been experienced in years—a space where actors could mingle freely with no roped-off area, no bouncers, no minders or personal assistants, and with a mix of other people thrown in. All were free to roam this celebrity Serengeti at will. Over the years, we included a sprinkling of people in the news at the moment, like Monica Lewinsky, General Tommy Franks, or Captain Sully Sullenberger. Already the following year, people were skipping the official Oscar party and coming to ours. We had our foothold in Hollywood.

—

That said, we still faced some real problems. For one, I was not the most popular figure out there. I had been at *Vanity Fair* for only a year and a half. *Spy* was still a recent memory, and we had treated many of Hollywood's biggest figures with what *New York* magazine once called "unfettered, delectable brutality." It was catnip to anyone who wasn't actually being attacked at that moment, so everybody read the stories. But for those in the crosshairs, it hurt. One of our more frequent *Spy* targets was Mike Ovitz, the head of CAA, who had been beside himself with fury at our intrusive coverage. And here I was, now at *Vanity Fair*, launching *the* Hollywood party. The single most powerful person in Hollywood would have preferred me dead. It was important that I win him over—or at least try to neutralize him.

We had lunch at his office. He had Eadweard Muybridge photographic prints on the wall that he was very proud of. Ovitz is not without charm and, obviously, is one of the great negotiators, which I am not. But we couldn't really bury the past. He told me then—something I hadn't known before—about how he and his partner Ron Meyer worried they might have to close down the agency after *Spy* ran its secretive client list. He said that it had destroyed so many confidences and broken down so many Chinese walls between the top clients. But Ovitz is a transactional person and wanted to make amends. A truce was put into place, though one where neither party trusted the other.

It was a bit like when S. J. Perelman was writing the screenplay for *Around the World in 80 Days* and Mike Todd was the producer. Perelman didn't trust Todd; Todd didn't trust Perelman. Perelman would come in with pages of script and Todd would have the money and they would exchange them across the table at exactly the same moment. Ovitz went down eventually—years later—in a blaze of name-calling, having lost millions in his own failed agency start-up, plus what remained of his reputation. In a swan-song profile by Bryan Burrough in *Vanity Fair* in 2002, Ovitz would portray himself as a victim—sabotaged, he said, by David Geffen, the "gay mafia," his former protégés at CAA, Disney's Michael Eisner, and *The New York Times*.

—

O ne thing I noticed about Los Angeles was that, despite the glories of its climate, almost nobody, aside from Bob Evans, George Hamilton, and a few other hearty souls, had a tan. My thinking was that tanning was considered very '70s, and that the lack of color indicated that you were chained to a desk somewhere and therefore working on something really important. During the weeks leading up to the Oscars, the only convertibles I ever saw with their tops down were driven by the New York–based *Vanity Fair* staff, who had escaped the East Coast cold and grayness for what they thought was a sort of sunny Nirvana.

I made a number of trips to Los Angeles in those early days, the purpose of which was to shore up the magazine's reputation. Well, to be honest, to shore up my reputation. *Vanity Fair*'s reputation was fine, but because many in the film business had been terrified of *Spy*, I assumed, by association, that they were terrified of me. I had to figure out a way to correct the image of me as a journalistic vulture.

The road trips my staff and I took out there were a lot of fun. We stayed at the Bel-Air or the Beverly Hills Hotel. I'd never lived like this before. I remember the first time Cynthia and I stayed at the Beverly Hills. We were going to meet somebody at the dining area down by the pool. It's sort of confusing how to get there from the ground floor, and all of a sudden there was a slight man in a trench coat walking ahead of us. We pulled up alongside him and I said, "I'm sorry, sir, could you tell us which way to the swimming pool?" The man turned around, and it was Fred Astaire.

I had hired Wendy Stark as our West Coast editor as I was first getting settled in at *Vanity Fair*. Her predecessor, Caroline Graham, for whom she'd worked as an assistant, had moved to *The New Yorker*. I had great affection for Wendy. She spoke without punctuation and could veer from one subject to the next without so much as pausing to catch her breath. But she had the advantage of being knitted into that world; she was, as they say, Hollywood royalty. Wendy's father was Ray Stark, the legendary producer. Wendy's mother was the daughter of the famed comedienne and singer Fanny Brice. Ray produced *Funny Girl* and *Funny Lady*, based on Brice's story, with Barbra Streisand in the lead role.

Ray was a banty fellow with pronounced front teeth that had earned him the nickname "Rabbit." He lived in Holmby Hills, in a house that had been owned by Humphrey Bogart and Lauren Bacall. And he kept a police car in the driveway. He had bought the car and parked it there with the thought that it would ward off the local criminal class. Ray was a serious art collector with a lot to protect. He had one of Monet's big water lily paintings on the wall in the dining room, and in the garden, he had one of the finest arrays of

Henry Moore sculpture in private hands. The thing is, Ray never updated the police car. And by the mid-'90s, it was a decade or two out of date—something even the dimmest among the local thievery would take note of. Still, I don't recall him ever being robbed. Wendy would be our West Coast editor for the next quarter of a century. After she got the job, Ray threw a dinner for me at his home. There were a number of movie stars at the table, but the only person I remember talking to was Sue Mengers, who was there with her husband, Jean-Claude Tramont. She was seated beside me and I was thrilled.

I knew exactly who Sue Mengers was. Anybody with any knowledge of Hollywood knew that she was the first female superagent. In the 1970s, she had on her roster the biggest movie stars in the world. She had Ryan O'Neal, around *Love Story* time; she had Barbra Streisand, who was her closest friend; and she had Gene Hackman. She also at one time or another had Tony Perkins, Candice Bergen, Michael Caine, Peter Bogdanovich, Faye Dunaway, Bob Fosse, Ali MacGraw, and Gore Vidal. Sue was the last of the old-school, live-on-their-landline agents. Success was built on personal relationships. She was popular when she was on top, and remained popular even after, because she never to the best of my knowledge ever screwed anyone over.

That's not to say she couldn't badger a director or a producer half to death. She shoehorned Gene Hackman into the lead role in *The French Connection* against the original wishes of its director, William Friedkin. Hackman went on to win an Oscar for the part. And William, or Billy to his friends, stayed Sue's lifelong chum. Her arguments with Paramount production chief Bob Evans were epic. And yet they remained close until the end. The thing that drew me to Sue was that she represented a more swingy, freewheeling Hollywood era. The corporate, top-down style of agentry as represented by

Ovitz and CAA was quickly becoming the new way of the movie business. The world was moving on from her. By the late '70s, she had lost many of what she called her "above the line" clients. And in 1981, she lost the biggest of all, Streisand.

Here I was, seated between Sue and Jean-Claude, and we just sort of hit it off. Her laugh was like nothing I'd heard before or have heard since. It came from way in the back of her throat and was more of a hard rasp than anything else. Making Sue laugh was one of the more rewarding experiences in life. Jean-Claude was a handsome Belgian-born director and writer. Their marriage was in equal parts a love fest and an episode of that old radio show *The Bickerson*s. They had an oval swimming pool that you could see from the living room. Sue told me she had never been in it. At one point, when she decided to get into shape, she and Jean-Claude visited one of those stores that sell gym equipment. As Sue was trying out a treadmill, wearing a caftan and with a long scarf hanging from her neck, Jean-Claude leaned over to the salesman and whispered, "You don't happen to have the Isadora Duncan model, do you?"

Sue took me under her wing, and I will tell you that having her imprimatur went a long way toward legitimizing me in the eyes of Hollywood. She was also good friends with Fran Lebowitz, and when she and I would come out to Los Angeles for the Oscars, Sue would rasp, "Let me give a dinner for you." My wife, Anna, told me once that most of the real movie stars she has ever met, she met in Sue's living room. And I know what she means. The room was a jewel, a calming mix of beige and aubusson. There were two sofas facing each other and two stuffed chairs at either end. That first dinner included Jack Nicholson and Barbra Streisand. Sue never represented Jack, but they adored each other. Both had an affection for pot, which helped, except when it didn't. When they went to see *Avatar*, they left the theater when the film was finished and threw their 3D glasses into one of the cardboard bins in the hallway. Once they got back to Sue's, Jack realized that the black horn-rimmed glasses he had thrown into the bin were his real glasses. They raced back to the theater and rummaged through the bin until they found them. One year Fran and I were out in Los Angeles, and here and there people would come up to us and ask, "Where were you the other night?" We were slightly dumbfounded. It seems that Sue had thrown a dinner for us, but in a haze of marijuana, had forgotten to tell us about it.

Aside from our first meeting at Ray Stark's place, I rarely saw Sue outside of her own living room. Sue was smart. She almost never left her home. If you wanted to see her, you had to go to her place. Dinner at David Geffen's was an exception. On Oscar night, she would never go out, preferring to watch the ceremony in her "screening room"—a small space off the living room with two sofas and an old Sony Trinitron. By the time I met her, agent Sue had become full-time hostess Sue—and she was even more successful in her new vocation. It was in this role that she became one of the more influential forces in Hollywood—a remarkable achievement in that she didn't write movies, act in movies, or direct movies. Sue became, in fact, the Elsa Maxwell of Southern California. She was most certainly a star snob, and she wanted only above-the-line talent at her table. Dinner at Sue's was like stepping into the Hollywood you imagined but almost never experienced.

Her house was a John Woolf gem within walking distance of the Beverly Hills Hotel. At Sue's, everyone was funnier, quicker, and smarter than they were anywhere else. For visiting friends from the East, such as Fran, Frank Rich and Alex Witchel, Maureen Dowd, Alessandra Stanley, or Lorne Michaels, she rolled out the single-name stars: Warren, Jack, Barbra, Elton, Ali, Anjelica, Marlon, Francis, Candice, Bette, and Jennifer (Lopez *and* Aniston). It was at her home that Mel Brooks told us he was going to take his film *The Producers* and bring it to Broadway as a musical—and that he was going to write the music and the lyrics himself. As we were getting into our cars at the end of the evening, I thought to myself that this was about the dumbest idea I'd ever heard. The next year, it was the sold-out hit of the Broadway season, with ticket prices edging above $400.

Sue directed the conversation from her command post at one end of the sitting area, and it moved like a freight train. Her food was also first-rate—a vital ingredient in a hostess's arsenal. One year she asked me if I liked brisket. To be honest, I don't. But I wasn't going to disappoint her. "Are you kidding me, Sue?" I said. "I love brisket." She must not have noticed me pushing the food around on my plate that night, because for years afterward she would pull me aside when I arrived for dinner and whisper, "I've got your favorite!" Her chicken pot pie, though, was out of this world.

She took credit for bringing Barry Diller and Diane von Fürstenberg together. "The von Dillers," she called them. Her big advice to young women was to "close the deal"—in other words, get the ring on the finger. As I say, old school. And she was funny. She had an asp-like wit that few professional comediennes could match. Her parents had escaped the Holocaust, settling first in Antwerp and then New York. She never lost the immigrant feeling of being just slightly on the outside. Nor did she ever lose her edge from growing up in New York and learning to speak English on the fly. Indeed, she relished it. When Tony Perkins and Stephen Sondheim wrote the screenplay for their mystery *The Last of Sheila*, they based the tough-talking character played by Dyan Cannon on Sue. She liked to say that she talked "like a gum-cracking Warner Brothers second lead." Walking into the Beverly Hills Hotel for an eighty-fifth birthday party for her mother, Sue surveyed the crowd and leaned toward

Jean-Claude and said out of the corner of her mouth, "Schindler's B-List."

Sue tended to see everything in terms of above-the-line and below-the-line talent. Above the line was movie stars and big-time directors. Below the line was pretty much everyone else. When the Manson murders took place up in Benedict Canyon in early August 1969, she tried to calm Barbra Streisand down. "Don't worry, honey," she told her. "Stars aren't being murdered. Only featured players." Sue famously tried to apply these gradations when, in 1979, she found herself on a Los Angeles to New York flight that had been hijacked. The hijacker, a woman, said she was wired with explosives and that she was prepared to blow up the plane. Passengers were on the floor praying and weeping. Not Sue, according to Joe Armstrong, then the publisher of *New York* magazine, who was also on the plane. Sue wanted the drama over so she could get to New York for dinner with Candice Bergen: "I'm keeping Candy waiting at Elaine's." The hijacker wanted Charlton Heston to read a manifesto on television. "Charlton Heston!?" Sue said. "I can get Streisand." Later she said, "With my luck, she would have said no anyway. 'Blow her up!'"

At one point, after six or seven hours of this, Sue lit up a joint. And then the actor Theodore Bikel, who was also on the plane, pulled out a guitar he was traveling with and began to sing. "And so I was thinking," she remembered, "I'm going to die listening to Theodore Bikel and he wouldn't fucking sit down and shut up. Like he's consoling us with these songs." In time, the plane made it to New York, the hijacker was overpowered, the explosives turned out to be fake, and Sue headed for Elaine's.

Fran joined us at the Oscars each year. The week before the party, we'd visit classic-car showrooms because we're both car nuts. She's got one of the last Checker Marathons, from the company that made the classic taxi cabs. One year we were at the wedding of

Heather Watts and Damian Woetzel, two principal dancers in the New York City Ballet. They were getting married on a lake near us in Connecticut, and I gave Fran a lift back to where her car was parked. This was the first time I had actually seen the cab. "Fran," I said, "I didn't realize your Checker was white." She looked at me and just shook her head. "Graydon, it's pearl. Any gay man would have known that."

Out of the blue one year, Sue told us that she wanted Anna, Fran, and me to take her to Bryan Lourd's party on the Friday night before the Oscars. Sue loved movie stars, and Bryan's CAA party had more per square inch than Forest Lawn cemetery. Bryan and his husband, Bruce Bozzi, live in mid-century splendor in a sprawling and glamorous low-slung Wallace Neff masterpiece a short drive away from Sue's.

Bryan is possibly the most charismatic agent in the film business, a throwback to Charles Feldman—who many said outshone his client Clark Gable in the suavity sweepstakes. Similarly, Bryan could more than keep up with his two principal male movie-star clients, George Clooney and Brad Pitt. Jerry Weintraub told me one night when we were having dinner with Bryan that he was the inheritor of Lew Wasserman's throne. By that he meant not only the most powerful person in the film business, but the chief moral arbiter in a town that had them in short supply. He had launched his Friday-night dinner a year or two after we kicked off the *Vanity Fair* Oscar party. That first night, there were maybe a dozen of us. By the next year, it had grown fourfold. And it just kept growing. By the time Sue wanted to go, the guest list was in the hundreds.

The scene outside Bryan's that night was already resembling a *Day of the Locust*–level frenzy. And it was starting to rain. Fans, who had camped out across the street, were packed three deep. Cops were directing traffic. Most people had drivers, who deposited their passengers and then hustled off somewhere else to wait until the evening was over.

I must point out that Sue was not the easiest person to pilot around, even in the familiar regions of her own living room. Movement was just not a big part of her lifestyle. Shuffling her from her home into the car, then out of the car, and then up the many stairs to Bryan's front door was a challenge. My mind kept turning to *The Wages of Fear*, where four men try to navigate two trucks full of nitroglycerine over hazardous mountain roads in South America. But we made it to Bryan's, and in a room that was wall-to-wall stars, Sue, who had been avoiding the public for years, was the hit of the evening. She sat in the library, and every movie star at the party—and there were a lot of them—stopped by to say hello. She still loved movie stars—she called them "sparklies" and "twinklies"—and I can't remember ever seeing her so happy as she was that night.

The rain had picked up by the time we were ready to head home. Curiously for a Hollywood agent, the cell phone reception at Bryan's house was spotty. After a few tries, Anna reached our driver. The departure system worked like this. The cars came down what was by now a one-lane roadway. You had to be there the moment yours pulled up. If you missed your chance to get in, the car had to move on, and it could be another half hour before you got another opportunity. Our car was just about there, and I was trying to get Sue down the slippery steps from Bryan's house. We were about to reach the departure area when Sue spotted Sarah Jessica Parker. Whoops of joy on both sides. I gently tried to pry Sue away so we could grab our car when it pulled up. And in a few minutes, it did. I begged the fellow in charge to let it wait a little longer. I managed to remove Sue from Sarah and we made it down to the car.

We got to Sue's house and made our way up to her front door. She rang the bell but there was no answer. Her housekeeper Virginia had gone to bed. It was raining. It was midnight. And we were desperate to deposit Sue so we could get back to the hotel. Anna, Fran, and I looked at each other in horror. Anna said, "Wait here." She went around back and knocked on the windows and was finally able to stir Virginia, who threw on a dressing gown and rushed to open the door. We almost collapsed with relief as we got into our beds that night, thrilled at being able to give Sue the evening of her dreams but almost weeping with joy that it was all over.

—

On one of my early trips west, I met with Sandy Gallin, then among the more notable and successful managers in show business. Sandy also happened to be very good-looking, with a great head of hair and one of the more forceful jawlines I'd ever seen. He was cheery and comforting. Which may have explained a client list that included Michael Jackson, Elizabeth Taylor, Neil Diamond, Barbra Streisand, Mariah Carey, Whoopi Goldberg, Cher, and his best friend, Dolly Parton. He and Dolly were so close they shared an apartment together in a building on the same block of Fifth Avenue as the Pierre Hotel. It was a vast white expanse, with white furniture, white rugs, and views in all directions. And it was as clean as any place I had ever been in. I had dinner there with them once, and had Dolly on my right. At one point I reached for my wine glass and my arm brushed up against her breast. I apologized and she said not to worry, that it happened all the time.

I'd never met Sandy before, and when I walked into his office, he was sitting at his large, spare desk with his shoes and socks off. There was a woman on her knees filing his nails and then soaking his feet and massaging him.

Sandy's first words were "Pay no attention to her, Graydon. Talk to me."

Sandy was as animated as any person I've ever met. If you've seen the movie *Wag the Dog*, I have to believe that Dustin Hoffman based part of his character on Sandy—with a healthy dollop of Bob Evans. He didn't read. The books in his many homes had drink rings on them. When he had to review a script, he had an assistant record it and he'd listen to it in his car on the way to the office. Running into Emma Thompson, Sandy asked what she was doing in Hollywood. She was making a film, she told him.

"What film?" Sandy asked.

"*Sense and Sensibility*," Emma replied.

"Mmm," Sandy said. "Very good title."

Sandy loved being loved and he was successful at this. He was incredibly popular, beloved by his Hollywood pals like David Geffen and Barry Diller. He told me once that when he and David would arrive in a new city on a trip, they'd search out the top real estate agent and say they were looking for a house. This, I thought, was inspired. They got a free tour, with all the gossip about each house while looking them over. Sandy not only wished his friends well, he enshrined them on the walls of his houses and offices. He had two-shots with everyone you can imagine, set in cheap little frames and all hung on the walls, cheek to cheek.

On this day in his office, Sandy shook my hand and then pressed the speaker box on the desk and called for someone. In a second, the person was there at the door. It was a floppy-haired, aristocratic-looking Englishman. He was a bit over twenty years old and very *Brideshead*-y.

"Have you got her on the phone yet?" Sandy said to the young man.

"No, not yet, I'm trying," he replied. The young man left, and

Sandy, the woman on the floor, and I were together for about a half hour.

As I got up to leave, Sandy said into the speaker box, "Do you have her yet?" And again, the poor young fellow answered no.

I said, "Do you mind if I ask who you're talking about?"

"I'm exhausted," Sandy said. "If I can pull this off, it will be one of my greatest productions. Michael [Jackson] wants to have a two-hour special on all three major networks. Without commercial interruption. And he wants it to end with him sitting on a bench between Liza Minnelli and Liz Taylor, and for the Queen to come onstage and knight him on live television."

As it turned out, the young Englishman was a distant relative in the royal constellation, and Sandy was pestering the poor fellow to get the Queen on the phone to discuss the Michael Jackson knighting. It was nuts. And Sandy, I believe, knew it was nuts. But if you're a Hollywood manager, this is what you did. Who wouldn't fall for someone like Sandy? As I was leaving the office, I looked down, and I have to tell you, his feet looked lovely.

Chapter 13.

Our Part in Hollywood's Big Night

During the first couple of years of hosting the Oscar party, an advance team would go out a month before the awards to chase up stars we wanted to invite. By about the fourth year, we had more or less seen off our competitors. But we faced a new problem: who *not* to invite. I'd usually come out two weeks beforehand. I'd bring my entire family and stay at the Beverly Hills Hotel or the Bel-Air. The phone in my room—in those days before cell phones—would never stop ringing. In desperation, I had the hotel screen the calls, so when they'd announce who was on the line, I could either take the call or have the operator say that I wasn't in. I was astounded by the number of people who happened to be out there that weekend and knew where I was staying and wondered if they could get an invitation. A few years in, it got to the point where if you hadn't been invited to the *Vanity Fair* Oscar party, it was best to be studiously out of town.

We had to go to great lengths to keep the numbers down. After two years of Oscar dinners, we'd outgrown Mortons. Our solution was to increase its size overnight by knocking out the back wall of the restaurant and building a passageway with latticework and topiary on the walls out into the parking lot, where we constructed a big marquee tent structure. This had carpeting, sofas, and more latticework and topiary. We'd rebuild the back wall of Mortons the following day. None of the add-on bits looked temporary. Even the bathrooms were exemplary. Despite the fact that Los Angeles is a big no-smoking city, and that it was forbidden indoors by the Beverly Hills fire marshal, a big hit each night were the cigarette girls. We outfitted them with costumes like those worn in nightclubs in 1930s movies. They roamed the premises with boxlike trays hung from their necks, passing out packs of cigarettes.

We also had *Vanity Fair* ashtrays and Zippo lighters—all of which were gone by the end of the night. One year we flew in a Cuban orchestra from Havana to liven the after-party up a bit. But Hollywood, I discovered, doesn't really dance. Why dance like a fool when you could be networking with someone who could say yes to your next movie? I like to dance, and at one point was out on the dance floor with Madonna, if you can believe it. I was a bit dismayed when her brother Christopher cut in. I was even more dismayed when I realized he cut in because he wanted to dance with me.

A word about seating. Male-female-male-female—yes, obviously. But there are different rules depending on geography. In Los Angeles, for instance, husbands and wives sit together. In New York, husbands and wives sit at the same table but not together. In Europe, husbands and wives sit at different tables—all the better, apparently, for post-dinner gossip picked up during the meal. You try to avoid putting people with a potentially antagonistic relationship too close to one another. This could mean a writer who gave another writer a bad review. Or two people who'd once had an affair. Or in the case of Hollywood, two actors who had been up for the same role and one of whom got it. There were times when we got the seating way off. Two writers who'd had an affair were seated beside each other at the Oscar dinner one year. With their new partners also at the table. Not good. Emilia Clarke, the charming young actress with the dragons in HBO's *Game of Thrones*, was seated in the vicinity of Brett Ratner and James Toback at one Oscar dinner. Their offensively florid behavior caused her to plead with Sara to change her seat. Which she did. When both Ratner and Toback were later corralled in the #MeToo roundup of sexual suspects, it didn't surprise any of us—least of all, Emilia.

The Oscars are a long night, often running to four hours. So when we were doing the seating, we wanted guests to be surrounded by compatible tablemates. The dinners were generally made up of fifteen tables of ten. My thought was to treat each one as a separate dinner party so that regardless of the dreariness of what was going on at the awards, the people at each table would have a good time. We built them around table leaders. The Jerry Weintraub table, for instance. Jerry Jones and his wife, Gene, were regulars at that one. Or the Hanks table. This is where we regularly sat Tom Ford and his husband, Richard Buckley, Martin Short, Jimmy and Jane Buffett, Tom Freston, and Eric and Lisa Eisner. My own table varied only slightly from year to year: Barry and Diane, Mitch and Kelly, Mick, Fran, Ronald Perelman and his then wife, Ellen Barkin, and a surprise guest or two. This could be Larry David, or Johnny Pigozzi, or Colin Firth and his then wife, Livia.

To get to the actual arrangements as to who would go where, we had a series of seating meetings in the days leading up to the big night. These were attended by close to a dozen staff members, all with their own areas of expertise. Seating meetings might sound like civilized tea-and-watercress-sandwiches sorts of afternoons. They were anything but. Each combatant had their favorites and fought for their table and placement. If the participant was in charge of a table, like Reinaldo, Bob Colacello, or Wendy, the negotiations got downright cranky. With Reinaldo and Bob, whose regions of social influence overlapped dramatically, there was especially heated discussion over who would get senior Hollywood chatelaines like Nancy Reagan, Betsy Bloomingdale, Connie Wald, or Denise Hale.

For the party afterward, the fire and safety officials had a maximum number of people they judged would be safe to have in the room. A fire marshal at the entrance would keep track of the number with a hand clicker, and stop anyone from coming in once capacity was reached. No one could enter until somebody else left. We didn't want a line of people with Oscars in their hands standing outside. So anybody with an Academy Award got in immediately—there was a speed lane for them. Because that was the job that night: to get as many of those Oscar winners as possible into our room. The rest of it—the control, the security, the knife-edge diplomacy—was planned and supervised down to the most minute detail by Sara. She was also the brick wall at which all attempts to cross the border without a pass—absurd and bizarre as some were, or just plain aggressive and threatening—were calmly repelled. She did brick wall very well.

We'd start out with a list of 500 potential dinner guests and then spend three months whittling it down to about 150. Various editors on the magazine got involved and everybody had their favored guests. The fashion editors—including, at various stages, Elizabeth Saltzman, Michael Roberts, and Jessica Diehl—were always colorful inclusions in these scrums. Once the invitations went out, the pleas flowed in from those not invited. I hate hurting anyone's feelings and was considered too soft a touch by the staff. A number of them— chiefly Sara—would redirect outside calls to their rooms so they had the chance to say no before I could say yes.

Sara was the object of bribery, threats, and even abuse. Gift after gift would arrive in her office, and she would write "Return to sender" on each one. There was once a five-figure offer from a Saudi prince. People would say to her, in the face of a refusal, "Do you know who I am?" and she would say calmly that she knew perfectly well who they were. I got a message once asking me if I had any pull with Sara. My kids found this really funny.

In the end, it hinged on having more movie stars per square inch than any party in the world. That was the business we were in that night. There were definitely As, Bs, and Cs for the after-awards invitations. But instead of referring to them by those damning gradations, we ranked them by the arrival times on their invitations. These started at 8:30 (right after the awards ceremony) and made their way in half-hour increments to the 12:00 category. It sounds horribly cruel, but it was the only way to handle eight hundred people vying for a place in a room that fit about half that. In order to get as many—or all—of the major Oscar winners, we had to invite all the nominees, many of them with partners or spouses. Some insisted on including their agent, or manager, or colorist. So that often meant in order to get that single Oscar in the door, we had to invite fifteen or twenty people. Multiply that across all the major categories, and the numbers start adding up.

Every aspect of the dinner and party was recorded by our photographers, a rotating cast that included Jonathan Becker, Peter Beard, Mark Seliger, and Larry Fink. I was reviewing things with Larry on the afternoon before the ceremony one year. He was dressed in what I can only describe as street camo. He had on a green flak jacket and cargo pants.

"When are you going to change?" I asked him.

"I'm not," he replied.

"What do you mean?" I said.

"I was planning to go like this."

"Larry," I said, "You aren't going to Cambodia. You're going to be working in a room full of men wearing dinner jackets. You'll have a much easier time blending in and getting great pictures if you look like one of them."

"But I don't have a tuxedo," he said.

Now this was about two hours before we were due to be at the dinner. I called Elizabeth, our then fashion editor, and explained Larry's situation.

"Have him meet me out front."

"Larry," I said, "Elizabeth's going to help you. Meet her out front of the hotel and be chop-chop-ish about it."

Larry beetled off, and two hours later, there he was in a splendid Armani tuxedo blending into the sea of other tuxedos. His photos from that night were particularly candid and memorable

Early on there were any number of gate-crashing attempts. Our vetting process was sharp but not infallible. A successful New York party planner named Bronson Van Wyck told me that he had bought an old Oscar at a pawn shop in the Valley and, brandishing it as he arrived, was whisked into the party. In 1996, the year the film *Babe* was nominated for Best Picture, a man in a tuxedo showed up with a small pig on a leash. He said it was the one that played Babe. Not being experts in barnyard livestock, we let them in. As you might have guessed, this was not the real Babe.

One year Martin Landau turned up with a dinner jacket but without an invitation. Sara beat her way through the crowd to ask me what she should do.

"It's Martin Landau!" I said. "From the *Mission: Impossible* TV show and *North by Northwest*. We have to let him in!"

The next year he showed up again. He had just come from the awards ceremony with his Oscar for best supporting actor for his part in *Ed Wood*. Good karma there.

Instead of hiring a security firm, we assembled our own team, led by Keith Duval, whose background was in the New York City Police Department's counterterrorism division and air/sea rescue team. Keith not only had the perfect résumé for the job, he was also a gentleman and family man. He was so confident of his authority that he could stop trouble in its tracks without ever losing his smile. This was our way. We were not bullies and we were not going to strong-arm uninvited guests. Sara had a box, like a complaints box, where a record of the expletives she received and of those dished out to other members of the staff were archived. After the party, "winners" were chosen, the names submitted to me for banishment.

Courtney Love made it into the box one year.

She had come up to me, with the party in full swing and people arriving from the Oscars, and said, "Graydon, Graydon, I need your help. You need to let in my manager."

I said, "Why?"

She said, "He's got my money, my car keys, and my drugs."

I said, "Courtney, I just can't deal with this now. Sara Marks is over there, go ask her."

So she went over to Sara, and Sara being Sara, said no. In the actual room we had TV monitors that showed the arrivals outside the party. There was a bank of about 150 photographers on risers and video crews and all the rest of the assembled media. Courtney went out to them.

"I've got an important announcement to make," she shouted above the din.

This not only got the attention of the press outside, it was heard inside the party and people turned to the monitors.

"I just want to say one thing," Courtney announced. "Sara Marks is a c**t!"

Sara was furious and I felt terrible for her. But I had to admire Courtney's novel use of the technology available.

Si had many friends in Hollywood, and as I say, he lived for show-business gossip. One year, before we were heading out to the Oscars, he said at lunch, "What about Abel Ferrara?"

"What do you mean?" I said.

"He'd be good," Si replied.

I thought, okay, and went back to my office and called in Jane. I said, "Okay, how do we get Abel Ferrara to the Oscar party? Also, his name rings a bell, but what films has he done?" Jane came back a few minutes later and told me that he had made the 1992 Harvey Keitel cop thriller *Bad Lieutenant*. "Ah yes," I replied. Jane said she'd look into it. So for the next two or three days she tried to get in touch with him. He didn't have an agent or a lawyer.

The search for Abel Ferrara took about a hundred man-hours. We enlisted staff in Los Angeles and in New York. Finally, after two weeks of searching, we tracked him down. Ferrara was a highly provocative, very gifted filmmaker and poet, possibly a genius, also notoriously hard living.

When Jane got him on the phone, she said, "We'd love you to come to the *Vanity Fair* Oscar party."

Ferrara replied, "Well, no, I don't want to."

There was a lot of to-ing and fro-ing. At one point, we offered him transportation to come and he was still resistant, and then he said, "I've got to bring my girlfriend."

Jane came to me and said, "He wants his girlfriend as well."

I said, "It's for Si."

We finally got it all worked out. When I saw Si at our next lunch, I said, "I've got some great news. I've got Abel Ferrara, he's coming to the Oscar party. I'll put him at your table."

Si said, "Oh, I don't want to eat with him, I just want to shake his hand." We'd already made all the plans, so we stuck by them.

When Si and Victoria came to Hollywood, their pugs came too.

And not without incident. Apart from their passions for books, art, film, and museums, the Newhouses' lives revolved almost completely around their pug, Nero. And later Cicero. Or maybe it was the other way around. They liked to name their dogs after Roman emperors or philosophers. At the Newhouse apartment at UN Plaza, on a table in the corner where you normally find framed photographs of family and especially children, there was none of that. Only photos of the pugs.

The Print Order meetings, which I have already described, were where before a half dozen stony faces, the editors would present their next issues. And as you were flipping through the pages, God help you if you had a picture of a dog and you didn't know the type of dog or the dog's name. Because Si would just stop.

"What kind of dog is that?"

And I'd say, "Gosh."

He'd say, "Can you find out?"

I'd say, "Absolutely, I'll get back to you right after this."

The Newhouse pugs hated Los Angeles, because, Si said, on the streets around the Beverly Hills Hotel, almost nobody walks their dog and therefore there are no dog smells. So the pugs were bored, which caused Si a fair amount of consternation. Before the Oscars, we had to book them a bungalow at the Beverly Hills Hotel. One year the bungalow we secured had a skylight. Si said that the rooms were fine, but Nero couldn't sleep unless it was really dark. The hotel painted the skylight black. Just for Nero.

—

I don't think I'm alone in being just a bit nervous before heading into a party or a big dinner. For something on the scale of our Oscar dinner and party, the anxiety just ratchets up considerably. If you're famous, I imagine that you worry that you're not going to receive the treatment and attention that other famous people are getting. And if you're not famous, you feel you're going to be ignored. I decided right from the beginning that I would suck up my own insecurities and be at the entrance of our events to welcome the guests and direct them into the room. We had 160 people for dinner and I would stand outside with Si and Victoria, and Donald and Sue Newhouse. Many nights I would have to introduce all four of them to the people coming for dinner. I'm pretty decent with names and, fortified with a beta-blocker and a glass of vodka, I would make upward of five hundred introductions in a little over an hour and a half. I also had an assistant standing behind me to come to my rescue if I couldn't remember someone's name.

The first year, we invited the "it" model of the moment, the busty and very pretty Anna Nicole Smith. At one point during the dinner, her tablemates on each side had slipped off to talk to others and Si came over to me and said he was going to keep her company. Which I thought was heroic of him. Because she was so much taller than him, her breasts and Si's head were at the same level. Someone took a snap, and with the three round elements alongside each other, it looked like a living pawnshop sign.

We had a mop-up meeting every year the day after the Oscars, when we'd go over what went right and what went wrong so that we would do better the next year. I wanted to get everyone's input while it was still fresh in their heads. The first time we did this, we were all sitting around by the pool at the Beverly Hills. Dana Brown was the first to speak up. He said, "No asparagus as a starter next year." Much time was spent discussing the enormous amount of thievery that went on. In the ladies' room we had decanter-sized bottles of cologne from companies like Dior and Chanel. By the end of the evening, they'd all be gone. And this with women all wearing barely-there dresses. It was a testament to their ingenuity. I remember catching Adrien Brody trying to smuggle out one of our electrified candle lamps on the tables, like the ones you see in old-fashioned nightclubs. I said, "Adrien, you can't do that. We had the shades all made up especially." He's a gentleman, and a charming one at that, and still apologizes any time I see him.

We had our own ashtrays made up with bas-relief lettering around the edge. We had them done for Los Angeles, for New York, for Washington, for London, and for Paris. And they'd all be gone by the end of the night. This didn't bother me. I thought of it as community outreach and effective advertising. I was at Disneyland with my kids one year and I noticed these little Oscar statuettes in one of the shops. I bought one and brought it back and said to Sara, "Let's put one of these with a little plaque, 'Vanity Fair Oscar Party 2009,'" or whatever year it was, "in front of every place setting." I thought people would steal them. They cost us about $2 each, and they would end up on everyone's desk or nightstand the next day. They all disappeared. But that was the plan.

Harvey Weinstein was a recurring issue. He regularly showed up with more guests than his invitation indicated and would bully the staff at the door. I finally had it out with him and told him that if he spoke rudely to any member of my staff ever again, I would bar him forever. It was both the correct thing to do and a foolish gesture, in that he was certifiably the reigning producer in Hollywood at the time and he could tell the stars in his films to give us a wide berth on Oscar night. This I did not want. The next year, he behaved himself. But three days before the actual awards, we had our own run-in. It was 1999, the year he was going to launch a magazine called *Talk* with Tina Brown. I was out having dinner with Mitch and Kelly, and as we were leaving, we spotted Weinstein at a booth with a number of young actresses. He called me over.

"I hear you're doing a big takedown on us in *Vanity Fair*," he said.

I thought for a moment, and nothing came to mind. "I think you're mistaken," I said.

Weinstein pointed at me and said that he had enough on our days at *Spy* to do a big exposé on the drugs and sex at the magazine. I knew this was an idle threat in that there weren't any drugs at *Spy*—for among other reasons that nobody made enough money to afford them. And as for sex, *Spy* was about as straitlaced a workplace I'd ever encountered up to that point.

Weinstein stood up and said, "Let's take this outside!"

Now, this was a whole new game. I hadn't been in a fistfight since my early teens, and other than maybe grabbing him in a head-lock, I had no idea how this could go. It was cool out that night, and the moment we hit the outside air, he changed completely, compli-menting me on *Vanity Fair* and saying that he hoped *Talk* was half as good. The "Let's take this outside" challenge was all for the benefit of the women at his table. I was surprised but I was also relieved. There were photographers outside the restaurant and two middle-aged men scuffling on the street is not a good look for anyone.

In time, a whole social ecosystem formed around Oscar weekend. Thursday nights, Ron and Kelly Meyer had a regular dinner at their beautiful house out in Malibu. Larry Gagosian held an annual celebration for one of his artists on a Thursday or Friday night at Mr. Chow. Saturday afternoons, Barry Diller and Diane von Fürsten-berg held a picnic on the parklike grounds of his house in Beverly

Hills. These afternoons and evenings were populated largely by the reigning monarchs of new Hollywood. I was intent on bringing old Hollywood to the party. Over the years, we had everyone from Artie Shaw and Nancy Reagan to Connie Wald, Kirk Douglas, Ernest Lehman, and just about every key figure from that era who was still alive. One person we took everywhere with us was Tony Curtis. He'd come to the White House Correspondents dinner. He'd come to the Oscar party. Tony was always there early with his little French Ordre des Arts et des Lettres tag in his lapel. His wife, Jill Vandenberg, a six-foot-tall equestrienne, was always at his side.

One of my great experiences was being in a restaurant with Bryan Lourd, Anna, and Jon Robin Baitz, the playwright and screenwriter. The restaurant was Les Deux Café and it was tucked away in the Hollywood Hills. We were talking when I heard somebody shout out to me, "Graydon!" I looked over and it was Artie Shaw. Artie was, in his heyday, considered the greatest clarinetist ever. He was also a famous stickman, as we used to say in Canada, and had been married to both Ava Gardner and Lana Turner. He came to the Oscar parties early, with his girlfriend Kay Pick. One time the decorator and man about town Nicky Haslam was at the party and needed to use the bathroom, and I said, "I'll walk you over there, I need to use it too." And as we made our way through the room, he mentioned Ava Gardner.

I said, "I just realized we have three men in here who slept with both her and Lana Turner: Artie Shaw, Bob Evans, and Kirk Douglas."

"Interesting," Nicky said. "And I've slept with one of *them*."

I had the idea one year of inviting all the actors who had played James Bond. I thought it would make for a great photograph. And having all of them in the same room would be exciting for the other guests. The invitations went out. Sean Connery was playing golf. Roger Moore was at his place in the South of France. And Pierce Brosnan and Timothy Dalton were working. We wound up with just George Lazenby. If the name doesn't ring any bells, don't feel too bad about it. He was a ruggedly good-looking Australian actor who played Bond in a single film, *On Her Majesty's Secret Service*. During the party, I spotted Lazenby at the bar drinking by himself. I felt a bit sorry for him in that I might have been the only person in the room who recognized him. *On Her Majesty's Secret Service* was not the hit that the other Bond films were. I went over and introduced myself as the host and told him how happy I was to have him there. He stared straight ahead during my brief monologue, then turned to me and said, "Fuck off!" He didn't get a lot of work in his later years. I suspect this might have had more to do with his off-camera manner than his on-camera talents.

There was one year that I decided to take a stab at getting both Olivia de Havilland and Joan Fontaine together at the Oscar party. They were sisters. Both had achieved great levels of success—de Havilland in, among other films, *Gone with the Wind,* and Fontaine in, among other great roles, two Hitchcock films, *Rebecca* and *Suspicion.* Hollywood was really only big enough for one of them, however, and they hadn't spoken in decades. I wrote long letters to each of them and attached the letters to their invitations. A few weeks later, a charming letter arrived from Fontaine declining my invitation. And on the same day, de Havilland called me to do the same.

It never fails to amaze me how Hollywood so often turns its back on its own history. It took outsiders—us—to remind Hollywood of its storied history. One time I gave a party for Billy Wilder and Cameron Crowe, for a book they'd done together on the making of *Some Like It Hot* and other episodes in Wilder's life and career. I invited all the major directors, thinking that they would want to pay homage to Billy, securely in the small pantheon of great American directors. I was surprised at how few of them turned up.

—

The year after the Bill Clinton–Monica Lewinsky scandal broke, I invited Monica to the Oscar party. I wanted her to feel good about herself. But I made the mistake of placing her at a table beside Jeffrey Katzenberg, the head of DreamWorks, who was also a Clinton friend and campaign finance bundler. When Monica was seated, he made a big thing of it and stormed away. I thought it was the height of rudeness. We moved him to another table and Monica stayed where she was. I thought she had been treated appallingly by members of the Clinton camp. She and I stayed in touch. In 2013, after she'd tried many things that didn't work—public appearances, handbag design, reclusiveness, finding a job, finding a partner—she called David Friend and asked if we could all meet.

The internet had by this time taken full flower, and Monica later argued that at this point she was the Patient Zero of public shaming. She was marginalized. We sat and talked for a long time, and she told me she wanted to reclaim her narrative. She wanted her life back. She wanted to stop being a punch line. "How come Bill Clinton is a superstar around the world and I'm a joke?" she said. "I was a kid when this happened." David and I were completely on board. I told her that I knew someone I thought could help. His name was Ant Gordon Lennox, and he was the brother of a friend of Anna's and mine, Lucy Cornell. Ant was a charismatic, bushy-haired Old Etonian and his business was to help heads of state and industry craft the messages they wanted to tell. He would help write the speech, if that was the goal, and—whether it was David Cameron, when he was prime minister, or Kate Middleton, when she was about to become the Duchess of Cambridge—he helped them deliver the speech. Ant lived in London and Monica was going to be there soon, so I introduced the two of them.

Monica and Ant spent about three weeks together, and they drafted a narrative, a way of addressing all that had happened. That redirection helped turn her into a voice and a combatant for others who had been similarly wronged. At that time, in 2014, my oldest daughter was twenty-one, and I thought if this had happened to her, I would have wanted to throttle Clinton. That he had preyed upon this impressionable twenty-two-year-old, and yet still traveled the world as a political grandee, was simply unacceptable. Working with Ant, Monica recrafted the story of her life. The facts didn't change, but the focus did. She had been preyed upon by the most powerful man in the world, not the other way around.

We gave Monica a platform and support. She did a TED talk and a big *Vanity Fair* story, and both got a lot of attention. Shame had been hung around her neck, she declared, "like a scarlet-A albatross." She continued, "Believe me, once it's on, it is a bitch to take off." Her story for *Vanity Fair* opened with a question that had once been shouted at her: "How does it feel to be America's premier blow-job queen?" The incident occurred in early 2001. She recalled: "I was sitting on the stage of New York's Cooper Union in the middle of taping a Q&A for an HBO documentary. I was the subject. And I was thunderstruck." Even then, Monica had balance and intelligence. She answered that it was hurtful and insulting. Then she said, "I don't actually know why this whole story became about oral sex. . . . The fact that it did is maybe a result of a male-dominated society." Turning to the "smirking guy" who had asked the question, she said, "You might be better poised to answer that."

It was with her *Vanity Fair* essay and her TED talk that she began to get her life back. I decided to make her a contributing editor, not unaware of the timing—Hillary Clinton was going to run for president. I've never seen anybody change the narrative on themselves quite the way she did. I later introduced her to Jemima Khan, who in turn introduced her to Alex Gibney, the documentary director, and they did a big three-part series on the impeachment. Monica not only got her life back, she became an inspiration for others who have been caught in the maw of the ruthlessness of the internet.

—

If the Oscar party was a big, splashy, exhausting work night, our annual dinner in the South of France was a luxurious holiday. Taking into consideration location, history, and sheer sophistication, when you come right down to it, there's really only one hotel in the world, and that's the Hotel du Cap in Antibes. From the late 1990s on, we held a dinner there on the first Saturday of the Cannes Film Festival. I promise you that these were evenings of such exuberance and glamour that had I not been the host, I would never have been invited.

I would regularly bring my entire family to the hotel. In fact, I almost never went on a business trip without all of them. Many years we'd stay for a week or two at the Ritz in Paris, the Connaught in London, or the Beverly Hills Hotel in Los Angeles. I figured my kids would learn a lot more about life watching things come together for these events—or just by being in Paris or London—than they ever would in the classes they missed. Also, I loved just being with all my children. They were then, and are now, the best company. And my philosophy was that family time was often more important than school time. At one point, I was going to London and I wanted to take Max, then a junior at Groton, to visit Oxford. When I called one of the school administrators to say I would be taking him out for a few days to see the school, she said that she'd rather I not do this.

"Why?" I asked.

"Well," she said, "it hurts the teachers' feelings when students don't attend their classes."

I was slightly dumbfounded by her reply. I said, "it's not as if I'm taking him to Disneyland. We're going to the college he thinks he might like to attend."

She huffed a bit and finally accepted the situation with an annoyed "Okay, fine then." And indeed, we visited Oxford and Max went to the school and it changed his life.

The Hotel du Cap is almost unchanged since Scott and Zelda and Cole Porter stayed there in the '20s, and it still radiates with the postwar glamour of Hemingway and Picasso and the libertine '70s of Serge Gainsbourg and Jane Birkin and John and Yoko and Peter Sellers and Michael Caine. Those dinners at the Hotel du Cap were magical evenings, filled with a mixture of film stars, continental aristocrats, tech moguls, fashion designers, writers, directors, and, on a single night, Harvey Weinstein. He showed up unannounced with what looked like a rented entourage, and we turned him around at the entrance. When he lashed out at Sara, I banned him for life from all *Vanity Fair* events—a ban that became universal a few years later.

We would have dinner for 150 in the dining room overlooking the Mediterranean and then the evening would spill out to the pool area, which Patrick Woodroffe lit in dramatic fashion. The big yachts of many of the guests performed as living scenery as they bobbed just beyond the shoreline, their lights reflecting on the water.

The only other person, aside from Weinstein, whom we banned

forever from our parties was Philip Green, the owner of Topshop, the fast-fashion retailer in the UK. The incident began when Elizabeth Saltzman, our then fashion director, who was staying on Green's boat, a bloated gin palace called *Lionheart*, asked if she could bring him to dinner. I told her that I didn't really want him there.

A key element to staging any big event: who you don't invite is just as important as who you do invite. But she begged me, and I finally relented. Green duly came to the dinner that night. When he looked at his place setting, he said, "I'm not sitting here. Who are these fucking people?" Green proceeded to rearrange the table placement. We always served good wine at *Vanity Fair* events, in a valiant effort to make sure guests didn't go home with splitting headaches. Green looked at what we were serving. "Swill," he announced, and ordered his own wine. The maître d' went to Sara, who had watched all this, and said, "What do you want me to do?" Sara said simply, "When he picks the most expensive bottle on the wine list, you're going to ask him for his credit card."

There were any number of incidents. This was the South of France, after all. The weather in May can be glorious one moment and then turn on a centime. One year a late mistral blew in from the north and caused havoc. The sky darkened to the color of charcoal and the sea turned nasty. The jetty became so swamped by water that boats had to dispatch their guests in the sheltered port of Antibes, where they were then driven to the hotel. Another year, just as dinner was ending, Sara came over and whispered in my ear: Isabelle Huppert, one of the grandest of the grande dames of French cinema, had collapsed. I rushed over. She was lying limp on a chaise and her skin was ashen. Oh God, I thought, she's died. When she moved, a silent gasp of relief went up. As we were to later discover, she had poured herself into a very tight dress and, not wanting to ruin the line, hadn't eaten a thing all night. But she had been drinking. And what with the combination of too much champagne and not enough food, she just collapsed.

Pierre Bérillon, who manages the dining room, arranged for her to be gently moved to an alcove, where a stretcher appeared. Very quietly, she was rolled out to a waiting ambulance and spirited off to a nearby hospital. So deft was the staff, and so calm was their approach to the situation, that not a single guest realized what had happened. It was as if this sort of thing occurred every night. I was just so relieved. Nothing can kill a party faster than a dead actress.

One year Henry Porter got stuck in the bathroom down near the Grill Bar when the party following dinner was in full swing. The door handle had jammed. He banged and shouted, but with the noise and the music, no one could hear him. He was about to give up when a man's voice said, "Stand back!" Henry hopped up onto the seat. There was a loud noise as the man on the other side kicked in the door. It was Jean-Claude Van Damme.

—

Needless to say, not everything can be pulled off with Gallic sangfroid or martial-arts precision. In the early days of my editorship, Reinaldo called and asked if we could have a chat. Reinaldo and I had been friends for almost a decade before I got to *Vanity Fair*, and I was thrilled that he decided to stay on as a fixer when I arrived. In addition to being an international sophisticate and a South American grandee of some standing, he is also the husband of Carolina Herrera, the go-to designer of dresses for first ladies, princesses, and Oscar-winning actresses. The Herreras had a wide circle of aristocratic and society friends, the pinnacle of this collection being the Queen, Prince Philip, and Princess Margaret. Reinaldo arrived at my office looking tanned. He told me that he and Carolina had just returned from Mustique, where they had been staying with Princess Margaret.

She was coming to New York, he pronounced gaily. "You should give a dinner for her! At home. She's so much fun. You will adore her!"

I confess I didn't know much about Princess Margaret, but my slim scholarship turned up any number of descriptions of her at that stage in her life, none of which included the descriptive *fun*. Her ex-husband, Tony Snowdon, was then on our masthead as a contributing photographer. He generally recoiled at the mention of her name. Tony never said anything downright negative about his former wife, but the look on his face when her name was brought up spoke volumes.

At the time, Cynthia and I had three young sons, Ash, Max, and Spike, all under the age of ten, and a one-year-old daughter, Bron. And to be honest, we weren't really prepared for a large dinner of any sort, let alone in honor of someone on the order of Princess Margaret. But Reinaldo pressed on, saying that having her on side would be key to the success of our European edition. I doubted this, but I was still too green to mount an effective defense. To be perfectly honest, I thought this could prove disastrous. Other, stronger minds prevailed, however, and I got together with Reinaldo, Sara, and Hamilton South to work out the arrangements. We were still living in the Dakota, in a three-bedroom apartment with a decent-sized living room and a small library off that, separated by a large pair of pocket doors. There was a foyer. But no dining room. We calculated that by putting round tables in the library and in the foyer, we could seat twenty-four. It would be tight, but we could do it. I called Brian McNally to see if the Royalton could handle the food.

Reinaldo went through a number of advance items that Margaret would require for the night. These included bottles of Famous

Grouse whiskey, Highland Spring mineral water, and barley water. She would be accompanied by Anne Glenconner, her lady-in-waiting, and Anne's husband, Colin Tennant, who had developed Mustique in the 1950s, having bought it from the Grenadines for about $50,000. They, too, were close friends of Reinaldo and Carolina's. Reinaldo exhaustively instructed me on protocol for the evening—including the proper way to address the princess. You were to lean forward from the waist, hold her hand gently, and say "Ma'am." That was it. After this was accomplished, you were to let her pick up the conversation. I had no idea what we could talk about, but I did know that the royal family's ice-breaking standby of saying "Have you come far?" couldn't be applied in this situation. I practiced my bow in front of the mirror a few times. We came up with a guest list that Reinaldo thought Margaret would find "amusing."

On the night of the big event, I instructed our three boys on the proper way to bow in case they bumped into the princess. Our apartment was not large, and the kids' bedroom was off the hallway that led to the bathroom. So there was an outside chance she could bump into them. I lined the boys up in their white cotton Bonpoint pajamas with black piping, bought especially for the occasion. I showed them the bend from the waist, the gentle holding of the royal hand, and the "Ma'am." I then asked each of them to perform the ritual. Ash, the oldest, pulled it off. As did the second oldest, Max. When I asked Spike to show me his bow, it was clear his mind had been somewhere else.

"Spike, what do you say if you bump into Princess Margaret?" I asked.

He looked confused for a moment, then said, "Hello, Margaret?"

I could have hugged him to death. But instead we rehearsed the whole rigamarole one more time.

The general anxiety was high. In fact, everyone associated with the evening was, under Reinaldo's detailed direction, hysterical with rehearsal fatigue. The evening was choreographed in a manner that would have made the master of the New York City Ballet tip his hat. I was to meet the princess and her entourage at the entrance to the Dakota and walk them to our apartment. Then the real strictures of protocol came into play. Nobody was supposed to sit for dinner until Margaret did. And nobody was to rise from the table until she did. Furthermore, no guest was to leave the apartment before the Princess herself.

As instructed, I met Margaret at the building's entrance and escorted her and Colin and Anne to the apartment. I introduced them one by one to the guests, all of whom had been given a quick primer in Reinaldo's etiquette of royal greetings. In time we sat down for dinner. Starter, main course, dessert. And then Margaret just stayed. And stayed. She wasn't being particularly festive. She wasn't being particularly un-festive. She was just staying. And smoking and drinking. Now I should tell you, as if you don't already know, that New York dinner parties generally break up around 10:00 p.m. because people have to go home, get to bed, and wake up early to go to work.

On this evening, 10:30 went by, and then 11:00. People were starting to panic. Margaret finally got up from the dinner table and we made our way the short distance to the living room. We were all waiting for her to start making her way toward the exit.

At 11:00, Barry Diller came over to me and said, "That's it, I'm out of here. This is ridiculous."

"Fine," I whispered. "I understand. But please go out the back door so she doesn't see you."

At one point, Peggy Noonan leaned over in a half curtsey to Princess Margaret, who was sitting on the sofa, and as she leaned forward I guess she nicked her gently in the shin, whereupon Princess Margaret shrieked, "You've wounded me. You've wounded me!" Finally, around 12:00 or 12:15, Margaret rose. The relief on the faces of the other guests was the sort of look that survivors of a difficult airplane landing have as they step onto the tarmac.

As per Reinaldo's dictate, he and I escorted Princess Margaret and the Glenconners out to the entrance of the Dakota. We were followed by the other guests. Sometime during the dinner, a horrendous rainstorm had started up. There's a porte cochere at the front of the building where cars can pull in out of the rain. By this time it was lashing hard, coming down at a dramatic angle. Finally, a gleaming black town car backed up into the portico and we collectively thought, *Oh, thank the Lord God.*

Princess Margaret turned and said, "Thank you so much," stuck out her hand to me, and stepped down to get into the car.

A little man jumped out of the driver's seat.

"No, no, not for you! Car for Mr. Hamilton South! Car for Mr. South!"

I thought I was going to have an aneurysm. Reinaldo gave me a filthy look.

"Hamilton, will you get that fucking car out of here!" I whispered loudly.

Princess Margaret climbed back out onto the sidewalk. Hamilton screamed at his driver to leave. By this time, the rain was getting people's legs wet.

A few minutes later, an older and slightly less polished town car backed its way in and Margaret and the Glenconners scrambled to get inside and out of the rain.

Reinaldo drew himself up and shot us another filthy look.

"You have ruined the party!" he spat at us. "This is a complete disaster."

Reinaldo didn't speak to Hamilton for three months.

Hamilton says I didn't speak to him for two weeks. He also claims that if you ever mention "Car for Mr. Hamilton South," I go into an apoplectic rage. I deny the charge.

But such is the mysterious and lasting power of the royal family.

Chapter 14.

Escape Velocity, at Last

B y my second year at *Vanity Fair*, I had the Oscar party in the rearview mirror. In Hollywood parlance, it looked like it might have legs. But in 1994, I still didn't feel I was out of the woods. Not quite. We were doing okay, but we hadn't kicked into proper gear. There were fewer rumors of my being fired. But I felt like I wasn't there yet. I don't know whether Si felt this as well. When he made a mistake or concluded that he had put the wrong person in the wrong job, he wasn't shy about ending it then and there. All an editor has, really, is confidence in his or her own judgment and taste, and as I've said, a lot of that comes from the proprietor. Looking back now, I can see that my escape from my perceived troubles came from two suggestions—one from my longtime friend David Halberstam and the other from Si himself.

I used to spend hours on the phone each week talking to Fran, Ellen Barkin, Halberstam, Christopher, and Michael Herr. Michael was one of the most magical men I've ever met. I have never fallen in love with a man's voice before, but I did with Michael's. Ours was a curious relationship in that for the first hundred hours or so, it was all on the phone. We didn't meet in person until two years into our friendship. Despite having written about battles of extraordinary horror during his coverage of the Vietnam War, he was the most peaceful of souls.

Michael and David were responsible for two of the seminal books about America's epic misadventure in Vietnam—Herr with *Dispatches* and Halberstam with *The Best and the Brightest*. And both wrote for me at *Vanity Fair* as they continued on with their careers. David was a writer of capital-*B* big books and was a commanding figure in American journalism and letters. He was a tireless gatherer of telling detail and won a Pulitzer Prize for his reporting from Vietnam for *The New York Times*. He had also been, in the early 1960s, one of the strongest proponents of the view that America was losing the war, which infuriated not only members of the Kennedy and Johnson administrations but his own editors at *The Times*. The generals and others were lying or deluded, he believed—a reality that his own paper as well as *Time,* the established broadsheets, and the television networks refused to acknowledge. Later he wrote *The Powers That Be*, on the media, a book that arrived in 1979, the year after I came to New York, and whose reception was seismic.

Michael, possibly traumatized by the epic 1968 Battle of Khe Sanh—out of which he produced one of the most astonishing pieces of journalism I have ever read—had retreated to upstate New York to live the life of a Buddhist and work on the odd screenplay for Francis Ford Coppola (*Apocalypse Now*) and Stanley Kubrick (*Full Metal Jacket*). He wrote a wild, original, almost hallucinogenic book about Las Vegas's golden age, called *The Big Room*, and turned an aborted screenplay about Walter Winchell into a fact-based novel. Michael wrote movingly for us when Kubrick died—the last magazine story he ever wrote. He was the only person I have ever known who used the interjection *man* in a way that didn't seem forced.

I remember very clearly a lunch I had with David early in 1994 at Patroon, which was owned by our friend Ken Aretsky. David and I got to talking about the changes taking place in American culture and business. The country, as he saw it, was going from being a heavy industrial economy that made physical things like cars and steel to an entertainment economy based around sports, information, technology, film, and television. Intellectual property, in all its various forms, was now what we exported to the world, rather than hard goods. America was becoming the world's first information and entertainment superpower—and we were at the dawn of this tectonic shift.

That night I started thinking that if the economic and cultural foundations had changed so radically, then the "establishment" must have changed too. I realized I could name the heads of all the major movie studios, but I didn't know the names of the head of U.S. Steel, or General Tire, or even General Motors—the sort of corporate elders who were once a fixture on the covers of *Time* and *Fortune*. In the business pages of *The New York Times*, a change at the top of Boeing or Chrysler barely rated a column inch. But if a number-two person at Disney left or was replaced, it warranted coverage. The establishment no longer consisted of gray men in Brooks Brothers suits at conference tables on Wall Street or in Washington—the small group of WASP men from St. Paul's and Groton, Yale and Princeton, who had dominated the monied class of America for most of the last century. Men like Averell Harriman and Dean Acheson, and going way back.

The "New Establishment" now consisted of dropouts, visionaries, artists, and tech oddballs and was located not only in New York but also in Los Angeles and Silicon Valley. They had their own planes; they dressed like college kids; and their bank accounts dwarfed those of the Old Establishment. I had always wanted to hang my hat on a big list story to rival the Fortune 500 or the Forbes 400. I thought that defining and then putting faces on this New Establishment would be not only great journalism but a turning point for both the magazine and me.

Over a number of nights, I developed a pretty clear idea in my mind of what I wanted to do to introduce this new class of inventors and entrepreneurs. The feature had to be visual, so that readers and advertisers could see and get a fix on all these new faces. I had an asset that no other magazine had in Annie Leibovitz. Annie was already a legend, a photographic visionary of huge gifts. Nobody ever worked harder. She spent about five months on this one portfolio, covering thirty thousand miles for portraits of two dozen members of the New Establishment—people like Barry Diller, Bill Gates, John Malone, Steven Spielberg, Ted Turner, and Oprah Winfrey. We photographed a lot of them in or alongside their toys, which is always pleasing and illuminating. Craig McCaw, a telecoms CEO, posed in hip waders alongside his gleaming sea plane near Seattle. David Geffen was shot while he was on the phone aboard his Gulfstream IV en route from New York to Los Angeles. Rupert Murdoch was photographed piloting his 158-foot ketch *Morning Glory* off the coast of Alaska. They really were like slightly beefed-up Slim Aarons portraits.

David contributed an article on the waning of the Old Establishment in the form of a cool, forensic portrait of Henry Kissinger, the wary and unrelaxed outsider, the lone operator—insecure, duplicitous, ego-driven, sycophantic to power, and lacking the easy, consensus-building confidence of his predecessors or successors. Kissinger marked the end of the gifted amateur, as Halberstam described it. He was prepared even to outdo Nixon in his hawkishness and belligerence. The secret bombing of Cambodia—when the Vietnam War was long lost—brought that country into the war, with catastrophic consequences, including the "killing fields" of Pol Pot. Kissinger remained a tiresome evil factor in American political life for the rest of his years.

Annie's portfolio was a tour de force that redefined the power centers of America and how this new breed of American business leader was markedly different from the generations that had come before. The New Establishment also allowed me to see what I could do with *Vanity Fair*. It could in large part cover the businesses and visionaries that powered the new American economy. People started looking at the magazine in a different way.

Annie became a household name and the de facto court painter of the ruling members of the creative classes. Maureen Dowd wrote that having your picture taken by Annie was an achievement in and of itself, like a portrait by Holbein or Van Dyck in their day. In more modern terms, she was the equivalent of Edward Steichen, who was the chief photographer during the Jazz Age incarnation of *Vanity Fair* in the 1920s and early '30s. An Annie Leibovitz photo treatment in *Vanity Fair* was a trophy coveted by many of the people the magazine covered. She was not always the easiest to work with. Anything I suggested would be reflexively nixed in a sort of default contradiction. It was not a collaborative relationship exactly, but it was a relationship. And it worked. When we disagreed on something, I would estimate that 75 percent of the time, Annie was right. She was most certainly the inheritor of the Steichen legacy, and I wasn't going to tell her where to put the camera.

—

T he second idea that helped *Vanity Fair* achieve escape velocity came from Si. After the first Oscar party, he and I were having lunch and he asked me if I'd ever thought of doing an entire issue on Hollywood. I've never liked special issues built around a single area of interest. My feeling was that people came to *Vanity Fair* for the variety of stories in each issue, and I resisted Si's idea at first. But he came back to it again and again. So one night I sat down at the kitchen table and thought about how I could create a Hollywood issue that would have the kind of variety where, even if you weren't interested in contemporary movies or film stars, there would be enough great stories of other kinds, though still connected to the movies. There would be a business story and a contemporary movie story and a crime story and an arts or architecture story to make it as varied as humanly possible, within the Hollywood bracket. I started assembling the first issue in my head and then I told Si we'd do it.

We needed a cover for the Hollywood issue, though. I loved old-fashioned group photographs of the kind that *Life* and a few other magazines used to do. One favorite, called *A Great Day in Harlem*, taken in 1958 by Art Kane for *Esquire*, showed the uptown jazz greats of the time, all in one photograph. Some were standing on the steps to a building, but there were so many they also spilled out onto the sidewalk. In the bar in our apartment, there's a Patrick Lichfield group photograph from the '60s of many of the notable figures of Swinging London, including David Hockney, Susannah York, Roman Polanski, David Hicks, George Weidenfeld, Antonia Fraser, Jocelyn Stevens, Terence Donovan, and Peter Wilson.

For our Hollywood cover, I wanted Annie to do portraits of contemporary stars over three unfolding panels, so it almost looked like a billboard. I didn't want to do a single panel built around a single actor or actress, because I felt no one in Hollywood at the time was strong enough to carry this big new idea. Annie composed the first one against a white background. There were ten actresses: Uma Thurman, Nicole Kidman, Gwyneth Paltrow, Angela Bassett, Sandra Bullock, Patricia Arquette, Julianne Moore, Jennifer Jason Leigh,

Sarah Jessica Parker, and Linda Fiorentino. All were on the high cusp of impending fame. And we did in fact take out a billboard of the cover over Sunset Boulevard, which we continued to do for many Hollywood issues thereafter.

Annie thought group shots were sort of a cheap trick at first, but then she started getting into them. In that same issue, we had some other photographers do group portraits. And most of them just had the shorter people in the front, the taller ones in the back, the way you do a high school group shot. Annie thought hers out with great attention to composition. I went to a couple of her cover shoots, and before the subjects got there, she had people roughly their size wearing roughly the clothes she wanted them to wear. She would pose them and light them and start building the picture the way old masters constructed their group portraits. Everybody would be perfectly lit, the whole thing figured out in advance. Then when the actual subjects came in, she knew exactly where they went, and she'd make slight adjustments in the lighting and probably wouldn't keep them there for more than an hour or two, because she'd done so many hours of work beforehand.

She might have the best taste of anybody I've ever met in terms of furnishings and real estate. She's got a good eye for architecturally interesting places. Her studios are always beautiful, and quite epic, the way Annie is epic. I think she always wanted to shoot more like Sebastião Salgado, to photograph vast plateaus and terrains. Artists of Annie's caliber often want what another talent in their field is or does. I think she envied Richard Avedon—the reigning photographer of the mid forty years of the last century. But the difference between her and Avedon was that Avedon had an unkind eye and Annie had a kindly one. Avedon developed his pictures so that a line on a face would look more pronounced than it did in real life. Even young starlets came out of an Avedon sitting looking like W. H.

Auden. Annie had a tendency to shoot with big box lights that could soften the subject's features. She was very good at making middle-aged average-looking men appear more heroic than they are. And she completely reinvented the magazine cover form with these group photographs.

The cover of *Vanity Fair* was the Mount Olympus of movie-star placement, but the annual three-page Hollywood-issue gatefold also became one of Jane Sarkin's biggest nightmares. Nobody wanted to be on the second or third panel; they only wanted to be on the first panel—the one you saw on the newsstand or coffee table. Convincing people to go on the second or third panel was like talking down a bridge jumper.

—

By the mid-'90s, with the Hollywood issue in the spring and the New Establishment issue in the fall, we had our tentpoles for the year.

Christopher called one day and suggested we get more involved with the White House Correspondents' Association dinner. It had for years been a dreary industry affair, and he felt that we could bring some life to it. The dinner was held every spring in the ballroom of the Washington Hilton. The room was noted for being the largest in the city without pillars to ruin sight lines. And so, in those first few years, *Vanity Fair* took two or three tables at the event. There was a raised dais up front, where the sitting president, the first lady, the headlining comedian, and assorted journalists sat and ate. After dinner, the comedian who had been booked for the night took the stage. And then the president spoke. The comedian was there to rib members of the administration. And the president was there to rib the journalists. Clinton, Bush, and Obama were pretty much on a par with the comedians they followed. All had great material and delivered it with impeccable timing. This is one thing both Republicans and Democrats did well.

The after-dinner entertainment aside, the correspondents' dinner was a long night of rented tuxedos and Rotary Club hair. The food was tragic. As were the refreshments. In the early days of our involvement, we invited a small number of those who'd be attending the dinner to a sort of *salon des refusés* the night before at the vast apartment in the Wyoming, on Columbia Road, owned by Christopher and his wife, Carol Blue. In time, the Hitchens-Blue apartment became the site of our after-party following the correspondents' dinner. Later we gave up the dinner altogether and staged our own at the French ambassador's residence, where on TV sets placed at either ends of the tables, we could skip most of the proceedings of the night and only watch the performances of the comedian and the president. Once dinner was done, invited guests from the Hilton would arrive for the after-party. Spring was a good time to be there, with the azaleas out. We did this every year until the Bush administration's invasion of Iraq, when we took a pause. We pulled out altogether during the Trump administration.

The way Tony Curtis and Artie Shaw proved to be our good luck charms for the Oscar party, Walter Cronkite proved to be one for the correspondents' dinner. When Dan Rather took over the *CBS Evening News* anchor chair from Cronkite, Walter was banished from the network's tables. So I invited him each year. And he and his wife, Betsy, were regularly among the stars of the evening.

A number of years before we got involved, Michael Kelly, then an editor at *The Baltimore Sun*—he would later become the editor of *The Atlantic* and die tragically during the Iraq War—brought along Fawn Hall, Oliver North's secretary, as his guest. This was during the Iran-Contra hearings, and Hall had been found to have shredded documents for North. She was the tabloid oddity of the moment. Her appearance was electrifying, which speaks volumes about Washington. After Fawn Hall, it became a tradition to invite not only actual guests—movie stars and luminous figures from the literary and music world, and people like the Cronkites—but also at least one novelty guest.

All the press organizations fought over who could bring the tabloid headliner of the moment. Now, the novelty guests didn't know that they were novelty guests. They just thought they were guests. At one point, I invited Trump to take this slot. I sat him next to one of the more prominent models of the day, Vendela Kirsebom. I thought she'd get a kick out of him. I could not have been more wrong. After forty-five minutes, she pleaded with me to move her. She said that Trump had spent his time assaying the "tits" and legs of the other female guests. Vendela said, "He is the most vulgar man I've ever met."

My durably contentious relationship with Trump had begun with the observation I made in my 1984 profile of him in *GQ*—his first major national exposure—to the effect that he had remarkably small (if neatly groomed) hands. This was ratcheted up to "short-fingered vulgarian" in the pages of *Spy*. When I got to *Vanity Fair*, the transactional Trump realized that a strategy shift was in order. Notes complimenting me on an article or a particular issue began to come my way. He sent me a couple of Trump ties. They were a basic blue and a basic red, and they were as stiff as a child's toy sword. He sent me bottles of Trump vodka. An invitation to Trump's wedding to the actress Marla Maples appeared. I went, out of journalistic curiosity—or at least that was how I reasoned it to myself and to my friends. It was in the Plaza Hotel, which Trump had recently bought, and we were in and out in a couple of hours. I've seen more honest emotion at an early morning Starbucks line. When I bumped into Trump in Palm Beach, he invited me to join him for dinner at Mar-a-Lago. We had "surf and turf"—something I hadn't eaten in twenty years.

Trump lived the way a poor person in a folktale might have imagined how a rich person lived—high up in gilded faux Regency and Louis XIV surroundings. In the early 1990s, he announced that he was making a comeback. In 1989, at his peak, at the height of the real estate boom, he had told *Forbes* magazine that he had a net worth of $3.7 billion, which *Forbes* adjusted to $1.7 billion. When the real estate market collapsed, Trump found himself almost $1 billion in debt. Now he was back, he said. He was taking his casinos public in a deal that he claimed would net him billions. I thought a story on this purported comeback might prove interesting and ordered up an article and a photo shoot. During the sitting, the stylist decided that the Loro Piana cashmere sweater she had given Trump to wear wasn't right. She asked him to remove it. Trump refused to pull it up over his head, not wanting to muss his elaborately assembled confection of hair. And continued to refuse. There was a standoff. Finally, one of the assistants on the shoot was sent to get scissors to cut the cashmere sweater up the back so it could be taken off.

The Trump-Carter truce was not to hold. Try as I might, I couldn't resist making fun of him, and thus vanished our days of bonhomie and transactional friendliness. In time, with his new Twitter handle, he fired back after every perceived slight. At first, the hurt was palpable: "Dummy Graydon Carter doesn't like me too much . . . great news. He is a real loser!" he tweeted in December 2012. And then, the next day: "Graydon Carter has no talent and looks like shit! Also, his food sucks"—this referring to the Waverly Inn, a restaurant I was a partner in. Trump has variously called me "no talent," "sloppy," "grubby," "dopey," and "sleepy." He wrote that my wife thought I was a "major loser." Just before he launched his campaign for the presidency—and I mean just days before—Trump sent me a tear sheet of a nearly twenty-year-old magazine ad for *The Art of the Deal*. In thick gold Sharpie he had circled his hands in the photo of himself and written, "See, not so short!" I almost admired the effort he put into his valiant attempt to show me the error of my ways. I wrote, "Actually, quite short," on a card, stapled it to the ad, and had it messengered back up to his office. This ignited another frantic flurry of tweets.

Trump provided inexhaustible copy—as did so many of his type. Wealth, in a few hands, was growing exponentially, and the people who had it were anything but shy about showing it off. Rich people were either stealing from each other or trying to kill each other, and it was a great period for journalism. When there's that much money at stake, it brings out the charlatans and the grifters, like worms after rain.

Many years after Trump's appearance as our novelty guest at the White House correspondents' dinner, he returned to the Hilton— this time as a guest of *Washington Post* heiress Lally Weymouth. It was around the time of Trump's lunatic "birther" campaign, in which he claimed that Barack Obama was not born in the United States and thus shouldn't be president. I was at the table next to Lally's and watched Trump seethe as he was mercilessly and cleverly ridiculed, first by the comedian for the night, Seth Meyers, and then by Obama. It was there and then, it is said, that Trump decided to extract his revenge by claiming the White House for himself.

—

Beyond Washington and Los Angeles, London, too, became a major part of our outreach program. We did a number of big dinners in London to boost the magazine's profile there and elsewhere in Europe. One memorable evening was at the River Café, the already legendary restaurant on the Thames in Hammersmith, run by Ruthie Rogers, the wife of the architect Richard Rogers (later Lord Rogers), and her partner Rose Gray. To celebrate a special issue we had done on London's return as the city of the moment—in terms of music, fashion, theater, literature, architecture, and food—we took over the entire restaurant. This was 1996, and I was still unschooled in the ways of mass hospitality. But Ruthie and Rose guided me through the evening, introducing me to the great and the good of the city. I came away with two things that night. A snapshot of everyone who was making London swing again, and the bud of what became an enduring friendship with Ruthie.

When the Serpentine Gallery in Kensington Gardens was looking for a partner for its annual fundraising dinner, Henry Porter suggested that *Vanity Fair* step in. I met with the museum's head, Julia Peyton-Jones, and we agreed to do it. That Diana, Princess of Wales, would be the cohost of the evening certainly had something to do with my willingness. The first time we did the dinner, in June 1994, the evening became immortalized by the arrival of Diana in her "revenge dress." It was a black off-the-shoulder number that was her way of responding to Prince Charles's recently televised admission of his infidelity in their marriage. The later dinners we did together at the Serpentine were lovely evenings. But nothing, in terms of impact, could compare with the night of the revenge dress.

—

B ig jobs can take their toll. Not only on your health but if you don't watch it, your marriage. In my case, both suffered. I never seemed to have enough time to do what successful people around me did: play tennis or golf, get on a StairMaster at 5:00 in the morning, or even do a few sit-ups every day. I put on weight. My hair grayed. And the hair that had grayed found itself with fewer neighbors. Now, a lot of that can be chalked up to aging. But a good amount had to do with the pressures of the job. Every month, putting out a big issue of *Vanity Fair*—even with all the resources at hand—was like building a locomotive on the fly as it barreled across the country. I was generally incredibly happy at home. I love the bourgeois comforts of hearth and family. But even that element began to change. Over time, Cynthia became disaffected with my life at the magazine. She wanted something quieter. Perhaps in Connecticut, where we spent our summers. We never argued over this sort of thing, but it did come up in conversation.

I didn't have to go out much for professional purposes, and so I spent most weeknight evenings at home the first three or four years trying to turn *Vanity Fair* into my *Vanity Fair*, through editing, story selection, and staffing. Once the kids were off to school, Cynthia found that being a mother was not the full-time, all-out job it had been. She finally had some time on her hands. And then we decided to move back downtown, not far from where my first apartment was.

We bought a house on a leafy street in the West Village, a few doors down from the Waverly Inn. Cynthia worked closely with Basil on the renovation. I honestly thought she could have done that full time, she was so good at it. She was always more health conscious than I was, and she threw herself into that too. She loved to swim and began waking up at 5:00 to get to the pool at Chelsea Piers so she could do her laps in an empty lane. She also did an hour or two of yoga during the day. This, along with looking after our household of four children, meant that she was tired by the late afternoon and started to go to bed earlier, often at 7:00, right after the kids were fed. The timing wasn't great because this was around the time that I had started seeing daylight in my quest to wrestle control over *Vanity Fair*.

When we broke up, I felt it was all my fault, and I was showered in guilt, wanting to begin the process of being a model ex-husband. Cynthia bought a house in Maine overlooking the ocean and was happy there. She has since moved back to Connecticut to be nearer the kids. She was such a magnetic force in my life that having her out of it was a shock. Cynthia was a peerless mother. I prided myself on being a good father, and I did my best with our kids. I learned to cook a few primitive dishes including chicken parmigiana, macaroni and cheese, and roast chicken, using a recipe I got from Anne McNally, Brian's ex-wife.

I had met Anna Scott in London years before when I first got to *Vanity Fair*. The head of the British wing of Condé Nast, Nicholas Coleridge, had thrown a lunch for me at the Ivy and I found myself sitting beside her. She was handling communications and advertising for Ralph Lauren in London. I found her captivating in all respects. I didn't see her again for seven years, when she came to work for a short term in the fashion department at *Vanity Fair*. I loved having her there, and over time, our relationship flourished. At a certain point, with our marriages in the past, we became engaged. Anna had an interesting and also tragic past. Her father, Kenneth Scott, had had diplomatic postings in Washington and Laos, and, being fluent in Russian, in Moscow. His wife developed breast cancer and died when Anna was nine. Ken later became the British ambassador to Yugoslavia and was on hand when the Dayton Accords were signed, settling the war between Serbia, Croatia, and Bosnia. He was then appointed to be one of the Queen's private secretaries. The job came with a grace-and-favor apartment in St. James's Palace, where Anna spent her teenage years.

I do believe that your success in a job is due in no small part to the work and temperament of your partner. Anna was terrific at calming me down during my frequent fits of worry. She was a great sounding board when it came to stories and staff. And her diplomatic skills, honed at the side of her father, went a long way toward making me look better in social situations. The same can be said for children. Mine were keenly attuned to different layers and currents in the culture—layers and currents that I might be indifferent to, but which I knew were of some importance to the readership of *Vanity Fair*. I constantly ran story ideas by them to gauge their interest.

Chapter 15.

The Writers Were
the Franchise

A round the time of our Oscar party debut, Dominick Dunne was covering what was the greatest global murder story in modern history—the trial of O.J. Simpson. Simpson had been arrested and charged with the stabbing death of his ex-wife Nicole Brown Simpson and her friend Ron Goldman. In the process of covering the trial in Los Angeles, which ran for eight months, Nick also became one of the most well-known reporters in the world. This was largely thanks to his almost pathological inability to say no when television bookers came calling—a trait that would later come to haunt him. But it also had to do with the way he managed to cover the trial that kept us ahead even of the weeklies, month after month, despite our long lead time. We put him up at the Chateau Marmont for the duration of the trial. We got a good rate for his room, but when you added in room service, laundry, and ferrying him back and forth to the courtroom and around town in the evenings, the cost was ruinous. We were hugely profitable in those days, and as hard as it is to believe now, it was all worth it. Nick was producing remarkable stuff and advertisers fell over themselves to secure pages near one of his dispatches.

It could be said that popular culture, particularly television culture, was changed forever on June 17, 1994, when Simpson, by then the prime suspect in the murders, went on the run in his friend Al Cowlings's white Ford Bronco, chased on the LA freeways by cops in squad cars followed by television crews in helicopters. People lined the road to witness the slow-motion spectacle. All three broadcast networks broke off whatever they were showing and, at the high point of this snaillike car chase, ninety-five million people were watching it. Years later, David Kamp wrote a superb essay for *Vanity Fair* about the '90s—"The Tabloid Decade," we called it. David was the first really to draw a line between the O.J. Simpson trial and a massive shift in American television-viewing habits. Simpson, remember, was a football legend. He was handsome. He was cool and smooth—at least on the surface. He had won the Heisman Trophy when he played for the University of Southern California. He then spent eleven years in the NFL and became a member of both the College and Pro Football Halls of Fame. And then he followed all of that with a long-time career as a commentator, including on ABC's *Monday Night Football.*

When the trial began, the networks interrupted their regular fare with live news reports from the courtroom. Soap operas, for decades the steady diet of bored American housewives, were giving way to a real soap opera. And that reality, in no time at all, gave way to reality television. Do not forget that one of Simpson's lawyers was Robert Kardashian, the father of all those other Kardashians; his wife, Kris, went on to marry the Olympic decathlete Bruce Jenner—later Caitlyn Jenner—the father of all those other Jenners.

We had a huge disadvantage going into the trial. With every

news outlet in the world on the story, we were the only major monthly covering the events in any sort of detail. And because of the time it took to close an issue, print an issue, and distribute an issue, we had a crippling lead time. CNN could break elements of the story live. The dailies could publish their stories on the trial the next day. Weeklies could present their summaries of the courtroom action the following Monday. Between the time Nick filed and the time the story appeared in an issue on the newsstand, a month or more could pass. What we offered was narrative, context, and behind-the-scenes elements of disclosure. We had to tell the arc of the larger tale in monthly installments. What separated Nick's coverage from that of the crime reporters assigned to the trial was he had the inside line on the high-grade dinner-table and courtroom gossip that surrounded this worldwide phenomenon. He, along with his editor, Wayne Lawson, had a riveting way of knowing, almost like Balzac, what to tell the reader and when to tell them. He made his pieces personal.

Nick was a complicated figure. The Dunnes were a well-to-do Irish Catholic family from Hartford, Connecticut, and Nick, among other family members, minded being overshadowed by the Kennedys, the first family of American Catholicism. Nick had a long-term animus toward Ted Kennedy and covered with great attention the periodic crimes and scandals that surrounded that family, including the Florida rape acquittal of William Kennedy Smith in 1991. Nick was awarded a Bronze Star as a corporal, aged just nineteen, for dragging a fellow soldier to safety during the Battle of the Bulge. He got into show business in New York as floor manager of the children's program *The Howdy Doody Show*. He then moved to Hollywood and produced a handful of films.

Nick was, with his wife, Lenny, an ambitious socialite and their parties in Beverly Hills featured the bold-faced names of the era, including Ronald and Nancy Reagan, Natalie Wood, David Niven, and Nick's on-again-off-again friend Truman Capote. One of Nick's five siblings was John Gregory Dunne, who had written a number of well-received books, including *The Studio*, about 20th Century Fox, and *True Confessions*, a detective story based on Hollywood's notorious Black Dahlia murder. When he married Joan Didion, they became the golden couple on the West Coast, the epicenter of everything that was literary and artistic and cool. They wrote books, they wrote films, and they lived in Malibu.

Nick began to unravel when John and Joan had a highly commercial success, though a critical failure, with their remake of *A Star Is Born* with Barbra Streisand and Kris Kristofferson. He was crushed by their achievement, and he was jealous. In succession, Lenny left him, he developed a serious drinking and drug problem, his career imploded, and he went broke, reduced to relying on government relief. He was shunned and humiliated in his adopted town, suddenly a pariah there, and he never forgot it. In the early '80s he cleaned up, moved to New York, and started trying to write.

In 1983, John Thomas Sweeney was about to stand trial for the murder by strangulation of Dominique Dunne. She was Nick's twenty-two-year-old daughter and he was determined to attend the trial. At a dinner party in New York, he had been persuaded by his friend Marie Brenner and her editor at *Vanity Fair*, Tina Brown, to take notes at the trial. What emerged was "Justice: A Father's Account of the Trial of His Daughter's Killer." It was the first piece he wrote for *Vanity Fair*, and it was powerful writing, a *J'accuse* directed at the legal proceedings that found Sweeney guilty of the lesser charge of manslaughter and that saw him out of prison in three and a half years. Nick said that he could only deal with the rage he felt at the proceedings by writing about it. And the process started him on a new career.

Nick wrote four bestsellers in a row, each of which became a television miniseries—then one of the shiny coins of the cultural realm. And he was writing regularly for *Vanity Fair*. All of a sudden, Nick, the down-at-heel left-behind, was more famous than his brother, the original writer—and this in a family that put great value on fame. I remember reading one of the reviews of John's books in a London broadsheet, and the critic opened by identifying him as Nick's brother. I'm sure that John stopped reading the review at that point. At a dinner party during the height of Nick's reporting and fame, Wayne was seated between John and Joan. John leaned across and said to Wayne, "Isn't there any way you can stop my brother writing these ridiculous pieces about O.J. Simpson? He's making a fool of himself." Joan snapped at him, saying, "John, please!" John and Nick didn't speak for years. John hated *Vanity Fair* and hated me as a result. That never really bothered me. But I always liked Joan, and I'm very close to Annabelle Dunne; she's my partner in documentary films. Nick was her great-uncle.

Nick was the only reporter on the staff who wasn't objective in approaching his reporting. Because of what had happened to his daughter, he came into a story from his own moral perspective: writing from the point of view of the victim. It worked for me and for readers as well. Nick believed that one of the things you had to fight in trials was the trashing by the accused's defense attorneys of the victim's character—"she took drugs; she was a mess"—which is what they did with Dominique. He was out to expose a system that he believed allowed killers to actually get away with murder, particularly if they could afford a polished legal defense. In the case of O.J. Simpson, Nick was convinced almost from the start that the former football star was guilty.

The judge in the trial, Lance Ito, gave Nick a regular seat in the courtroom, just behind the prosecution and defense. He was in court every day. His real reporting ground, though, was outside the court, in the hallways, where he gabbed with the witnesses and the trial lawyers and their assistants. And also at the dinner parties. Nick was not only back in favor, he was the toast of the town. He'd gone suddenly from being a washout to the most sought-after guest. He suited up for dinner party after dinner party in Beverly Hills, Brentwood, and the Palisades, where he became the floorshow, spilling the inside details of what was really going on at the most talked-about trial of the decade. Hostesses hung on his every word. And his dinner mates in turn would spill their secrets about figures on the periphery of the case. Often, Nick would dart to the bathroom to write down some particularly tantalizing tidbit.

He wasn't averse to baring his soul for the purposes of his Simpson narrative, recounting his own troubles, how he became hobbled with his drug habit when his career stalled, and how he knew what it was like to be a nonperson in Hollywood. Later, he wrote in open sympathy about an actress named Lana Clarkson, Phil Spector's murder victim, who had fallen on hard times in Los Angeles, and whose character was being traduced in court to save Spector. "Having once been a failure in Hollywood myself," he wrote, "I totally understand the kind of despair that Lana Clarkson felt." Nick appreciated the makings of a great narrative over a good narrative—and a great narrative when you're on top of the world is so much better if eight chapters before you were scraping along the bottom.

It wasn't always easy to get the copy out of him. His dispatches were generally the last to go into the magazine, and often right down to the wire. This, in spite of Wayne sitting with him and going over every word, listening to Nick read his copy aloud to see if it sounded effortless. Many times, Wayne flew west and camped out at the Chateau and spent a week or so working feverishly to get the story out of Nick, and then sent it back to New York by fax. Wayne had a huge hand in structuring Nick's remarkable, if at times jumbled, drafts. He would break up the narrative with interspersed quotes Nick had picked up in his social victory laps—from a studio head, a restaurant owner, a Bel-Air matron—and so on. Everyone wanted to be quoted; they became part of the story. It also made the reading of the piece—the grim details of the murder—easier to digest.

—

Like Nick, Christopher Hitchens became a popular talking head, the contrarian commentator of the day, constantly on the cable channels CNN and MSNBC, which had just exploded into life. And he did it brilliantly and fearlessly. He loved dogging the other side, mostly because he was so good at it. It served him well and he liked being known outside the bitter circles of the establishment Left. I relished and admired his wit and his social fearlessness, his willingness to be "the man who," for example, in a live Bateman-cartoon-like gaffe he performed one lunchtime at the Everglades Club in Palm Beach. A group of us, including Christopher, was down there on a visit, and a friend, Betsy Kaiser, invited us to lunch at the Everglades, where she was a member. The Everglades Club is a high WASP temple, beautiful in that sort of baroque, byzantine style reminiscent of Mar-a-Lago or Beverly Hills in the 1920s. It's also monstrously exclusionary. I don't think they allowed anybody who wasn't white and Episcopalian—although I'm sure some Catholics and Presbyterians have snuck across the threshold. When the waiter came over, Christopher asked for the kosher menu, which I thought was both very funny and very rude. The episode got Betsy banned from her own club for six months, though having eaten the food at the Everglades, I don't think it was the worst punishment.

The only time I saw Christopher almost on the canvas was during a particularly nasty spat with Sidney Blumenthal, a friend of his who was also a Clinton aide. Christopher famously didn't like the Clintons. He, and other reporters, had all heard the Clinton White House's whispered talking points about Monica Lewinsky—that she was a stalker, unstable, blackmailing the president into sex. Christopher had heard it from Blumenthal himself, though Sidney claimed he had spoken the words off the record. When the White House sought to deny its campaign against Monica, Christopher wouldn't play. He gave evidence against the White House version to the House Judiciary Committee. All hell broke loose and it unspooled over columns of ink and long stretches on cable news. Central to the discussion was what was and was not "off the record."

On television, Christopher began to look ragged and unkempt— or at least more unkempt than normal. He was becoming an undesirable in Washington journalistic circles. He confessed to Martin Amis that he was in some pain. He had grown a beard, and rather than looking like an aging hipster, he was nudging into Gabby Hayes territory. Aimée and I cooked up a plan to bring him to New York and get him freshened up. The fashion department at *Vanity Fair* got him a new suit, a shave, and a haircut. Fresh underwear, socks, and shirts were brought in. At one point, Elizabeth Saltzman looked at the shoes he was wearing.

"These need to go. What size are they?" she asked.

"I don't know," Christopher said. "They're borrowed."

In this cleaned-up version, Brian McNally and I took him to Elaine's, where the crowd was not so censorious as his comrades in Washington. It restored him and cleansed him—and he rose from the canvas to battle on.

Christopher was not just a polemical columnist, though. He was also a serious reporter. His profile of Henry Kissinger was a forensic revelation, using declassified materials that documented his horrifying complicity in torture, rape, and "disappearances" under the right-wing dictatorships of the '70s in Chile and Argentina. Christopher went to Vietnam for us with the great war photographer James Nachtwey to investigate the unending effects over succeeding generations of the sadistic U.S. deployment of Agent Orange, which attacks the nervous system. A half century after the end of the war, Vietnamese babies continued to be born with birth defects and malformations. Entering the debate about U.S. interrogation methods following the U.S. invasion of Iraq, he underwent waterboarding for a column, and wrote, quite simply, echoing Lincoln, "If waterboarding does not constitute torture, then there is no such thing as torture."

He survived an equally painful experience, on assignment for the magazine, in an unlikely area. A friend and Connecticut neighbor of mine, Tom Hedley, who had been an editor at *Esquire* during the celebrated Harold Hayes years in the 1960s, suggested we send Christopher on a series of self-improvement regimens and have him write about them. One such enhancement involved a waxing operation called "the sack, back, and crack" that had been developed by the J Sisters, seven women from Brazil who had pioneered the technique. They'd become the premier waxing operation in New York— and people came from all corners of the world to get their hair removed at the hands of these masters. When I suggested he try the procedure, Christopher thought for a bit, shuddered, and then said, "Well, in for a penny, in for a pound." He said it was more painful than the waterboarding and he did look drained afterward, his skin a sickening pallor. Poor Christopher, he was almost undone by it.

⌁

When Marie Brenner came back to us from *The New Yorker*, having initially followed Tina there after her departure, she wrote stories that shook the world of journalism and the corporate and financial worlds she reported on. She was just one of a group of writers at *Vanity Fair* who achieved a level of disclosure and narrative thrust that gave us our high reputation for investigative journalism. Marie was a wonderful writer and a phenomenal reporter. In 1995, I put her onto a story—based on a leak to the *Daily News*—that a *60 Minutes* segment about a tobacco-industry whistleblower was being killed by CBS. There were murmurs in the trade about bullying corporate interests, feuding between producers, and the death of investigative journalism. What emerged was "The Man Who Knew Too Much," Marie's story about the whistleblower Jeffrey Wigand, who had gone public with evidence that Brown & Williamson, a big southern tobacco company, had long suppressed: that nicotine was addictive and that cigarettes contained added carcinogenic material.

Wigand had been chief of research and development at the company and his scientific information was never in doubt. His revelations were lethal and big tobacco mounted a multimillion-dollar campaign not just to discredit Wigand but to destroy him. They also by then faced many thousands of plaintiff actions. Several former Brown & Williamson executives would be indicted for perjury. Wigand's testimony ultimately led to a $206 billion settlement in 1998 between big tobacco and forty-six states. Marie spent a long time on the story—many months—time that I knew was crucial. She didn't see herself as an investigative journalist. She wrote about the people in the drama. She made them her teachers, and she needed time to get their trust. She had come to the central whistleblower story through a friend of hers, Lowell Bergman, a veteran producer for *60 Minutes*. It was he who had persuaded a reluctant Wigand—facing harassment, lawsuits, and the loss of his family in a divorce—to go public on CBS. Marie discovered that the man orchestrating the vicious public relations campaign against Wigand on behalf of the tobacco company was a friend of both of ours, John Scanlon.

Scanlon had worked for New York City mayor John Lindsay's administration in the late 1960s and early '70s. After that, he became a legendary hand at crisis management. I had met him through his best friend, John Leo, my colleague at *Time*, and we developed a deep and affectionate friendship during summers in Sag Harbor and winters in New York. Scanlon—almost nobody referred to him as John—produced a dossier on Wigand discrediting him and full of truly damaging falsehoods: allegations about breaking into hotel rooms, beating his wife, and filing false insurance claims. He dropped copies of this dossier off with reporters at *The Wall Street Journal* and with producers at *60 Minutes*.

At that time, Scanlon was on contract at *Vanity Fair* as a public relations consultant. Marie came to my office and told me that "Scanlon is the guy who is trying to smear Wigand." He was reportedly being paid a million dollars by Brown & Williamson to do this. She couldn't do the story, she said, unless Scanlon was put on leave from the magazine. I agreed immediately and called him to say so. I always felt I was never going to go after a friend intentionally, but it was very hard to avoid writing about someone close if they'd stuck their hand in the news-cycle wood chipper. Scanlon had done this, and it wasn't his finest hour. I told Marie to write what she had. When her story came out, Scanlon was furious, both with her and with me. There wasn't much I could do about it. It was painful. And Marie is good—she does the reporting and then she tells it straight. I've generally found that if the story's true and accurate, however hurtful, the rage subsides pretty quickly. It's only when it's hurtful and *inaccurate* that the outrage on the part of the subject goes on long-term boil.

The thing here was that Scanlon's campaign of disinformation had backfired on him and he had been called out on it. His campaign of hammering Wigand's credibility, as reported by Marie, became part of CBS's story—that he'd tried to discredit this otherwise honorable, but complicated, whistleblower. And it wasn't quite in Scanlon's character. After the Lindsay days, he'd worked for left-wing causes and handled the press for films like Richard Attenborough's *Cry Freedom* and Sydney Pollack's *Absence of Malice*. He was very much an advocate for press freedoms and was hugely popular with journalists. He was dishy with a quote and loved a good gossip. At the same time, he lived large. He had a sprawling apartment on the Upper West Side and a huge mansion built for a nineteenth-century whaling captain in Sag Harbor with a living room the size of a ballroom. There was also a house in Ireland. Friends worried that he had taken on dodgier clients than he would have liked in order to cover his financial nut.

Tobacco companies still advertised in magazines in those days, and after Marie's story, the big American ones collectively pulled $4 million worth of advertising from *Vanity Fair*. Which was not an ideal outcome. But we got through it. They stayed away for about six months and then they came back. I mentioned it to Si over lunch one day, and he was typically philosophical about the loss. If the story was good, then that was the most important thing. Marie's article led to the Michael Mann film *The Insider*, with Al Pacino as Bergman and Russell Crowe as Wigand. (Scanlon was played by the incomparable Rip Torn—which I imagined eased the pain of the whole episode for him somewhat.) Just before the film was finished, I got a call from Mann. He said that he would rather not have the "Based on a *Vanity Fair* story by Marie Brenner" in the credits. I said that I thought it should be there, given his reliance on the source material. Mann leaned into the conversation and in an almost conspiratorial voice said, "Please, as a personal favor to me." Which I found strange. I told him that I didn't know how I could do it as a personal favor given that we had never met. The credit remained.

With these big stories you need some luck, and sometimes a break. Marie got both in her subsequent exposé in 2002 of the collapse of Enron and the fraudulent accounting of its directors, which cost investors billions of dollars and wiped out the retirement savings of twenty thousand employees. With the disappearance of $63.4 billion in assets, Enron was the biggest bankruptcy case in U.S. history up to that time. Like the tobacco story, it was an example of a general assignment reporter starting from scratch and having the time to pursue it. Just to make the assignment more difficult, Marie had little knowledge of accounting procedures on which the frauds were based, procedures that baffled even the battalion of bankruptcy lawyers who tried to unravel the Enron mess. I nevertheless had a hunch Marie would be well suited to this story. For one thing, she came from Texas, where so many oil companies were based. And she knew some lawyers there—always a way in.

Quite often, early in pretrial proceedings, reporters can be useful for lawyers in setting up the optics of a case. One day, in federal court in Houston, where Marie had decided to go to get a briefing, the prosecutor mentioned that some former employees of Enron would be witnesses for the prosecution. Marie told me that a woman, dressed unlike the attending press corps, had hurriedly left the small courtroom. Marie followed her, made contact, discovered that her name was Jan Avery. She had been a key accountant at Enron, and she was also the secret witness in the case. She had left the courtroom because she didn't want to be photographed and identified by the television news reporters who were stationed outside. Like anybody else who got on the wrong side of the company, she was afraid of intimidation. From that first meeting she began to fill in Marie on how the fraud had worked. Marie called me from Houston that day and said, "Graydon, you're not going to believe this." She had her guide and her mole; potentially she had the whole story.

The other break she got was the kind that reporters usually only dream of. One of the big secrets of the case, which Jan Avery knew, was that Ken Lay, the CEO of Enron, had demanded that employees hand over all their records, which he then had destroyed to hide the original fraud. As the story was almost going to press, Marie got a tip that one of Enron's accountants had copied the records, taken them to his house, and hidden them in his attic. Marie tracked him down in Corpus Christi, Texas. He confirmed that he had the files, and that the files proved the fraud. Her contact was by telephone, her piece had more or less gone to press, and the early pages were unchangeable. So we tacked this new element of the story onto the end and dropped a page of ads to get it in. All this took place amid a blizzard of midnight calls and a lot of excitement, with our legal editor, Robert Walsh, continually working with Marie to confirm the facts (and talking on his own to the accountant in Corpus Christi). On this story, we seemed to be literally following the truck to the printing press.

———

I do think people got the wrong impression of me with regard to going out at night. The truth is, I delineated my life pretty firmly. Daytime was for work and nighttime was for family. Once I had gotten my feet under my desk at *Vanity Fair*, I generally peeled out of the office at 5:00 or 5:30 in the afternoon so that I could be at home with my kids. I had a rule never to discuss the office or the magazine after hours unless the story was funny, or if I could use some advice on something. We would all have dinner together and then I would edit at the kitchen table while the children did their homework. Dinners at home were often highlighted by rounds of what we called

"Quizmasters," a game I made up to get the kids digging into the things I thought they should be digging into. "For ten points, what was the name of George Lucas's first film?" (*THX 1138.*) "And for fifteen points, in what other Lucas film was this title used?" (It was the license plate of Paul Le Mat's dragster in *American Graffiti.*) We never tallied the scores or anything. But it got the young brains whirring in an engaging way at the end of a long day of schoolwork. We also had our own film festivals. We'd run through a half dozen Hitchcock films over a weekend when the weather was bad, for instance. It got them on a road that has informed both their personal and professional lives, centered around film, books, music, and art.

It was a rare evening that required me to put on a dinner jacket. Aside from the Oscar party, I did this perhaps once or twice a year. Some years not even that. Most nights out were at Da Silvano, Sant Ambroeus, or Il Cantinori. We'd have dinner with another couple and I'd book a second table for our four kids right beside us. They weren't allowed games or toys or anything. It was just the four—and later five—Carter kids. Cynthia and I started this tradition when the oldest, Ash, was, say, eight. That would make Max six and Spike three. During those first nights, they sat there and didn't speak a great deal. Then Ash and Max would begin talking, then Spike, and then, as the group grew, Bron and Izzy. Within a few months of our sidecar dinner arrangement, the Carter kids became a veritable talk-fest. And they have never stopped. Newcomers think the Carter children have their own special language. And they do, in a way. It's an animated stew of current events and film and music and books and television and, when they were younger, made-up table games. When other kids were potted at the table with them, it would take the newcomers a while to figure out what the Carter kids were talking about, so wide and diverse were their reference points. I don't know any other siblings who are as close, and I attribute a lot of that to their dinners together one table away from the adults.

Da Silvano became something of a second home. The small Italian restaurant down on lower Sixth Avenue was an art-world hangout. I had a regular table, on the left by the window as you came in. I was there maybe three times a week. On many of those nights, across from me at a table that could have held six, was a slim, nice-looking man with world-weary eyes. He regularly ate by himself; occasionally, he'd be joined by someone else. He had an effortless cool about him and his hair was combed in a sort of DA style popular with television stars in the '50s. We'd nod to each other, but we never exchanged a word.

Back to the office for a moment. In those days, issues were demonstrably thick. With 200 to 250 pages of advertising, I had upward of 140 editorial pages to play around with each month. And once that number was set, you couldn't go over it. You could get about eight hundred words to a page. I always felt that filling those pages was a great opportunity and not an obligation. I think that made a difference in how I approached each issue. Although I generally started out each month with a blank slate, the pages filled up quickly and I wanted to make every one count. Each and every one of them was its own separate opportunity. To make the whole jigsaw work, I tried to keep the writers to the word count they were assigned. Turning in a ten-thousand-word story when the assignment was for five thousand was a problem. It was a bit like getting a four-seater sofa delivered when you only ordered (and had room for) a loveseat.

But every once in a while, a piece would come in that made you want to change the size of the room. I had an idea in the mid-'90s to do a story on Sidney Korshak, the Chicago mob's lawyer in Holly-wood in the '40s and '50s and right up to the '70s. He lived in the shadows and was rarely photographed. But those who knew, knew that he was, in his own way, the most powerful man in the movie business. And there was, pre-internet, nothing about him—no book, no pictures, almost nothing in print. I assigned the story to Nick Tosches, who was already something of a legend. Nick had started in the rock press and had grown into a major writer. I'd read his book on Dean Martin, *Dino: Living High in the Dirty Business of Dreams.* He'd also written biographies of Jerry Lee Lewis and the Vatican banker Michele Sindona. This would be Nick's first piece for *Vanity Fair*, and it was a tough assignment.

He accepted the commission and then just disappeared for about a year. It was on our planning board, but kept moving, when month after month the story failed to materialize. And Nick wasn't responding to his editor's calls. One day a bulky envelope arrived at the office for me. It was a typed manuscript, a half inch thick. (By this point, Christopher and Gore Vidal were the last contributors on the *Vanity Fair* writing staff who still worked on typewriters.) It was the Korshak manuscript, and it was seventeen thousand words long. The story had been assigned at half that length. I sat down and, without a break, read it through in one sitting. It was a masterpiece, and so beautifully written that I felt my eyes welling up with tears. I expected something great from Nick, but this was truly magnificent. The introduction: "This is the story of a boy, a dream, a law degree, and a gun. It has no beginning and no end, but opens in the American desert on an October day in 1961, with a car emerging as a shimmer in the sun. In the car is Sidney Korshak." We are led slowly and historically and with brilliantly researched detail to Korshak's arrival an hour or so later at the Riviera hotel in Las Vegas where the all-powerful teamsters boss Jimmy Hoffa has to move out hastily from the Presidential Suite to accommodate Korshak's unexpected arrival.

It was all that good.

I called Nick up and I said, "Nick, this will be the most wonderful thing I will have published up to this point. And I want to pay you twice what we agreed on because it's so much better than I ever imagined."

He got a bit emotional.

I said, "Plus, I'll get the check over to you as soon as possible. Where should we send it?"

He said, "Da Silvano."

I was confused. "You mean the restaurant?" I figured he might owe them money.

"Yeah," he said. "That's where I get all my mail. That's where I eat."

I thought for a moment and then said, "Wait a minute. Do you sit at the table across from me?"

Nick said he did.

"Why didn't you ever say anything?" I asked.

"Oh, I didn't want to bother you," he said.

⌐

On the planning board for an interminable time was a card that read "The Collapse of Lloyd's of London." The writer was David McClintick, who had done a number of pieces for me. He was a significant figure in the world of financial journalism. David had been a star at *The Wall Street Journal* but he had truly made his name with *Indecent Exposure*, his 1982 bestseller about David Begelman, the flawed but popular head of Columbia Pictures. Begelman had a gambling addiction that got the better of him, and he ended up siphoning money not only from the studio, but from the Oscar-winning actor Cliff Robertson.

In 1995, Begelman ran into another fraud situation, and I assigned David to write a piece about his new batch of troubles. During his reporting, Begelman committed suicide. I remember a detail in David's story that involved a friend of Begelman's turning up at his house to start planning a memorial for him. She looked in the fridge and found that it was completely empty. Begelman was broke. Just as his friend was leaving, a team of detailers showed up—the sort who go over cars with Q-tips—to clean his Rolls-Royce. Begelman would spend the money to detail his car—a Rolls, no less—but didn't have money for food. That, in a nutshell, is Hollywood.

When I met with David, he told me he wanted to do a story on the possible collapse of Lloyd's of London, the world's leading insurance market. I told him that I didn't know much about the organization beyond the 1936 Tyrone Power film, *Lloyd's of London*. I did know that its members, or "names," made extraordinary profits but were also subjected to unlimited liability. Meaning that they could be completely wiped out if things went horribly bad. Such was the extent of my Lloyd's scholarship.

In the 1990s, Lloyd's, which I was also to discover is a syndicate rather than a company, was on the edge of collapse. Huge losses resulting from insurance claims from oil spills, hurricanes, and asbestos lawsuits were crippling many of the partners. The names were largely a collection of wealthy individuals who introduced each other to the syndicate. It was like a private club. David said that should Lloyd's collapse, "it could affect the wealth of nations." I thought it was right up our alley, so I gave him the go-ahead. He said he would have to go to London for a few months to integrate himself into the Lloyd's ecosystem of wealthy names in London and the shires. We settled on two months. A plea for more time came through, and two months became four months and four months became six months. Between David's expenses and his fee, we were in for about $180,000. And he hadn't written a word. Chris Garrett and I would just reel when the bills arrived.

When David finally turned his story in, it just didn't work. Many of the names had been brought to bankruptcy, but the syndicate seemed to hold, and the wealth of nations appeared to be secure. It wasn't the great opera of aristocrats bringing the world to its knees that David, and I, had hoped for. He said he needed more time in London. I didn't know what to do. I couldn't invest more, but I couldn't run what we had. I told him that if he wanted, he could take it elsewhere. Norman Pearlstine, David's former boss at *The Wall Street Journal*, had become the editor in chief of Time Inc. David sold him and Jim Kelly, by then *Time*'s editor, on the story and he continued with his investigation. Eventually, David's Lloyd's piece ran over twenty-three pages in the European edition of *Time*.

Stories founder for all kinds of reasons, mostly unpredictable. When a military coup overthrew the government of Jean-Bertrand Aristide, the president of Haiti, in 2004, I called T. D. Allman. He was quaintly named on our masthead as "foreign correspondent"—as if foreign stories could only be written by him. Tim (the *T* in T. D.) was a formidable historian and journalist who had exposed the CIA's secret involvement in the war in Laos and whose books had put the phrases "rogue state" and "secret war" into the lexicon. But he was also slightly eccentric. At a party once he had gently bitten Aimée Bell's face—after *Forrest Gump* had won the Oscar for Best Picture. I can't recall if that was a bite of happiness or of outrage. He had a sweaty charm that completely surprised me. One night in the 1990s, Bob Colacello and I were in Paris and bumped into Tim. We were on our way to São Schlumberger's vast, almost hallucinogenic house at the foot of the Eiffel Tower, and we invited him along. There were a half dozen grand Parisian women there, and we watched as Tim slowly came to have them leaning in on his every word. Bob and I might well have been furniture.

Tim was game for a fresh assignment. He was an old Haiti hand, and in a previous dispatch, in 1989, he had seemed entranced by the specter of Baron Samedi, the voodoo king. He quoted a friend of his: "I have seen the zombies laughing and dancing awake. There were tens of thousands of them. . . . I'll never forget the rage in those eyes." He had also praised the proprietor of the Hotel Oloffson, in Port-au-Prince—the hotel made famous by Graham Greene in his novel *The Comedians* and the only place to stay in Haiti's capital that offered reasonable safety—for his forbearance during his stay. "For one month," Allman wrote, "this stranger had shown me kindness and given me help with a graceful stoicism it was beyond my capacity to repay." Had he been a demanding guest?

He set off, and I heard nothing from him for more than two months. This was in the days when not everyone used cell phones. I was in my office a few weeks later when a registered letter arrived. It was from Richard Morse, the proprietor of the Hotel Oloffson. The letter ran to four pages, closely typed. I no longer have it, but it started something like this: "Dear Mr. Carter, My family has been through hurricanes, wars, and revolutions, but nothing, nothing, could have prepared me for the arrival of your Mr. T. D. Allman." Allman, he wrote, had spent a month and a half at the hotel. The details of the letter are unprintable here, but it did include the sentiment that Morse would rather have had the Tontons Macoutes to stay than our correspondent. And after all that, Morse wrote, our man had left without paying his bill. I was horrified and walked over to Chris's office and showed her the letter. Chris called the hotel to ask for the complete invoice so we could pay it. And then I called the owner to offer our most abject apology. Tim must have ventured once too often into that heart of darkness.

Looking back, there were some clues in that earlier report from

Haiti: "All I'd wanted was to get out of Haiti," he had written. "Now I could not imagine leaving, because each day I saw things that once would have been unimaginable to me." Had he been a Victorian explorer and this his discovered diary, one would have said, "Poor All-man. Let's hope the wretch got a Christian burial."

Chapter 16.

The Smell of Grease Paint

For those of you who don't waste your time prowling the credits section of IMDb film listings, I should perhaps say a word about my own time in the film business. It started when I was at *Spy.* I was in the office one day tinkering with a manuscript when I got a call from a woman who said that she was a casting director. It seemed that Dick Wolf, then beginning his ascent as a television producer, was making a show called *H.E.L.P.* She said that the series would star John Mahoney and David Caruso and that it was about a New York City effort to combine police, fire, and emergency services in Harlem. I gently asked what this had to do with me.

"Well," she said, "we have a scene in which a WASPy editor is caught hunting rats in Central Park. And I wonder if you'd be interested in the part."

I asked if I was the first person she had called.

She paused for a bit and then said, "Well, no. We asked George

Plimpton, but he was busy. And we asked Lewis Lapham. He said it was beneath him. So we're reaching out to you."

Not being as busy as George or as high-minded as Lewis, I said sure. I did warn her that I had never acted beyond grade school theatrics. Don't worry, she said. "You only have one line."

On the day of the shoot, I found myself in wellies and a Barbour jacket standing on a knoll in the park with a fake shotgun in my hand. I had never been on a television set before and I was astounded by the number of people it took to film this one scene. I had memorized my line, trying all manner of delivery. The thing is, like an idiot, I never bothered to memorize the line that came before it. So this simple scene went through about a dozen takes as I slowly began to respond to my prompt with my memorized line at the proper moment. Dick went on to become perhaps the most prolific producer of cop shows in history. This part of his vast procedural empire, alas, was canceled after six episodes. And I only partly blame myself.

Ron Howard cast me in his film about the newspaper business, *The Paper*. In that one, Cynthia and I had a scene with the editor of the fictional paper, played by Jason Robards. Then came a part in the remake of *Alfie*, with Jude Law and Susan Sarandon. I was playing a Wall Street asshole being cuckolded by my driver. At one point, we were filming at the Chanel boutique on Madison Avenue. When I arrived, one of the hands led me to a trailer parked on a side street around the corner with my name written in masking tape on the door. It was huge and had a living room and bathroom. I was about to get settled in when a crew member knocked on the door and said that I'd have to move—the trailer was needed in New Jersey. I gathered my things and was escorted over to another. It was so small that I had to duck when I stood up inside it, and could touch both sides if I stretched my arms out. I got dressed for the scene. On the way to the Chanel boutique, I noticed that my old trailer was still in place, but new masking tape had been put on the door with the name of one of the stars of the film, Jane Krakowski.

Then came a part in a thriller called *Arbitrage*, with Richard Gere and, again, Susan Sarandon. Once more I was playing a Wall Street asshole. I was beginning to worry about being typecast. I had a number of lines in this one, though. A Canadian critic gave me high marks, but in the most backhanded of ways. "Surprisingly good," the reviewer said. Sometime later, Peter Bogdanovich called and asked if I would play Owen Wilson's driver in a romantic comedy he was making with Owen and Jennifer Aniston. The film had a not altogether promising name: *Squirrels to the Nuts*. Again, I said why not. By this time, I was experienced enough to memorize not only my single line ("Welcome to New York!") but the one that came before it. Although the title was later changed to *She's Funny That Way*, the film was not a success. But on this one I could take no blame. My scene had been cut.

My *Vanity Fair* office in the Condé Nast Building near Times Square fared slightly better than its occupant. It was used by Robert Redford in his 1998 film *The Horse Whisperer*, which he both directed and starred in opposite Kristin Scott Thomas. At one point, "Bob," as he insisted I call him, was examining my office with his set decorator. I was working at my desk editing something.

"Would you mind excusing us?" he said.

"Absolutely," I replied and went back to my manuscript.

And then he said, "No, I mean could we have the office to ourselves?"

I was a bit put out but grabbed the manuscript I was working on and decamped to Chris Garrett's office while Bob and his colleague scoped my desk area. Cameron Crowe also used the office for his 2001 film *Vanilla Sky*, with Tom Cruise and Penélope Cruz. Neither film did particularly well at the box office. After *Vanity Fair* had moved out of the building, my office had a featured role in HBO's *Succession*. Finally, a hit! I think the rental fees to Condé Nast for use of my office certainly topped the paltry amounts for my acting work. Although every six months or so, I do receive residual checks in the high single digits for my film career.

—

I fell into producing documentaries completely by accident. In the mid-1990s, I was driving out to spend the weekend with Mitch and Kelly at their desert house in Lone Pine, a little over three hours northeast of Los Angeles. I had a Volvo convertible for the trip. The one the rental company delivered was candy-apple red with white leather interior and red piping. I had been hoping for something that looked a little less like the sort of car that Joan Collins's hairdresser would drive. But this was the only one the agency had. Mitch and Kelly were driving out in his more masculine 1969 black-on-black GTO, and I was going to follow them. I had bought the book on tape that had just come out of film producer Robert Evans's memoir *The Kid Stays in the Picture*. He read the book himself, and along the way there and back, I listened to it. Something about Bob's oaky voice recounting the stories of his remarkable life in the film business made me think that perhaps we could make a *Vanity Fair* documentary out of it. I had no idea how to make a documentary. I didn't even know any nonfiction filmmakers. But I love documentaries, and I thought one narrated by Bob would be entrancing.

I had met Bob a decade earlier at a lunch at Mr. Chow organized by Peter Bart, his second-in-command during his remarkable run at Paramount—the late 1960s and '70s, the period of *Chinatown, The Godfather,* and *Love Story.* By the time I met him, Bob had gone through what can gently be called a rough patch. He'd been arrested for trying to move cocaine into the country during a broken period in his life. He lost his job and his standing in the community. He didn't go to prison, but his reputation was highly tarnished. He couldn't get work. He'd even spent time in a psychiatric hospital. Struggling to find his footing, he made two films in the next decade, but both were poorly received by critics and audiences. The moment you lose your name on your studio-lot parking space, Hollywood just erases you from its memory. And that is what had happened to Bob. None of this mattered to me. I liked him. I admired all that he had accomplished as well as his cheery presence, despite his being surrounded by the smoldering remnants of a once illustrious career. After that first lunch, every time I was in Los Angeles, I would go to see him at his house, Woodland, up behind the Beverly Hills Hotel.

Aside from his years of bringing glory to Paramount, he'd had some famous liaisons. He'd already been married a number of times, the longest—four years—to Ali MacGraw. The shortest was to the actress Catherine Oxenberg. That one lasted two weeks. And there were more to come. It wasn't surprising. Bob was certainly the best-looking studio executive ever. I know, a low bar. But he had also mastered the art of seduction, with both women and men. Anna and I bumped into him at the Caprice in London a few weeks after one of his marriages. Bob was there with a leggy brunette, whom he introduced as his "niece," and a man, whom he introduced as his clairvoyant.

I begged him to come to the Oscar party, but he didn't want to go out. He wasn't a recluse, but he'd see only a few friends, like Jack Nicholson, Warren Beatty, Dustin Hoffman, and Sue Mengers. Through Bob himself, I met a talented young pair of filmmakers, Brett Morgen and Nanette Burstein. They wanted to do a documentary about him while he was working on his next film. I wasn't sure about this idea. Not only did Bob not want to be on-camera, I thought he had only a slim chance of ever getting another film made. Also, Bob wanted to be remembered the way he looked when he looked good. I suggested a biographical documentary based on his book, one where we could use his narration as the backdrop to his remarkable story. Brett and Nanette came around and we sold the idea to October Films, an independent distributor that was then a part of Universal Pictures.

While we were making the documentary, Brett, knowing that I had worked at *Life*, called me to see if I could get my hands on a copy of an issue that featured Bob on the cover. He had mentioned it in his book. I called the archives, and, after a search, they called back and said that they simply couldn't find it. We moved on. When the film was done, I arranged to show it to Bob in one of the screening rooms on the Paramount lot where he still had an office. I picked him up and when we went through the gate, it was "Hello, Mr. Evans!" "Hey, Ernie, how are you?" I felt like I was living that scene in *Sunset Boulevard* where Norma Desmond comes to the studio for her close-up with Mr. DeMille. Bob sat beside me in the screening room and we watched the film. I glanced out the corner of my eye at one point and there was a tear running down his face.

Afterward, he took me to his almost unused office. There was a dusty smell about it; everything was framed—scribbles on a napkin from Lana Turner and, lo, the issue of *Life* he had mentioned in his book. When he went to the bathroom, I stepped over to look at the *Life* cover. And I realized that it wasn't real. It was a black-and-white photograph of Bob with the red *Life* logo stuck onto it. And knowing Bob, I realized that he'd seen it on the wall for so long that it had become real to him. He was the master of invention: when I'd visit him at Woodland, there'd always be a phone call from Jack Nicholson. Alan, his butler, would glide in and say, "Mr. Nicholson is on the line." Bob would go to the phone in his screening room and pick up the receiver with a conspiratorial "Irish!" My hunch was that the calls from Jack were the audio version of the *Life* cover.

The Kid Stays in the Picture came out, and thanks to Brett and Nanette's visual artistry, it was a huge success. It premiered at the Sundance Film Festival in January 2002. A number of *Vanity Fair* hands came out for it, including Chris, Sara, Jane, Aimée, and Krista. Bob was there, and he got a standing ovation. We took the documentary to the Cannes Film Festival that May, where it was shown at the Grand Palais. The film made Bob current again in Hollywood. And I even got him to finally come to the Oscar party. I conscripted Minnie Driver and her sister, Kate, to go to Woodland and bring him as their date. A whole new generation of filmmakers and musicians came to appreciate Bob. He very sweetly dedicated his next book to me, writing, "You saved my life." Bob died at age eighty-nine after a lifetime of God knows how much sex and cocaine. They should have donated his heart, and perhaps one other organ, to the Smithsonian.

—

One documentary led to another. *9/11* was directed by the French filmmakers Jules and Gédéon Naudet and a former fireman, James Hanlon, who were in the World Trade Center making a documentary about a rookie member of a firehouse in Lower Manhattan when the towers came down. (Jules got the only clear footage of the first jet, American Airlines Flight 11, hitting the North Tower.) The Naudets were the sons of a photographic correspondent at *Paris Match*. He reached out on their behalf to David Friend, whom he had known for some time, and David brought the Naudet brothers to me. I took all three of them to see Les Moonves, the CEO of CBS. He was impressed by what they had shot and agreed to do the documentary. I said that we would do it with them on three conditions. That it be broadcast on a Sunday night; that it have limited commercial interruptions; and that it be introduced not by a CBS news hand, but by Robert De Niro, inarguably the de facto mayor of Tribeca and that part of Lower Manhattan.

That was fine with Les, and he was good on his word. Susan Zirinsky, the dynamo whom the Holly Hunter character in James Brooks's *Broadcast News* was based on, stepped in to handle the actual production. When it was broadcast, *9/11* got almost Super Bowl–sized ratings. It also won a Peabody Award and an Emmy. I'm not much for awards ceremonies, so on the day of the Emmys I skipped the event and went out to a dinner at a friend's house in Malibu. When I returned to the hotel, the man at the front desk called me over. He reached down and gave me a note letting me know that I had just won an Emmy.

I was brought into the HBO orbit in 2002 by my chum Richard Plepler, who was then running the company, and whom I had first met when he was working with Scanlon. I produced *Gonzo*, a biographical documentary of Hunter S. Thompson, directed by Alex Gibney, and *Public Speaking*, consisting of interviews with Fran, directed by Martin Scorsese. There was *Surfwise*, Doug Pray's film about the Paskowitzes, the legendary surfing family. I produced a documentary on the Chicago Seven conspiracy trial with Brett Morgen that, for reasons too complicated to even remember, we had to call *Chicago 10*. And there was one on Ralph Lauren with Susan Lacy called *Very Ralph*.

Annabelle Dunne, an old *Vanity Fair* hand, came on as my partner and we did two documentaries about the new culture: *Swiped*, about dating in the digital age, directed by my *Vanity Fair* colleague Nancy Jo Sales, and *Fake Famous*, about Instagram influencers, directed by another *Vanity Fair* hand, Nick Bilton. Annabelle and I have made a number of films with Nick Hooker, including *Agnelli*, a documentary about the Italian industrialist and playboy, and *AKA Mr. Chow*, about Michael Chow, the remarkable impresario behind the restaurants. Recently, we were producers on a documentary Nick directed about the life of Karl Lagerfeld.

Everything Is Copy, about Nora Ephron, the journalist, screenwriter, and director, was a special project. Nick Hooker codirected that one with Jacob Bernstein, Nora's son with Carl Bernstein. After her marriage to Carl fell apart, Nora married Nick Pileggi, the former crime reporter who wrote *Goodfellas* and who had been a collaborator with Marty Scorsese for decades. Nora knew the answers to everything, and Nick was a god among journalists and screenwriters. One day in 2012 we were scheduled to go to a friend's birthday party. Nora called earlier that day and said, "No, no. You must have dinner with us." She was pretty insistent. So we skirted the birthday and went to dinner at La Grenouille with Nick and Nora and David Geffen. The dinner was wonderful, but we didn't realize that Nora had intended it as a farewell. She knew she was fading, and three weeks later we got a call from Louise Grunwald saying that Nora had just died. She wanted to say goodbye to all her friends but didn't want to burden anybody with what was going to happen. She was just seventy-one.

Almost on a par with the reinvention of Bob Evans was the documentary we produced for HBO in 2011 on the movie and music industry legend Jerry Weintraub. Jerry had, by that time, been a part of my life for many years. A Jewish kid originally from the Bronx, he claimed that Woody Allen's *Broadway Danny Rose* was based on him. He had started out promoting circus acts in New York and worked his way up to Hollywood. His enviable career had left an imprint on a half dozen decades. He'd worked at one end with Elvis

Presley and Frank Sinatra (claiming credit for Sinatra's many come-back concerts). And at the other end he produced all three *Ocean's* remakes, with Brad Pitt and George Clooney.

Jerry was a gifted storyteller. He famously retailed tales about people who were helpfully dead and couldn't talk back or contradict his versions of events. At Oscar time, a bunch of us would have a Jerry dinner at La Dolce Vita, the charmingly boozy, red-sauce Ital-ian restaurant in Beverly Hills. He'd tell many of the same stories, and Susie Ekins, his devoted girlfriend of many years, would listen as if she were hearing them for the first time—a performance wor-thy of an Oscar. Jerry was attractive to women, but he was a real magnet for men too. Guys simply loved him and loved being around him. I've never met any man whom more men had man crushes on.

He was also almost comically self-involved. Years ago, at a din-ner in my honor in Brentwood, he stood up, rested his hand on my shoulder, and said, "I'd like to say a few words about my friend Gray-don." My innate anxiety about becoming the sudden focus of atten-tion wound down quickly. Once he had said those words, Jerry spoke for more than half an hour—about himself. He could get away with it, though, because his friends knew he could drop his favorite topic in a heartbeat if he thought you needed something, anything, or just wanted to talk.

Realizing that the best stories are sometimes right under your nose, I assigned Rich Cohen, a great narrative writer, to do a big piece on him for the Hollywood issue. I thought Rich would appre-ciate Jerry's singular Jerry-ness. And he did. The piece ran in the 2008 Hollywood issue and the attention it got only elevated the Jerry Weintraub myth, much of which had been created by Jerry himself. Cohen then cowrote Jerry's subsequent memoir, called *When I Stop Talking, You'll Know I'm Dead.* A year later, Doug McGrath directed our documentary about Jerry for HBO. We called it *His Way*, a play on the title of the Sinatra song. The public at large hadn't really heard about Jerry Weintraub before this, and it said something about the power of *Vanity Fair* and HBO that it turned him into a significant and more widely known cultural figure.

A good part of the film centered on Jerry's somewhat unique living arrangements. For many years he was a manager of musical acts, including Bob Dylan, Led Zeppelin, John Denver—and the singer Jane Morgan. In time, Jane and Jerry got married. When she caught Jerry with another woman, she took a different tack than most other wives do in that position. She told him she would stay married to him, but he'd have to shoulder her living costs for the rest of her life. Jerry agreed. Jane moved to their house in Malibu and Jerry stayed in Beverly Hills and in time took up with his girlfriend Susie, the daughter of the stuntman who performed Steve McQueen's memorable motorcycle chase scene in *The Great Escape*.

When Jerry died in 2015, his friends struggled to find words to express what they were thinking. Leave it to George Clooney, a man with a knack for always saying the right thing at the right time: "To those who didn't know him, we send our deepest sympathy. You would have loved him."

—

Sometime in 2012, I was having drinks at home with John Logan. It was a meeting set up by our mutual agent at CAA, Brian Siberell. John has an impressive array of screenwriting credits, including *Gladiator*, *Any Given Sunday*, *The Aviator*, and two Bond films. He also wrote the hit play *Red*, about Mark Rothko. We got to talking and he mentioned Sue Mengers, who had died the year before. I told him that I was surprised that no memorial service had been held for her. John said, "What about a one-woman show?" I told him that I thought it was a brilliant idea and proceeded to introduce John to a number of Sue's friends so he could soak up some Mengers history and color. Four months later, John sent me the finished play. It captured Sue about as closely as was possible. John asked me if I would produce it—a perilous gesture of goodwill given my nonexistent theater résumé. Fortunately, he also asked his *Red* producer, Arielle Tepper Madover, to sign on, and we were soon joined by Jimmy Nederlander and the Shubert Organization. We went after just one director, Joe Mantello, the Tony Award–winning director of *Wicked*, *Other Desert Cities*, and countless other esteemed productions.

Once Joe accepted, we needed a star capable of capturing the essence of Sue and bringing her alive onstage. We all agreed that there was one actress who was perfect for the part: Bette Midler. Bette adored Sue, and Sue adored Bette. In fact, Anna and I first met Bette at Sue's place. To Bette's legion of admirers, this production would be welcome news, inasmuch as she hadn't been on a Broadway stage in more than three decades. It took a bit of persuading—her chief worry, and I can fully sympathize, was having to memorize ninety minutes of dialogue. But she accepted. *I'll Eat You Last: A Chat with Sue Mengers*, starring Bette Midler and directed by Joe Mantello, opened at the Booth Theatre in April 2013. For someone who had worshipped Moss Hart's theater memoir, *Act One*, I felt part of something that I had only up to then read about.

Bette was magnificent, ruling the stage from a sofa for the entire ninety-minute performance. Her introduction—"Forgive me for not getting up. Think of me as that caterpillar from *Alice in Wonderland*, the one with the hash pipe"—set the mood for the evening. John's script told many of the wicked techniques Mengers used, the aggression, the minor deceptions. It told of her dinner parties, where the gossip was uncensored, without limit of indiscretion; Sue was very much in the Alice Roosevelt Longworth school: "If you can't say anything nice about someone, come sit by me." A profile of Mengers that Mike Wallace did for *60 Minutes* in 1975—and which Sue would play regularly for guests—quoted Bob Evans: "Four years ago, Sue Mengers would call me six times a day and say, 'Ryan O'Neal for *The Godfather*.' 'Ryan O'Neal for *The Godfather*. Are you crazy, Sue? Ryan O'Neal is blond, blue-eyed. We want an Italian.' The next morning, there'd be flowers at the door. 'Ryan O'Neal for *The Godfather*.'"

At one meeting with the producers, Jimmy Nederlander expressed worry about how Ben Brantley, *The New York Times*'s chief drama critic, would review the play. He didn't have the clout of his legendary recent predecessor, Frank Rich. Frank could kill a bad play in an evening. But if he loved something, he could fill the house for months. Ben was a good critic, but he just wasn't in that league. That said, a middling or damp review in *The Times* could really hurt business. I thought for a moment and said that I wasn't sure Ben could review the play.

"Why not?" said Jimmy.

"Well," I said, "he worked for me for about three weeks when I took over *Vanity Fair*, and knowing the rules at *The Times*, he probably has to recuse himself from reviewing anything I'm associated with."

Jimmy's mood, which had been bordering on blight, lifted considerably.

"So you mean to say that if you are involved with a play, Brantley can't review it?"

"I don't think so," I said.

A devilish smile broke out on his face.

"So if you become a part of *all* our productions, he would have to bow out?"

I could see where he was going with this. As it happens, the Nederlander-Carter collaboration became a friendship rather than an ongoing professional partnership. But Ben did bow out and Charles Isherwood took his place on the aisle.

On opening night, I invited a lot of friends and the staff from *Vanity Fair* both to the play and to an after-party at the Russian Tea Room. And as I had seen in movies and had read in *Act One*, we waited on tenterhooks for Isherwood's review in *The Times* to come in. It did—not in the form of newspapers, as it would have done a decade earlier, but through pings on our phones. Everyone pulled out theirs to see the review. And it was more than positive—it was a complete rave. Isherwood called the play "a delectable soufflé of a solo show" and wrote that Bette gave "the most lusciously entertaining performance of the Broadway season." I was so incredibly happy for Bette and John and Joe. It was sold out for the next three months, and then Bette took it to the Geffen Playhouse in Los Angeles for another sell-out run.

━

One other foray into the world outside *Vanity Fair*—though still atmospherically connected to it—came in the form of a restaurant. In 2006, I was having dinner at Elaine's with a neighbor, Roberto Benabib, a successful television showrunner. We had both noticed a for sale sign on the Waverly Inn, a restaurant on Bank Street in the West Village, a few doors down from my house. Over far too many glasses of wine and scotch, we decided to buy it. I thought it could be a place where friends and neighbors could coexist in a neutral zone alongside the odd movie star. Since neither of us had run a restaurant, and I can't even cook, we brought in partners who did know their way around—Sean MacPherson and Eric

Goode. When I was in London, I asked Emil Varda, an old restaurant hand in New York and London, to join us as the managing partner.

I knew little about how restaurants operated, but thanks to the expansiveness of the Time Inc. and Condé Nast expense accounts, I knew what I wanted as a customer: good food, good cocktails, good lighting, white tablecloths and napkins, and brisk but friendly service. At the time, there were few American restaurants in the Village. Most of them were Italian, in part because Italian food is the most profitable food you can put on a table. If a restaurant serves you a $75 steak, the chances are they've paid $35 for it. If they sell you a $30 plate of pasta, chances are it cost them around $5. We wanted an American restaurant that looked like it had been around forever—as indeed the Waverly Inn had been. We settled on American comfort food—creamed spinach, chicken pot pie, a hamburger, macaroni and cheese, and the like. American grub for a cold winter's night, even in August.

The Waverly was on the ground floor of a former carriage house and tearoom that had been around since the 1920s. In the late '20s and early '30s, it had been a speakeasy owned by the secretary to Clare Boothe when she was the deputy editor to Frank Crowninshield at *Vanity Fair*—a coincidence that I thought pleasingly closed a circle. The restaurant has low ceilings and four working fireplaces. And everybody who had lived in Greenwich Village had been through its front door at one point or another. Basil Walter, Sean, and I worked on redesigning the inside and I persuaded the great illustrator and caricaturist Ed Sorel, who had been publishing work in every magazine you've heard of for half a century, to do a mural of the Greenwich Village all-stars over the decades: Edmund Wilson, Anaïs Nin, Dorothy Parker, William Burroughs, and scores of others.

In the first months, there were paparazzi outside hoping to get a shot of an exiting and inebriated movie star. I paid careful attention to the seating. My feeling is that when you return to a restaurant, you want a table similar to the one you had the last time you were there. So I did the seating with an assistant—at the beginning, that would have been Jon Kelly. It would take an hour at first, but then I got better and faster. I still do the seating.

Around the time we took over the Waverly, Harvey Weinstein bought the house directly across the street from us and immediately began an extensive renovation. One night at about 8:00, Anna and I were preparing dinner when our conversation was drowned out by a lot of noise on the street. I went to the window and saw that a crew was unloading scaffolding for the renovation. Now, New York City building laws stated that tools had to be laid down at 6:00 p.m. at the latest. This was in direct violation. I told Anna I was going to go ask them to stop. "Please don't!" she said. I ignored her pleas and went out onto the street and asked the fellow who looked like he was in charge what was going on. When he brushed me off, I grabbed a length of scaffolding and threw it into the street. Then another one. Feeling somewhat pleased with myself, I went back into the house.

"And how did it go?" Anna asked, her arms folded.

"Okay, I think. Although I did notice some flashbulbs going off."

The next morning, I was in the office praying that none of the paparazzi outside the Waverly had recorded the scaffold incident for posterity. By 10:30, I thought I was in the clear. Then I got a call from Col Allan, the editor of the *New York Post*. I picked up the receiver.

"Hey, mate," Col said. "I've got some pictures of you throwing some scaffolding. Can you talk to our reporter?"

I called in Beth and she showed little in the way of sympathy. "You better call him" was her only advice. Which I did and gave some flippant quote to the effect that scaffold tossing was a venerable sport in my Canadian homeland.

The next morning, the *Post* came out with not particularly flattering shots of me throwing the scaffolding onto the street. I got a note from Morley Safer, a fellow Canadian and one of the stars of *60 Minutes*, congratulating me. He also sent me a T-shirt with the words *World Scaffold-Tossing Champion* on the front.

The menu at the Waverly is still labeled "Preview Menu." And just below that comes the endorsement "Waverly Inn, 'worst food in the city'—Donald J. Trump." This was a quote from one of the four dozen rude tweets I received over time from his tiny hand. Sometime later, we did a story in *Vanity Fair* on the Trump Grill, a restaurant in the bowels of Trump Tower. The piece went into some detail regarding the wretchedness of the food and the gilded gaudiness of the surroundings. The next week, Trump sent his son Eric to eat at the Waverly. Eric came with his wife, Lara. It was a Saturday night, and Emil called me and said, "What do you think we should do?" I said, "Let's give them the best table, treat them royally, and then send them on their way." It happened to be a great, packed night. They couldn't have had a bad time, and I heard no more of it.

Emil, it must be said, was prepared for most surprises and mishaps. These included dustups between ex-spouses, removing garlic from the kitchen on nights when Si was dining, and escorting well-known people out the back door to avoid photographers. He had, in his younger days, been a Polish theater director and dissident who had marched with Lech Wałęsa. Only once did he call me in something of a fluster. It was after Mayor Mike Bloomberg had decreed that all New York restaurants be nonsmoking. Snitches were everywhere, and the city even had smoke police making their night rounds. Emil called and said, "Toni Morrison and Fran are here, and Toni wants to smoke. What do I do?"

I thought for a moment.

"Emil," I said, "you've got a seventy-something Nobel Prize winner there and one of the great wits of our age. For God's sake, let them smoke!"

Chapter 17.

Meltdowns and
Valedictions

Successful magazines have to be able to turn the corner when the world experiences a seismic shift. The early *Vanity Fair*—founded in 1913 and thereafter the monthly bible of the international smart set—failed to take the rise of fascism in Europe seriously. By the mid-1930s, it seemed hopelessly out of touch, and in 1936, Condé Nast was forced to close it. *The New Yorker*, on the other hand, although also catering to the smart set, did turn the corner, and indeed made its name with its journalism during the buildup to war in the late 1930s, then cemented a reputation for excellence with its reporting on World War II.

Our *Vanity Fair* had turned a corner once already, following the attack by al-Qaeda on September 11, 2001. Overnight, our editors and writers turned their attention to the Middle East and then to the Bush administration's ill-fated response to the attacks. I do believe that, among the big-league magazines, we alone wrote month after month about the looming disaster that the invasion of Iraq would prove to be. Almost every other male editor I knew was pro-invasion. The women I knew in the business were more measured. Christopher Hitchens, on the other hand, who was cheering on the neocon invaders in our pages, was not. More on that later.

The need for another pivot came with the devastating recession following the financial crisis of 2008. And we absolutely flourished journalistically during this period. We were getting scoops, particularly financial scoops and big revelatory stories on a regular basis. Doug Stumpf, who read the business pages with some regularity, was a star editor in this respect. As was Cullen Murphy. We had on staff William D. Cohan, a former banker at Lazard, Merrill Lynch, and JPMorgan Chase, and Bethany McLean, coauthor of the best book on the collapse of Enron, *The Smartest Guys in the Room*. We had Bryan Burrough. We also had Sarah Ellison, a deft reporter who had come to us from *The Wall Street Journal*, and Nicholas Shaxson, the Berlin-based financial investigator. Cullen brought in Nobel Prize–winning economist Joseph Stiglitz, who popularized the term "the 1%" in the pages of *Vanity Fair* to describe the insanely rich few at the top of the American wealth pyramid.

And if all that wasn't enough, Michael Lewis arrived, a surprising addition to the magazine. Years before, Marjorie Williams had written a profile in *Vanity Fair* about Michael, who was already a risen star. He was working at *The New Republic* in Washington, then being edited by Michael Kinsley at the height of his gifts. Michael Lewis had written *Liar's Poker* in 1989, a huge bestseller about his experiences as a bond salesman at Salomon Brothers, on Wall Street. He was ambitious and exceptionally talented, but Marjorie dented his image in her profile with quotes from angry former romantic partners. Michael hated the story, steered clear of me for the next decade and a half, and refused to write for us. Then, out of the blue, in late 2008, he made contact and had lunch with Doug, who specialized in tough business narratives. If anybody could have led him toward a change of heart, it was Doug. He was dedicated to, and adored by, the writers under his wing, including Bryan, Bethany, Bill Cohan, and Sebastian Junger. Michael told Doug that he was still angry with the magazine, but he also said, "When they write about the golden age of magazines, this is the center, and I want to be part of it."

Michael was, and still is, one of the most versatile magazine writers alive, and probably the finest nonfiction narrative writer there is at this moment. His way into stories was like nobody else's. More sideways than direct. His articles became bestselling books, and his bestselling books became hit films: *The Blind Side* in 2009, *Moneyball* in 2011, and *The Big Short* in 2015. He'd summed up his journalistic viewpoint this way in a *Vanity Fair* article: "The behavior of our money people is still treated as a subject for specialists. This is a huge cultural mistake. High finance touches—ruins—the lives of ordinary people in a way that, say, baseball does not, unless you are a Cubs fan. And yet, ordinary people, even those who have been most violated, are never left with a clear sense of how they've been touched or by whom. Wall Street, like a clever pervert, is often suspected but seldom understood and never convicted."

When the Great Recession hit, kicked off by the collapse of the subprime-mortgage bazaar, Michael set out to find his own way into the catastrophe. With Michael, you agreed on his approach to a story and then he set off and returned with a dispatch that was breathtaking in its originality. His first report on the global economic collapse was on Iceland's de facto bankruptcy, an unexpected sidebar to the bigger drama in New York that almost nobody expected.

After Michael wrote his remarkable story on Iceland's bankruptcy, he reported, always with a mix of wit, stupefaction, and almost comic disbelief, on the financial collapse in Greece and then Ireland. On his way to the mysterious Vatopedi monastery at Mount Athos in Greece, whose property-dealing monks had brought down the Greek government, he mused:

> The tsunami of cheap credit that rolled across the planet between 2002 and 2007 . . . offered entire societies the chance to reveal aspects of their characters they could not normally afford to indulge. Entire countries were told, "The lights are out, you can do whatever you want to do and no one will ever know." What they wanted to do with money in the dark varied. Americans wanted to own homes far larger than they could afford, and to allow the strong to exploit the weak. Icelanders wanted to stop fishing and become investment bankers, and to allow their alpha males to reveal a theretofore suppressed megalomania.

On Ireland, he wrote:

> Ireland's financial disaster shared some things with Iceland's. It was created by the sort of men who ignore their wives' suggestions that maybe they should stop and ask for directions, for instance. But while Icelandic males used foreign money to conquer foreign places—trophy companies in Britain, chunks of Scandinavia—the Irish male used foreign money to conquer Ireland. Left alone in a dark room with a pile of money, the Irish decided what they really wanted to do with it was to buy Ireland. *From one another. . . .* The numbers were breathtaking. A single bank, Anglo Irish, which, two years before, the Irish government had claimed was merely suffering from a "liquidity problem," faced losses of up to 34 billion euros. To get some sense of how "34 billion euros" sounds to Irish ears, an American thinking in dollars needs to multiply it by roughly one hundred: $3.4 trillion. And that was for *a single bank.* As the sum total of loans made by Anglo

Irish, most of it to Irish property developers, was only 72 billion euros, the bank had lost nearly half of every dollar it invested.

Michael continued to cause problems for the kingpins in the financial markets with a *Vanity Fair* story that eventually became *Flash Boys,* his bestselling exposé of high-speed, algorithmic trading. These young men had jeopardized a multibillion-dollar slice of the market and made some of Wall Street's wealthiest people very angry, as the Securities and Exchange Commission and others reacted to Michael's piece and moved in.

Most of our correspondents were basically general assignment reporters who would go off to a strange industry or a strange place where they didn't know a lot and each time they'd have to start from scratch. It's not easy. Some had fallen into specialties, though they still had the ability to write outside them. Michael cast his net wide with a variety of other superb reports: a profile of Tom Wolfe as seen through his papers at the New York Public Library and the trafficking of Cuban baseball players. Bryan Burrough would write about the Bush government's blunder into war and the battle between the fashion giants LVMH and Kering (then known as PPR) to buy Gucci. Bryan grew up in Texas and knew nothing about fashion, but you wouldn't know that from his report on the Gucci fight—a perfect *Vanity Fair* story.

The recession of 2008 did little to help *Vanity Fair*'s fortunes—or any other magazine's, for that matter. There were a few bright spots. My former assistant, Jon Kelly, who had risen to senior editor, left the magazine for a job at *Bloomberg Businessweek* and then at *The New York Times Magazine*. He returned a few years later and, once he got settled, suggested that we start a new digital-only dispatch that would be a daily reflection of the areas of interest that members of our New Establishment were involved with: Hollywood, Washington, Wall Street, and Silicon Valley. Jon and I drew up a plan of attack and a proposed budget. We presented all this to the company and they gave us half of what we were asking for. I still thought we could do it, and so we set to work. I came up with the name *The Hive*, and Jon, along with a gifted veteran editor, John Homans, began producing daily dispatches that almost immediately caught on. We assembled a number of stars to report for *The Hive*, including Gabe Sherman, Bill Cohan, and Sarah Ellison. After we all left the magazine in 2017 and 2018, Jon built on the idea for *The Hive* and created a new journalistic enterprise called *Puck*, which again was an immediate hit.

I was proud, too, of our art-world coverage in this period—where stories of grift and corruption mirrored those on Wall Street. We had a number of sure hands in this arena, including Ingrid Sischy, Amy Fine Collins, and Bob Colacello. We had scoops on some spectacular scams, such as Michael Shnayerson's report on the art-forgery scandal that ultimately brought down the 165-year-old Knoedler gallery in New York. The gallery had a world-class collection of Abstract Expressionist masterworks; as it happened, many of the pictures had been created by an amateur painter in Queens.

Amy Fine Collins, the scholarly art critic who was on our masthead the whole time I was there, wrote a searing and memorable mini biography in our pages of Frida Kahlo, based on her emergent diaries and Amy's own delving, which put Kahlo into much-needed perspective at the time. As she wrote, "a whole cross section of marginalized groups—lesbians, gays, feminists, the handicapped, Chicanos, Communists (she professed Trotskyism and, later, Stalinism), hypochondriacs, substance abusers, and even Jews (despite her indigenous Mexican identity, she was in fact half Jewish and only one-quarter Indian)—have discovered in her a politically correct heroine." Most pertinent to the diaries, she wrote, "is an understanding of how the daughter of a lower-middle-class German-Jewish photographer and a hysterically Catholic Spanish-Indian mother became a celebrated painter, Communist, promiscuous temptress, and, later (during the diary years), a narcotic-addicted, dykish, suicidal amputee afflicted with a bizarre pathology known as Munchausen syndrome—the compulsion to be hospitalized and, in extreme cases, mutilated unnecessarily by surgery."

Amy led her piece with an extraordinary image of a last sighting of the artist: She wrote:

> As frenzied mourners watched the earthly remains of Frida Kahlo roll away into the crematory, the artist, known in her day for her macabre sense of mischief, played one last ghoulish trick on her audience. The sudden blast of heat from the open incinerator doors blew the bejeweled, elaborately coiffed body bolt upright. Her ignited hair blazed around her head like an infernal halo. One observer recalled that, deformed by the phantasmagoric, flickering shadows, her lips appeared to break into a grin just as the doors closed shut. Frida's postmortem smile—a last laugh if there ever was one—is echoing still. Half a century after her death, Kahlo, around whom a whole industry has sprung up like a garden on a grave site, grows more alive with each passing decade.

We were always on the lookout for covers that would fly off the newsstands and, in years to come, go viral on the internet. Sometimes the quest took us down unexpected byways. If the unmasking of Deep Throat was the biggest journalistic scoop of my time at *Vanity Fair*, the biggest scoop with regard to the overall culture was our cover exclusive about Caitlyn Jenner. I remembered Jenner as an Olympic decathlete who as Bruce Jenner had appeared on Wheaties boxes—once among the highest accolades an athlete could aspire to. Jenner was tall and still good-looking—later, with a bit of help from colorists and surgeons. There had been a minor and desultory film career early on, and by the time of transition, Jenner was a stepfather getting ordered about by sundry Kardashians on their reality television show. Jenner had become a slightly tragic figure. But word began to seep out that there was going to be some dramatic news.

One day I called Jane into my office and said, "What about Bruce Jenner?" There were stories floating about that Jenner was going through reassignment surgery. I said, "At some point Jenner's going to make an announcement. Why not in *Vanity Fair*? Why don't you see if we can get it?" Our initial approach was turned down flat. Then Jenner switched to a public relations person Jane was friends with. After a lot of to-ing and fro-ing, Jane had some news. Jenner was game to do it with us, she said.

To get the cover and the inside pictures and the story, we went into deep-secrecy mode. As we had done with Deep Throat, we set up a special room at the office and covered the windows with kraft paper. Nothing suspicious about that! We had one key for the room, and a computer to handle traffic on a server separate from the one that handled the rest of the magazine. Only eight people in the office knew about the project. I assigned Annie to do the pictures and Buzz Bissinger, a Pulitzer Prize–winning journalist and the author of *Friday Night Lights*, to do the story. I thought Buzz would be ideal. He could talk sports, and given that he had dabbled with a bit of cross-dressing, he could converse in the language of women's finery as well.

Buzz made a number of trips west as Bruce began the process of transition. The plan was that Bruce would have surgery and then recuperate in isolation at his home in Malibu. Our agreement was that no one else was allowed to visit him during this period. Only Buzz. As the reporting progressed, we had issues to contend with, including finding women's clothes for a six-foot, two-inch former athlete and then smuggling the most famous photographer in the world into a house that was surrounded by paparazzi. Word had gotten out about Jenner, and there were even news helicopters circling overhead. We put security guards around the perimeter. And then we put the entire staff for the shoot in two large vans with darkened windows. Jane and Buzz were in one of them, as was Buzz's editor, Dana Brown. Later, Jane described walking in with Annie's team. "The house looked out at a beautiful vista of Malibu. Very modest house. But a beautiful pool. You walk up the steps, and as I come up, this person is coming towards me in a silk robe with marabou feathers, and kitten heels with marabou feathers. Her legs are glistening with satin oil. The hair is down, and the hands are huge. She says to me, 'Hi, I'm Caitlyn.'"

Once we had the story and the shoot, it was time to pick the cover and figure out what to say on it. We toyed with any number of options. Finally, I just wrote the line "Call Me Caitlyn." I figured that, by the time the issue hit the newsstands, her name would be everywhere, and we wouldn't have to say much more than that. We were still in relatively primitive digital times, but we decided to make it the first cover we ever released online. No waiting around for the printing and binding and delivery trucks—all constant sources of leaks. We prepared a brief description and a short video that had been filmed during the shoot. At noon on the appointed day, we released our story to the world. A dozen or so of us sat at a long borrowed conference table, watching the traffic on a big TV monitor. It started slowly and then, as the minutes clicked by, the graph arm just began to climb until it was completely vertical. I have no idea whether you can "break" the internet or not, but if it is possible, we surely came close.

The next morning, our story was on the front page of newspapers around the world. President Obama tweeted congratulations to Caitlyn. She joined Twitter that day and got to a million followers faster than anybody else ever had. The previous record holder had been Obama himself. What made the whole effort so gratifying was that a legacy print publication—a monthly one, at that—had arranged, produced, and released a story that had global impact.

—

You could build a sterling magazine just around the great writers, artists, and photographers who died during my twenty-five years at *Vanity Fair*, many of them still in the flower of their lives and careers: David Halberstam, Christopher Hitchens, Dominick Dunne, Ingrid Sischy, Marjorie Williams, A. A. Gill, Snowdon, Frederic Morton, Bruce McCall, Tim Hetherington, Michael Herr, Helmut Newton, Herb Ritts, and Nick Tosches. Tim Hetherington, who had won World Press Photo of the Year for us in Afghanistan, was killed by shrapnel in Libya in 2011. David Halberstam died in a car crash on his way to a journalistic appointment. Helmut Newton also died in a car crash, in the garage of his beloved Chateau Marmont. I added an In Memoriam section on the masthead to recognize some of the great talents who had done so much to make *Vanity Fair* the magazine that it was.

Marjorie Williams was already at the magazine when I got there. But she quickly became one of my favorites. She had an angel's face and a smile that could melt the toughest combatant. But beneath the flawless skin lay a devilish wit. She wrote a devastating profile of Barbara Bush, the wife of former president George H. W. Bush, that just leveled Washington. A few years in, she told me that she was ill, and she died soon after.

Ingrid Sischy, a specialist in the worlds of fashion and art and all the intersections between them, was another favorite. She was funny and conspiratorial and always delivered a story that brimmed with sharp writing and fresh insights. She and her wife, Sandy, were great friends with Karl Lagerfeld and would have him to stay at the grand Stanford White house they owned out in Montauk. She was very funny about the measures Karl would take to get himself assembled before coming down from his bedroom. There was the Herbert Hoover collar, the tie, the jacket, and the powdering of the white hair. After he left, Ingrid told me, his bedroom was covered in white dust from the powdering. She had been up and down with a lingering illness. The last time I saw Ingrid was at Louise Grunwald's house in Southampton. I could tell that she was not well. But she had made the half-hour trek from Montauk, and I was overwhelmed that she did that. The next week I got a call from her. She wanted to say goodbye. I wept over the phone as we said our farewells. A day later she was dead.

The last trial Dominick Dunne covered was that of record producer Phil Spector, for the murder of Lana Clarkson, for which Spector went to prison. Nick had seemed to be in full form—taking the side of the victim, scattering names, anecdotes, and riveting detail. "It's a very peculiar position to be in," he wrote, "knowing personally the defendant in a murder trial about which I am writing, especially when I am publicly a victims' advocate. My sympathies in this case are with Lana Clarkson, who was found shot dead in the foyer of Phil's castle in Alhambra, California, on February 3, 2003. She is being trashed by the defense." And, reported Nick, also trashed by her own friends. "After their declarations of friendship and love, they took their poor dead friend apart, with anecdote after anecdote making it appear that Lana was in such a state of abject despair over the failure of her life that shooting herself in the mouth in a stranger's house was a totally logical step for her to take. I mean, talk about false friends."

But Nick, too, was deteriorating at this point. He had replaced his earlier addiction to drugs with an addiction to fame. He was never off television. I've always been leery of television appearances and have done my best to avoid them. But I do know that for some people, it's like crack cocaine. It fills some part of their core that little else can. Nick had become print and social famous, but he wanted that ultimate level of American fame—television famous, the sort of fame that gets you noticed in airports and affords you upgrades and the best tables in restaurants.

As this addiction progressed, he became more and more difficult. He developed an imperious, overbearing manner. When he'd call the office and an assistant didn't immediately jump to attention, he would lacerate them with statements like "Do you know who I am? I'm Dominick-fucking-Dunne!" I can see that reddened face now, along with his uniform: the Turnbull & Asser shirt, the Hermès tie, the Gucci loafers, the blue blazer and gray flannels. And the manicure, with the nails trimmed to a point. In the 2016 television series *The People v. O.J. Simpson*, Robert Morse (a dream in *How to Succeed in Business without Really Trying*) played Nick so well it gave those of us at the magazine chills. The more the real Nick appeared on television, the more difficult he got. Most press requests for writers at the magazine went through, or were forwarded to, Beth Kseniak's office. But Nick just took the calls and booked himself, generally without telling us. He said yes to almost anything, TV or radio, big audiences or small.

In the years after the O.J. Simpson trial, as the notoriety of courtroom dramas diminished, the more important programs stopped calling. My hunch was that, to stay in the public eye, Nick began upping his claims on various cases that were in the news. In late

2001, Nick appeared on TV and radio telling a story about Gary Condit, a married congressman who was alleged to have had an affair with a government intern. Her name was Chandra Levy, and she was then missing and presumed dead. Nick cited a source he called "the horse whisperer," whom he said informed him that Levy had been taken away by someone on a motorcycle as a favor to Condit. The story turned out to be false.

Condit vigorously denied any involvement in or knowledge of Levy's disappearance, and he filed two lawsuits accusing Nick of slander. He blamed his election loss on the false accusations and sought millions in damages. Nick was shattered. He asked me if *Vanity Fair* would pay his legal fees. I went to see Si. He suggested that we could cover what Nick's insurance wouldn't. I thought this was more than fair, in that this didn't have anything to do with what Nick wrote for the magazine—and that he had made the appearances on the *Laura Ingraham Show* and *Larry King Live* without even informing us. Nick was outraged that we wouldn't support his legal fees in full. He settled one of the suits with a financial payout and an apology. The second one was dismissed on legal grounds. Condit was never identified by police as a suspect, and eventually another man was convicted of Levy's murder. After all this, my relationship with Nick deteriorated. This I could understand—I don't think he ever completely took to me. But then he fell out with Wayne, who had not only edited every word of his over the past decades but had been his friend and champion. Nick further complicated things by writing me a deeply insulting letter about Wayne. Nick wasn't done, though. He fell out with his longtime book editor at Crown, Betty Prashker. He fired his agent, Owen Laster. He then learned that he had prostate cancer and even fired his doctor because it was the nurse, not the doctor, who had first told him of the diagnosis.

Nick's funeral was complicated by his long-term animus against

Teddy Kennedy—the last of the Kennedy brothers. Ted died on August 25, 2009. Nick died the next day, and I worried that his death would be buried in the coverage of Ted Kennedy. I called his son, the actor and director Griffin Dunne, to tell him how sorry I was for the death of his father. I also suggested, half in jest, that he pretend his dad was still alive so as to give a bit of separation for obituaries in *The New York Times*. It would have crushed Nick to have Kennedy's obit on the front page of the paper and his own way back on page D12. So a superannuated version of *Weekend at Bernie's* began to play itself out. Griffin managed to keep his father's death a secret for the next twenty-four hours. At the office, Beth began getting calls from reporters about rumors of Nick's death. She didn't want to lie, so she simply didn't return their phone calls. When the media send-off for Kennedy finally died down, Beth took a call from *The New York Times*. She confessed that, yes, Nick had indeed died. The word was out.

His obituary was tagged on the front page of *The Times* the next day. The memorial was as Nick would have liked it, star-filled and elegant. Although he had eliminated having Wayne as a pallbearer in his written instructions, for some reason he had kept me on the list. I shared the duties with a number of much more distinguished men, including Nick's old college roommate, Stephen Sondheim. A half year later, Griffin sent me a play he'd written. It was about two squabbling brothers who die on the same day and the efforts the children of one of the brothers go through to make sure their obituaries are separated.

—

Christopher Hitchens, too, had a weakness—and a talent—for television, but in his case it played well to his contrarian nature, and thus was not always predictable. Aimée, Christopher, and I had dinner shortly after the Columbine mass shooting of 1999.

I said, "What about doing a piece about gun control?" I thought that Christopher was just the sort of person you'd want to hear on the subject.

He said, "Yes, I'd love to do that, but I'll warn you in advance that I'm anti–gun control."

I took a breath and said, "Okay, let's think of something else then."

With the beginning of the Iraq War in 2003, his contrarian nature became a sticking point, at least for us at the magazine. Here you had this all-encompassing political subject and we had the most prominent liberal public intellectual in the country who was pro-war.

James Wolcott had written in the June 2003 issue that "since September 11, much of the press has dropped to both knees before George W. Bush to take dictation." Washington officials nevertheless seemed to open up to *Vanity Fair* writers, notably to Sam Tanenhaus, who created worldwide news when he quoted Paul Wolfowitz, then deputy secretary of defense, on the subject of the pretense for the invasion of Iraq: "For bureaucratic reasons we settled on one issue, weapons of mass destruction, because it was the one reason everyone could agree on."

The invasion of Iraq was clearly dishonest, but it was also cynical and strategically catastrophic. We reported that the White House under Bush had co-opted the CIA, cherry-picked intelligence, deceived Congress, deceived the American people and the United Nations, and pushed the weapons inspectors to the wall. And yet Christopher remained dogged in his support for the war. It was something none of us could understand. He was particularly close to Wolfowitz, whom I remember seeing at Christopher's apartment at a cocktail party and being slightly shocked. Christopher himself was very much welcomed into the living rooms of the ruling party for eight years. Whether it was calculated or not, I don't know, but I think some voice in the back of his mind must have said that one of the most prominent public liberal intellectuals being in support of the Iraq War is going to get a lot more television airtime than a liberal who is antiwar.

One evening in 2010, I was to introduce Christopher and Salman Rushdie for a conversation at the 92nd Street Y—that uptown haven of intellectual liberalism and cultural discourse. I met them backstage, and Christopher looked haggard. I asked him if it was "cocktail flu." He shook his head. He and Salman went on and gave the audience a spirited evening of talk. The next day, Aimée came into my office. She told me that just before going onstage, Christopher had received some devastating news—he had been diagnosed with esophageal cancer. It is often caused by a combination of scotch and cigarettes. Humphrey Bogart reportedly died of it. So, apparently, did Christopher's father. His illness took him to various hospitals, but in the end he went to Texas, where he was attended to by doctors and his friends Michael and Nina Zilkha.

Aimée, who had been his editor at both *The New York Observer* and *Vanity Fair*, visited him on a regular basis—we should all have such friends—up until his death in 2011. He was just sixty-two. We organized a memorial at the Cooper Union, which was attended by a wonderful collection of old hands and Hitchenites. (I probably shouldn't be mentioning this in a book that is dependent on my memory, but as we were planning Christopher's send-off, I said to Aimée, "Wait, did we do one for Nick?" She looked at me and said flatly, "You were a pallbearer!" I thought for a moment and said, "Right." A few years later, I was presenting Martin Amis with an award at the National Arts Club on Gramercy Park and bumped into an old friend of mine, Rob Searle. I asked where his wife was, and he pointed across the room. I told him that she looked lovely and that I was looking forward to meeting her. Rob looked at me and said, "Graydon, you were my best man.")

Last to speak at Christopher's memorial was Martin, his closest friend, who began, "I'm Martin Amis, or 'Little Keith,' as Hitch always called me. 'My dear little Keith,' he used to call me, and I used to call him 'my dear Hitch.' The most salient and striking thing about Christopher is how widely he was loved. Not just by us, family and friends, but by you. And one struggles to think of a public intellectual with a following half as passionate." I do not believe such a one existed.

We all went to the Waverly after the ceremony and took over the whole restaurant. People stayed until one o'clock in the morning. It was an old-fashioned New York day in so many respects. A month or so later, Salman asked me if I would come on a PEN panel to talk about Christopher. It was me and Katha Pollitt, one of his old colleagues from *The Nation*; Victor Navasky, a dear friend of both Christopher's and mine who had been the editor for some years of *The Nation;* and Ian Buruma, who in a few years would become the editor of *The New York Review of Books*. About forty minutes in, I came to the conclusion that the three of them—even Victor, which surprised me—were jealous of Christopher. They had all tried to be public intellectuals but none of them achieved Christopher's level of wide influence. He was the most famous public intellectual in the country at that point. And the venom that poured out just astounded me. I had found myself in a cauldron of acetous leftist politics and was the only one defending Christopher. It got so bad that Salman stood up in the audience and said we weren't there to bury Christopher, we were there to praise him. I think that sort of settled things down, but I left with a very bitter taste in my mouth.

—

A. A. Gill—Adrian to his friends—also died young, also of cancer in 2016, and, like Christopher, at the age of sixty-two. He was writing almost until the day he died. He had been one of the more recent additions to the magazine's stable. I had been reading his reviews and journalism in the London *Sunday Times* for years. Two reviews in particular made me pick up the phone to see if he would write for us. One was of the Connaught Grill, on the ground floor of the hotel. And the other was of the Hempel Hotel. The reviews were knowing and funny and just outrageously rude. I desperately wanted that voice in the *Vanity Fair* ensemble. His first story for us—a bracing review of a new restaurant in New York—made news for its shocking irreverence toward the city's food-obsessed culturati. Adrian was to restaurant reviewing—though he was also an acclaimed, and prizewinning, foreign correspondent—what Christopher was to conventional liberal wisdom. He was, in short, a raider who took no prisoners, and whose weapon, as with Christopher, was as much wit as knowledge of his subject.

That first review was for 66, the union of chef Jean-Georges Vongerichten and architect Richard Meier, on Church Street in Tribeca. "The first thing you notice about 66 is that it's difficult to notice anything," Adrian wrote of Meier's interior. "The lighting is nighty-night nursery dim, as if keeping it crepuscular will stop you from noticing that it looks like every creperie in Berlin, and that the babe in the corner isn't Claudia Schiffer but a Serb television producer on steroids." Next, he trashed the welcoming committee:

> "Have you eaten here before?" they ask. "Do you understand how this works?" "What—I order, you serve, I pay, you give me my coat back?" "Ha ha ha . . . No, we bring you the food when and in the order that it's prepared." This talk-to-the-chopstick attitude implies one of two things: either after a lifetime of experience I'm still not to be trusted to feed myself, or, like edible thongs, the food is really only an amusing addendum to social intercourse.

This was merely a warm-up to the fare itself:

> To say the food is repellently awful would be to credit it
> with a vim and vigor and attitude it simply can't rise to. The
> bowls and dishes dribble and limp to the table with a yawning
> lassitude. A vain empty ennui. They weren't so much pre-
> sented as wilted and folded to death. It was all prepared with
> that most depressing and effete culinary style—tepid whimsy.
> Tell me, off the top of your head, what two attributes should
> hot-and-sour soup have? Take your time. It was neither. Nor
> anything else much. How clever are shrimp-and-foie-gras
> dumplings with grapefruit dipping sauce? What if we called
> them fishy liver-filled condoms? They were properly vile, with
> a savor that lingered like a lovelorn drunk and tasted as if your
> mouth had been used as the swab bin in an animal hospital.

The article caused a storm in New York because this kind of trashing was unheard of. No one had seen anything like it. *The New York Observer* did a front-page story, longer than the review itself, quoting half the piece. Meier, understandably upset, was quoted in the *Observer* piece, saying, "I thought it was a very odd thing for them to do." He went on to say he was going to invite me to dinner at 66 to discuss the matter. Whether we had that conversation or not, I can't recall. I felt badly because Meier was such a tower of architectural vision and imagination.

Adrian later took on L'Ami Louis, in Paris. I had been a number of times and found the place to be overrated and overpriced. It was beloved of Hollywood figures, New York financiers, and internet moguls, but few actual French people. Given its cherished status with Americans in Paris, it should have been off-limits. But not for us; Adrian's review was brutal. "It's undeniable that L'Ami Louis really is special and apart. It has earned an epic accolade. It is, all things considered, *entre nous*, the worst restaurant in the world."

A few years later, David Zaslav, then running the Discovery channels—which included the rights to tennis in Europe—invited a dozen or so friends to Paris to watch the men's finals at Roland-Garros. As part of the weekend, he booked L'Ami Louis and took over the whole restaurant for a big dinner. David had a number of tennis stars under contract to provide commentary on his broadcasts, including Mats Wilander, Boris Becker, and Chris Evert. They were there. I worried that one of the members of the restaurant staff—particularly the beefy head waiter who was in charge of the front of house—would recognize me and organize the kitchen to perform a collective urination on my food. As it turned out, the dishes all came out family style, which was a huge relief. They weren't going to poison us all. But the head waiter kept looking at me as if trying to place me. Only as we were leaving the restaurant did his eyes widen and I heard him whisper in horror the words "*Vanity Fair!*"

Chapter 18.

Letters from Admirers

When it comes to stories written about us, we all have our sensitive spots. Evelyn Waugh once said that you could say pretty much anything about a man so long as you said that he was good in bed. And I have indeed found that mention of someone's abilities in this regard generally finds a welcoming recipient. I was at a dinner party early in my *Vanity Fair* residency, seated with the actor Michael York and his wife, Pat. At one point Pat told me that she had gone out with Si during her days as a single woman in New York. I don't know what compelled me to say this, but I asked how he was in bed. "Fantastic!" she replied. This didn't surprise me. I do believe that good sex is about 80 percent enthusiasm, and Si was enthusiastic about his enthusiasms. The next time I saw him at lunch, I relayed Pat's assessment of his nighttime skills. I don't recall ever seeing him so pleased by a bit of news.

I have also found that just a single word can tick off a subject. A story that lavished thousands of words of veneration could be undone if a single sentence alluded to the fact that, say, the subject's ears were too big for his head. For all her toughness and resilience, Sue Mengers could be surprisingly touchy. (I should say here that Sue was perhaps the most devoted reader of *Vanity Fair* I ever met. "It's like Proust," she would say. She read every word of every issue.) Peter Biskind wrote a profile of her in 2000 and we put it in the Hollywood issue. After the story ran—a love letter, really—Fran and I went over to Sue's house for dinner. I walked in, and she just sat there, making no effort to get up. She was staring straight ahead.

I said, "Hi, Sue," and bent down to give her a kiss on the cheek. Nothing.

I said, "Are you okay?"

She turned and waved her arm around the room: "You call this *modest?*"

"What do you mean?" I said.

She replied, "This house! You call this *modest?* That pisher Peter Biskind called it a 'modest' John Woolf house."

David Kamp, an old *Spy* hand who had come to *Vanity Fair*, wrote a profile of Tom Wolfe that was incredibly flattering. And how could it not be? We worshipped Tom. The story included this passage: "Now that he's 68, the years have caught up somewhat: he's thinner than he used to be (155 pounds, he will say), his hands tremble slightly, and his orange-yellow hair, still cut in that familiar Eton flip, is going white. All things considered, though, he's an impressive specimen, handsome and spry, especially when you learn that, as of this meeting, he's racing to finish the book in time to get it published this fall." Tom hated that the word *spry* had been applied to him. He rang me up to gently complain. He wasn't "spry," he said. My guess is that he took it to mean old but still functioning in a Mr. Burns sort of way. But it was the perfect word to describe Tom. He told me once that he did 5BX exercises every day. It was a program developed by the Canadian air force, and to my eyes he was in amazingly good shape.

A profile of Bob Evans by another *Spy* hand, Matt Tyrnauer, may have helped usher in the comeback of the former Paramount chief, but it also included the following: "This is a man so thoroughly put together he seems assembled from disparate parts. The hair is a blackened frizzy pompadour, swept up in front and silver at the ends; his face is wide and puffy, colored an otherworldly shade of brown." A few days after the story came out, one of my assistants said that Bob was on the line. I picked up the phone. He got right to it. "Puffy?" Bob said. "You called me puffy!" He hung up. He was furious with Matt. Furious with me. He didn't speak to me for months.

Few complaints marshaled the levels of venom dispatched in my direction by Linda Bruckheimer. She was the wife of Jerry Bruckheimer, who with Don Simpson had made up one of the most powerful producing partnerships in Hollywood during the '80s. "Don and Jerry" had a dark side, though—mostly related to Don's excessive use of cocaine, for which then Paramount chairman Barry Diller had fired him as head of production. He kept him on as a producer for the studio, though, and in tandem with Bruckheimer, they became responsible for a good number of Paramount's hits. The pair made *Beverly Hills Cop I* and *II*, *Days of Thunder*, *The Rock*, and *Top Gun*, among other high-testosterone smashes. It wasn't just the cocaine, though. Several memoirs have recorded what was then an open secret—Don's forays into bondage and sadomasochism, his exploitation of prostitutes, and his routinely self-destructive lifestyle. He died in 1996 in his early fifties, leaving Jerry on his own.

I didn't know the Bruckheimers, but I thought it would be a nice gesture to invite them to the Oscar party, which they accepted. The next year, in the Hollywood issue, we ran a funny one-page chart by

Richard Rushfield and Adam Leff on the characteristics of Hollywood types over the decades. In the column for the '80s, we made mention of the drugs. Harmless, I thought. I returned to my hotel one evening to find a letter of epic outrage and vitriol from Mrs. Bruckheimer. Peeling away the adjectives, the gist of her complaint was that I had used the Bruckheimers as bait to attract others to our sorry little Oscar party and that they were doing me a favor by attending. The invitation to that year's party was in the envelope—torn up into quarters. Not quite knowing what to do, I suggested blowing the letter up and mounting it on the doors of the ladies' rooms at the party. And I would have, had wiser heads—in the form of Chris, Aimée, Beth, and Sara—not talked me out of it.

No less venomous was a missive I received from John Gregory Dunne. John could never quite come to grips with the fact that his older brother, Dominick, had become the more successful writer, when for years John had been the literary darling of the Dunne family and Nick had been written off as a sorry drunk and a Hollywood failure. As Nick wrote after John died: "I was, after all, moving in on turf that had been his for 25 years. I was the upstart. He and Joan were the stars. But I wrote four best-sellers in a row, all of which were made into miniseries, and I wrote regular features for this magazine. Was John jealous? Yes. Our books came and went, but we never mentioned them to each other, acting as if they did not exist." John hated *Vanity Fair* for being the platform for his brother's elevation, and he disliked me as an extension of that. I always admired Joan and her writing, but John could be quite unpleasant. Wayne, Nick's editor, had been John's contemporary at Princeton, and had found in him, as I did, an unattractive mixture of insecurity and arrogance.

In our first Hollywood issue, we assembled a group shot of all the greatest screenwriters alive at the time. Eighteen in all, including

Julius Epstein, who had cowritten *Casablanca*; Paul Schrader, who had written *Taxi Driver*; *Ordinary People*'s Alvin Sargent; and *Chinatown* author Robert Towne. It was a highly distinguished group— and we had assigned Richard Corman to take the photograph at the old Dolores Del Rio mansion in Los Angeles. When the issue came out, word reached me that John was livid that he and Joan were not included. In truth, their names never even came up when I met with the staff to compile our long list of candidates for the shoot. They were both successful in print, but their screenwriting credits were for films that even by then were mostly forgotten or lamentable, including *The Panic in Needle Park* and the remake of *A Star Is Born*.

John wrote to me in a rage. His letter was vile and operatic in its pettiness. I wish I could find the original. It is hard to do it justice from memory or even imagination. Some highlights, as I recall them: that the magazine's covers were populated with a lineup of hookers; that the actresses featured were dressed like sluts; that I was deeply second-rate, provincial, culturally unlettered, and ignorant; that I knew nothing about good writing; and that I had excluded him and Joan from the group shot in support of Nick's malice toward him. I was stunned by his letter. I was almost embarrassed for him. About twenty years later, I bumped into the couple at Da Silvano. As John brushed past me, Joan came over to my table. I stood up and she put her hand gently on my arm. "John," she said, "forgives you."

I received a letter in somewhat the same vein not from a reader, but from one of our own writers, Alex Shoumatoff. Alex was a great, if at times, chaotic writer. He wrote stories of far adventure, political reports from bad republics, and environmental horror tales. His dispatch on the murder of the primatologist Dian Fossey became the basis for the 1988 film *Gorillas in the Mist*, with Sigourney Weaver as Fossey. Alex had studied poetry at Harvard, tutored by Robert Lowell. In a way, his problems began with his previous employment at

The New Yorker, which, under the encouragement of its longtime editor William Shawn, published pieces of great research and Miltonian length. The greater the number of words, the greater the writer's fee. At *Vanity Fair*, Alex used to turn in 70,000-word drafts of a story that was assigned at 7,500 words. He used to say, "Here's my vomit draft." His editor, Dana Brown, would then spend the next two weeks trying to find the right 7,500 words out of this mountain of copy.

Often his stories—it almost didn't matter what the subject was—would include long digressions into Alex's White Russian heritage. These, too, would have to be surgically removed from the actual story. When an assignment was not forthcoming, or a completed assignment didn't run as soon as he wanted, he would turn his guns on me. His missives would make the Unabomber blush. Alex would tell me the magazine was a dreadful mess and that only by publishing more of him could I save it. He was not sparing in his opinions, following much the same path of invective that John Gregory Dunne had set. I rarely replied to these explosions, and a few months later, Alex would write again, saying that he was willing to extend an olive branch. And I would take him back.

Alex was out of control in a good and bad way. Although he dressed like a dissolute preppy, he could be quite grand. He would tell me on a regular basis that he was the greatest living magazine writer. I should say now that he is indeed a fabulous writer and reporter. But I felt he should have left it to others to elevate him to the Pantheon. On one occasion, he called Dana to praise a dispatch we'd published by someone else. "That writer's really good," he said. "Shades of me and Kapuściński." The story that brought an end to our relationship was about Ukraine and the 2014 Russian invasion of Crimea—a chilly echo of later events. He turned in another vomit draft of around 30,000 words—a third the length of the average novel. It almost reduced Dana to tears. The story was less about "the

Russian soul," as Alex put it, than it was another history of his own family. It was a memoir more than anything. And for the purposes of the magazine, it was unpublishable. Alex took to his typewriter.

> *I was trying to tell you a year ago: the American policy about Russia and Ukraine was incredibly inept and hypocritical. But you didn't have the balls to publish it. . . . The problem was not that I turned a rough draft of the piece in at 30,000 words, which I ended up cutting to 20,000 words myself and Dana did the rest. . . . Then, Graydon, you wanted more about Putin—the usual Putin bashing, which Masha Gessen has done so well. We all know that Putin is a very nasty piece of work. That was not what the piece was about, which was to convey the Russian point of view, "the secret of the Russian soul." So you fucked up, Graydon, or were too scared to criticize America's at this point largely bankrupt foreign policy. . . . Which brings me to the point that you are fucking up with, not to mention fucking over: ME, Graydon . . . I don't need Vanity Fair, and Vanity Fair doesn't need me, but it would be a shame for you to lose arguably the greatest writer this incarnation of the magazine has had, certainly the only one with any lasting artistic value. But what are we anyway but specks of dust in the universe? It's up to you boys. All the best, as ever, Alex*

At one point during the long and tortuous stretches of Shoumatoffia, David Kamp came up with a character he called Ed Coaster, a fictitious contributor to *Vanity Fair*. The Coaster Correspondence became a recurring feature—we must have run more than thirty installments over the years. Each one generally centered on Ed's attempts to wheedle money out of the magazine for ever more preposterous assignments. Alex's general disdain for me filtered through the features. At one point, after we published a particularly disturbing hate letter from Ed, my mother called to say that she was worried for my safety. I told her, "Mom, Ed's a fiction. He's made up. A fake." I'm not sure she believed me. Indeed, so clever were David's constructs for the feature that a number of other readers took Ed to be a genuine contributor. As for Alex, I'm not sure he read *Vanity Fair*—or at least not The Coaster Correspondence, because in all his complaints, he never mentioned this character who, to the rest of the staff, cut so close to the White Russian bone.

— ⌐

Donald Trump is not a man who is easy to ignore. But I assure you, it's well worth the effort. That said, his constant self-puffery, and his eventual run for the White House, made ignoring him all but impossible. It is a given that the one thing a narcissist can't bear—any more than a vampire can bear garlic—is being ridiculed. And because most autocrats are narcissists, ridicule is one of the most effective weapons against them. It punctures the unreality they have created about themselves and dissolves their aura of authority. A joke against a tyrant, in some of the autocracies across the globe, could be reliably predicted to end in death for the joker. Within this multiplying cohort of thin-skinned strongmen, I do believe that Donald Trump is in a narcissist class of his own. He might have been the most easily baited person I've ever met.

Vanity Fair used to do big round-up extravaganzas on the secretive enclaves of the rich, places like Mount Desert Island in Maine, and Palm Beach. These were built around current histories of the places and of the people who lived there. Each expedition required a good deal of wrangling to get residents not used to posing for photographs to sit for Jonathan Becker, who took most of the pictures. One of the enclaves we profiled was Bedford, New York, the town in Westchester County that is now the weekend home of monied New

Yorkers like Ralph Lauren. Alex Shoumatoff, who had grown up in Bedford, wrote the story, and Jonathan took the pictures. In 1998, when we were preparing the article, another name came up on our list of whom to photograph: Donald Trump. He had just bought the Seven Springs estate, a great pile of stone from the end of the Gilded Age that had been built in 1919 by Eugene Meyer, publisher of *The Washington Post*.

As Jonathan discovered when he went to see him, the WASP surroundings were getting to Trump. Somewhere on the hundreds of acres of the estate, Trump wanted to build a golf course, but the town wouldn't let him. Trump believed that they wouldn't let him build it because they were WASPs and he was from Queens. In fact, the problem was a concern about local drinking water. The nitrogen used to fertilize the fairways and greens could poison a nearby reservoir. At their meeting, Jonathan suggested that the problem was that he hadn't tried to blend in with his WASP neighbors. He said Trump needed to dress like a WASP—and Trump agreed. Jonathan went a bit over the top, bringing in plus fours, Argyle socks, and brogues, along with a big floppy tweed hat and walking sticks. It was the sort of outfit a small theatrical touring group would use to denote a member of the English gentry at play in the years between the wars. Trump loved the photo and agreed to an arrangement: covering the repairs to Jonathan's car, damaged in a Trump-owned parking garage, in return for two hundred copies. Then, of course, he reneged— "Call your lawyer," Jonathan was told—but a little too soon. Trump never got his photos.

In 2013, I assigned Bill Cohan to do a story on Trump University, his fraudulent self-help racket. After serial lawsuits, Trump paid $25 million to the poor souls who had bought into his scam. Bill was halfway into his research when I got a call from Trump's daughter Ivanka. She said, "My father doesn't know I'm calling, but I hope you'll go easy on him." I said, "Well, give him my regards and I'll certainly edit the story with the utmost care when it comes in."

I didn't tell Bill about the call until after the story was published. And Bill is nothing if not thorough and fearless. Word about his investigation began trickling out in the press. Trump wrote to me directly: "I just heard you are trying to put yet another 'hit' on me through writer William Cohan. You've been trying since the terrible GQ cover story you wrote in May of 1984. After that, with your failed (which I predicted) SPY Magazine (I actually have very long fingers) and then Vanity Fair. . . . At least you don't give up!" But then, as ever, he went a tad overboard: "Let me tell you one thing that you can count on with great certainty—if you hit me, I will hit you back 100 times harder—harder than you've ever been hit before!" Even the massacre by Islamist militants of the journalists, policemen, and security personnel at *Charlie Hebdo* magazine in Paris in 2015 caused Trump to reflect only on his own suffering. "Charlie Hebdo," he tweeted, "reminds me of the 'satirical' rag magazine Spy that was very dishonest and nasty and went bankrupt. Charlie was also broke!"

As Trump bullied his way along toward the Republican presidential nomination, the "short-fingered" observation from *Spy* days went from schoolyard calumny to campaign talking point. It became the stuff of late-night punch lines and novelty gifts. In a *Washington Post* interview in 2016, Trump couldn't stop bringing up how big his hands were, calling them "normal," "a good size," "great," and "slightly large, actually." In one of the televised Republican debates, Marco Rubio, the trifling Republican senator from Florida, said, "You know what they say about guys with small hands . . ." He paused for effect, then continued: "You can't trust 'em." At the *Fox News* debate days later, Trump responded to Rubio's taunt. "He referred to my hands: if they're small, something else must be small. I guarantee you, there's no problem." *The Hollywood Reporter* had obtained a copy of Trump's handprint, cast from his own hand at Madame Tussauds. A study commissioned by the U.S. Army indicated that Trump's hand length of 7.25 inches hovers around the lower 25th percentile of hand length among military men. According to *The Hollywood Reporter*, Trump "does indeed have hands just below average size, particularly for a man standing 6-foot-2."

During his presidential campaign, I wrote an editorial saying that I didn't think Trump would make it to the White House—though I registered my astonishment that his carny act had gotten as far as it had. The narrative arc was now clear: "The presidency of George W. Bush was an eight-year warm-up act for the final stage of a dumbed-down America: a Trump presidency. You can draw a relatively straight line from the Florida recount of 2000, which took Bush into office, right through to the shambolic Trump campaign. The election of Bush led to the invasion of Iraq, which led to the destabilization in the Middle East (Libya, Egypt, Syria), which led to the migrant crisis, which led to European nationalism, Brexit, and, at the tail end of all these disasters, Trump."

It's chilling to go back and hear the lies in his inauguration address: "We are transferring power from Washington, DC, and giving it back to you, the people. . . . We will bring back our jobs. We will bring back our borders. We will bring back our wealth. . . . We will build new roads and highways and bridges and airports and tunnels, and railways, all across our wonderful nation. . . . A new national pride will . . . heal our divisions. Hear these words. You will never be ignored again." And on it went. Trump survives on crowd approval, and to get it he continues to engage in what the Yale historian Timothy Snyder calls "sado-populism"—you promise the people things you have no intention of delivering, making them angrier when they don't appear, then you direct their anger at others. After he was sworn in, early in 2017, I enlarged and then printed all of Trump's negative tweets about me. Some highlights:

> Graydon Carter, whose reign over failing @VanityFair has been a disaster, has acted in two movies—both bombed & got bad reviews.

> I have watched sloppy Graydon Carter fail and close Spy Magazine and now am watching him fail at @VanityFair Magazine. He is a total loser!

> Sissy Graydon Carter of failing Vanity Fair Magazine and owner of bad food restaurants has a problem-his V.F. Oscar party is no longer "hot"

> Has anyone looked at the really poor numbers of @VanityFair Magazine. Way down, big trouble, dead! Graydon Carter, no talent, will be out!

I had them framed and then hung on a large wall outside my office. When guests marveled at the installation, I would tell them that it was the only wall Trump had ever built.

I was generally careful in bringing new editors into the mix. I don't like office drama, and would often have *Vanity Fair*'s editors spend some time with prospective hires to make sure they would fit in. On the two occasions I skipped this vital step, I failed miserably. A young journalist named Toby Young had a London-based magazine called the *Modern Review*, which I admired. When it folded, I thought he could use a job and I offered him one in New York. His time at *Vanity Fair* was limited, but he nevertheless saw fit to write a not particularly flattering book about his days at the magazine. As the saying almost goes, no good deed goes unpublished. I never read it, but I did see the film version that was made. I was played by Jeff

Bridges. Which was both flattering and at home mortifying when I began to suspect that my wife, Anna, would have preferred him in the job over me.

I made the same mistake with Vicky Ward, a former *Daily Mail* reporter who had gone to work for Tina Brown at *Talk* magazine. As I was to discover, her former office mates regularly referred to her as a mini-Tina. Ward approached me and said that she'd love to work at *Vanity Fair*. I thought a sprinkling of *Daily Mail* spice could freshen up the magazine's pages and, forgoing the usual vetting process, hired her. The staff was nonplussed. A number of them didn't like her. More important, there were some who just didn't trust her. At one point Bruce Handy said to me, "I wasn't around when Toby was here. I sure hope I make it into Vicky's book." Fact-checkers regularly expressed concern about her reporting. I was also getting word that she was going around town saying that I had appointed her as my heir apparent—if this was true, it was a figment of her imagination, in that the only one who could determine who would follow me was Si himself.

One of her efforts caused me a good amount of grief years after it had run. I had been reading in the *New York Post* about a slightly mysterious former Bear Stearns banker named Jeffrey Epstein who had been flying Bill Clinton around on his private plane. This was relatively early in the private-plane-in-every-wealthy-person's-garage period and was therefore somewhat unusual. In 2002, I assigned Ward to write a profile of him. She turned in a fairly perfunctory story and then, as we were about to send the Epstein piece to the printer, early the next year, she said that there might be some sexual improprieties in his life, specifically involving a young woman and her sister. Because Epstein was then a private citizen, the evidentiary burden of proof on a publication is much greater than it is when you're writing about a public figure. Ward was instructed to go back to the young women to see whether they would be willing to stand up confirming their story in court, should Epstein sue us. Both understandably said no. They were terrified of him. That being the case, we agreed that these details could not be included in the story.

The article ran in the March 2003 issue. The extent of Epstein's monstrous behavior would be definitively documented fifteen years later in a series of stories by Julie Brown in the *Miami Herald*. In that intervening decade and a half, Ward could have taken her story elsewhere. She did not. Instead, she wrote glowingly about Jeffrey Epstein and his enabler Ghislaine Maxwell on numerous occasions, including on the *Vanity Fair* website in 2011: "'Jeffrey knows a good deal about most subjects,' newspaper publisher Mort Zuckerman told me last week. He was certainly preaching to the converted. The truth is, Epstein does know a lot about a lot of things. Just a few moments in his company and you know this to be true." She was at the same time even more gushingly a fan of Maxwell's. "She is always the most interesting, the most vivacious, the most unusual person in any room." Ward continued: "I've spent hours talking to her about the Third World at a bar until two a.m. She is as passionate as she is knowledgeable. She is curious. She has spent weeks at the bottom of the ocean, literally going deeper than anyone else. She has sent me a DVD of the fish there. Her Rolodex would blow away almost anyone else's I can think of—probably even Rupert Murdoch's. She is very well read and can talk about most things for hours. She is passionate about Bill Clinton, with whom she is close friends."

In 2018, when the Brown series was published, Ward jumped on the Epstein bandwagon with relish, churning out stories, a podcast, and even a television documentary that portrayed her as the truth-seeker and us at the magazine—and me in particular—as malign gatekeepers keeping truth at bay. We all found this a bit rich. As indeed did the two sisters whom Ward wanted to include in that original story. One of them told the *New York Post* that she was so fed up with Ward "profiting" from their stories that she sent her a cease-and-desist letter. "I am horrified," the woman said. "Just leave us alone! Can't she make money off of other victims? She's a 'presstitute' and vulture. . . . She won't stop torturing us, and it is hurting so badly. Whenever we hear the name 'Vicky Ward,' we cringe."

Chapter 19.

The Long Arm of the Law

L ibel battles are prolonged, expensive, and draining slogs. And brutally time-consuming. I have been through two of them.

The biggest libel case of my editorship at *Vanity Fair* was brought by Mohamed al-Fayed, then the owner of both the Harrods department store and the Paris Ritz. From beginning to end, the whole affair lasted two years. And I must tell you, spending a portion of every week coming up with evidence to fight a serious libel action isn't as fun as it sounds.

Maureen Orth had written a profile of Fayed (the "al" was tagged on in the '70s) for the September 1995 issue of the magazine. The title of her report was "Holy War at Harrods." When it came out, Fayed sued us for our allegations of his sexual harassment of female employees and his use of charitable donations to stifle official criticism of him. He also sued us for our allegations that he used a secret surveillance apparatus to keep an eye on staff and visitors. And he sued us over our allegations of his racism. In her story, Maureen had cited numerous cases of unfair dismissal, enforced HIV tests for female staff, the bugging of phones, and his general "management by fear."

When I commissioned Maureen to write the story, I'd been reading a lot about Fayed. And I was generally on his side. (It wasn't then public knowledge that he had been using Britain's famously plaintiff-friendly libel laws to stifle any negative comment about him or his family.) I felt he was the subject of institutional racism in Britain, both from the establishment and the London broadsheets. I felt he was being held at arm's length because he was not like them. He hadn't gone to Eton. He didn't have a cut-glass accent. He didn't know the rules. He was Egyptian, and to the ruling Oxbridge set, he looked funny and spoke funny. Fayed tried desperately to ingratiate himself through philanthropy, straight cash donations to politicians, and finally, and tragically, by pushing his son Dodi into the arms of Princess Diana. He had been furious when Conservative prime minister John Major's government had refused his request to become a British citizen. His revenge? He divulged the names of three ministers in Major's cabinet who had taken cash from him in return for asking questions on his behalf in Parliament or who had stayed for free at the Ritz. The establishment's response was that it was Fayed's fault that so many British politicians were venal. The whole thing was laughable. I saw Fayed as the classic British outsider and perhaps not the monster that the British press was portraying him as.

Halfway through her assignment, Maureen called to say that we had a very different story on our hands. The British papers, she believed, had actually been overly generous. The man was a monster. And a litigious one who had buried accusations against him with flurries of libel writs. Maureen had the story of a racist and a serial sexual harasser, a man surrounded by goons and enforcers who had cowed his victims into silence or bought them off, and who had muzzled the press with gag orders and threats of withholding Harrods' considerable advertising budget.

Fayed couldn't believe that the British Conservative Party, to which he had made so many donations, official and unofficial, had turned against him. There was a time when its mandarins purred in his presence, hoping for scraps from his bank account. Margaret Thatcher's government had waved through his audacious coup to buy Harrods in 1985 with little scrutiny from the Monopolies and Mergers Commission. Later, enough evidence of impropriety reached them to trigger a report by the Department of Trade and Industry, whose conclusions were devastating. "The Fayeds [Mohamed had two brothers, Ali and Salah] dishonestly misrepresented their origins, their wealth, their business interests and their resources," it stated.

This was damning stuff. The British government suppressed the report for as long as it could—no doubt out of fear that it would reflect as badly on itself as it would on Fayed—and never prosecuted him based on its disclosures. Instead, it refused Fayed citizenship, which requires evidence of "good character." When she interviewed Fayed for the story, Maureen put to him the rumor that he wanted to become a member of the House of Lords. "I don't want that," he said. "But they didn't also say thank you for everything I have done. It's the opposite. They just could shit on me, everyone." He had named the cabinet ministers who accepted cash to ask questions on his behalf in order to take his revenge, he said, "to show people who really runs this country, what quality they are. . . . These days it's only the trash people." The Department of Trade and Industry report drove him crazy; he called it worthless and shocking. "I make revolution," he told Maureen. "The devastating thing is the class system, created of people who think they are above the rest of the human race. They think they can shit just on anyone. They think I'm a wog." Members of the British establishment who had accepted his favors were astounded by the recitation of facts in Maureen's piece.

As it turned out, we only knew a portion of it. We learned so much more about Fayed during discovery, as we built a case to defend ourselves. One of our barristers at the time, who would become an appeals court judge, later told our London editor, Henry Porter, that Maureen's story was so well done and backed up that, in his opinion, our case was won before we ever began this process. But that's not what we believed at the time.

British libel law is markedly different from libel law in the United States. In America, the burden is on the person suing to prove not only that an allegation is false but that the news organization knew that what it was printing was false or at least probably false and published it anyway, with malice aforethought. In Britain, the burden is on the news organization to prove that what it said was true. The plaintiff need not prove anything other than harm. That's why winning libel cases in Britain is so much easier than it is in the United States.

For eighteen months, we prepared to defend ourselves. Henry was instrumental in gathering our defense, digging up fresh evidence, finding witnesses, and attempting to nail it all down. He did little else during that period. We'd have a weekly chat when Henry would bring me up to speed—information I would deliver to Si during our fortnightly lunches. We were in good hands on the legal front. In London, we had David Hooper, from Biddle & Co. And in New York, we had an astute lawyer in Jerry Birenz, who worked for the firm that handled all the Newhouse businesses. Robert Walsh, our legal editor in New York, and Rich Bernstein, a partner at *Vanity Fair*'s legal firm, were involved every step of the way. As the trial date approached, we examined our findings. It was a wealth of new material. We had new witnesses and thousands of pages of fresh evidence.

What we discovered was truly shocking. It was a mistake for Fayed to have sued on four counts. It meant that we could legitimately investigate four areas of his life, and if in one of those areas we could prove our case, it would compromise the rest of his libel suit. Sexual harassment was almost the easiest. Fayed had been serially abusive and predatory to a host of young women who came to work for him. If they refused his advances, he would persecute them or fire them. Any who walked out were followed by threats to muzzle them.

Fayed settled harassment cases out of court with money and gag orders. Women who came to work for him were subjected to medical examinations to see if they had HIV or any other diseases. Once hired, they would be plied with gifts, then pounced on. Women in his employment would frequently be subjected to abusive, misogynistic language. One affidavit described Fayed asking a female employee in his office, "Who did you fuck this weekend?" When she refused to answer, he asked her whether she was "into girls." Fayed terrorized his staff, keeping them in a constant state of fear. Henry found many female former employees who were willing to sign affidavits about his behavior. He tracked down one of them—a hearty New Zealander nanny who was working as a hiking guide—to a fax machine in the Himalayas. She was a key witness and willingly agreed to describe Fayed's repellent advances. We also got testimony from many of the managers he'd fired—one of whom ended up in prison in Dubai, in the United Arab Emirates, after Fayed had written to the Crown Prince of Sharjah, Sheikh Al Qasimi, falsely claiming that the former manager had embezzled millions of dollars from Harrods.

Employees and managers were electronically bugged by Fayed.

There was surveillance equipment everywhere: in the elevators and the bathrooms. There were hidden cameras on desks. As to our reporting about Fayed's racism, we had eyewitness accounts of his daily walks around Harrods, where he would loudly proclaim his pathological hatred of Black and Asian employees when any came into view. At times he tried to get them fired on some pretext, such as contravening the dress code. One manager described "an almost constant stream of invective hurled towards Black and Asian people, primarily towards the cleaning staff." As employees, they were never given jobs on the shop floors, only on the floor below for menial work, all in contravention of British antidiscrimination laws. Fayed's manager, in his statement to us, described Fayed during one foray around the store walking over to a Black cleaner and telling her she was "fucking too fat." He asked the manager, loudly, "What's a fucking Black woman who is too fat to clean doing here?" He told the manager to get rid of her.

There were dozens of unfair dismissal cases pending. Many were settled, with cash, only after weeks and months of distress and intimidation toward the employees. There was a case where a female employee had been pressured to take a drug rap for Fayed's brother Salah. When her testimony didn't stand up and Salah came under suspicion, one of the former managers told us how he was introduced to a former employee of the Metropolitan Police who acted as a "consultant" to Fayed. Shortly afterward, all charges against Fayed's brother were dropped. We got help from Roland "Tiny" Rowland, chairman of the mining company Lonrho, who had been passed over by the government in his bid for Harrods in favor of Fayed and had ever since been using his newspaper, *The Observer,* and intelligence-gathering companies to discredit his former opponent.

Then came the dirty tricks. Fayed saw the evidence further mounting against him and unleashed his security personnel, the ones he regularly called "fucking donkeys" to their faces. He had them intimidate witnesses who had spoken to us. On Fayed's instructions, they subjected witnesses to anonymous phone calls. "You've been a very naughty girl" was a typical warning. Two witnesses had to be hidden away by Henry and David Hooper, one at a health farm, before protection orders could be issued. Henry, who is a successful writer of thrillers, had his own contacts in the spook world, and through them discovered that he was being followed. He, too, received threatening calls. "You're up against some very serious people," he was warned at one point.

They tried to set Henry up with false evidence. A bodyguard who claimed he'd been fired by Fayed came to see Henry and offered to sell him a videotape he supposedly had, purporting to show Fayed having sex in his office with a member of staff. Henry suspected the bodyguard was recording them, and said loudly, "But that would be stolen property. I'm not going to receive stolen goods." Henry, too, had recorded the conversation. He also warned our lawyers, one of whom, incomprehensibly, went ahead and made an offer for the tape. Furious, Henry called a meeting with Condé Nast's managers in London. But it was too late. Fayed had leaked the story to the *Mail on Sunday*, which reported that "at a clandestine meeting," Henry (no mention of our English lawyer) had offered £5,000 for the stolen tapes. When the *Mail*'s lawyers heard the concealed tape of the conversation between Henry and the bodyguard, they realized that the paper itself was exposed to a libel action from Henry and quickly printed a retraction.

At one point during discovery, I had to go to London and then on to Paris. Nicholas Coleridge, the managing director of Condé Nast in England, gave a lunch for the Princess of Wales, and given my relationship with her—we cohosted the Serpentine dinners each year—he invited me and seated me on her left side. I must have caught an infection of some sort, because during the trip a boil had developed on the right side of my neck along the line of my shirt collar. And it was so raw and painful that in order not to chafe it with the collar, I had to move my whole torso in the direction of the princess to speak to her. Which she must have found incredibly odd.

I went on to Paris, for reasons that now escape me, and Sara Marks had flown over as well. She came up to my room at the Ritz one morning with a hi-tech-looking gadget. She reminded me that Fayed owned the hotel and that there was a good chance he was bugging my room. I make no excuses for my stupidity in not factoring the libel case into my choice of hotel. The gadget was something she'd bought at a "spy" shop on Madison Avenue—a machine used to detect the presence of bugging activity. We began going around the living room of the suite listening to the Geiger-counter-like monitor. It buzzed a bit near the phone and near the television set. We moved into the bedroom. The machine was largely silent as we made our way around the room. Until it came to the wall-sized tapestry over the bed. Then it just went berserk. I spent the next day and a half getting dressed and undressed in the dark and not talking to anyone on the phone.

Back home, the bills were mounting, and Si would get a bit teetery from time to time. As it continued, I'd remind him that Rupert Murdoch would fight these things on an almost daily basis. I wasn't actually sure about that, but I knew that Si revered Murdoch—the great buccaneer of Si's generation of media moguls—and it would get Si back on the train. When Fayed tried to set up Henry, Si just said, "Go for him. You can have whatever you need."

A few weeks before we were due in court, Henry found a piece of evidence that we knew would terrify Fayed and his legal team. An acquaintance had told Henry that he'd seen a 150-word letter written by a friend of his—a senior government official—to Fayed, warning him that accusations against him by the official's stepdaughter were shocking and totally believable, and that any further contact with her would have very serious consequences. Both Henry and I met with the stepdaughter, a young woman in her late twenties. She was about to get married and therefore didn't want to sign an affidavit that could publicly connect her name to Fayed's. She told us that she had been hired to do some work on his 208-foot yacht, the *Jonikal.* After she came aboard, he jumped her in her stateroom. When she rebuffed his advances, Fayed locked her in the room, turned off the water and air conditioning, and kept her there for three days. In other words, kidnapping and imprisonment. The young woman added that one of his requests to her before he locked her up was for her to relieve herself in his presence on a glass coffee table. She was obviously traumatized by the experience, but her father hadn't wanted her name to be associated with Fayed—in the same way that there are no doubt more women who could have come out against Harvey Weinstein but didn't want their names mentioned in the same sentence as his. We knew the letter was in Fayed's possession. And so we asked for it in discovery, a bombshell request for Fayed's lawyers to receive. Our lawyer's letter referred to the "assault" on the official's stepdaughter, and included the line: "It relates precisely to the conduct complained of in this case albeit in a rather more serious form than usual." He did not know that we did not have the stepdaughter as a witness.

About a week before we were due to walk into court, Fayed announced that he wanted to settle. He said that he would drop the suit and that he would restore advertising to the Condé Nast magazines, advertising that he had pulled after Maureen's story had run. But he demanded that we destroy all the evidence that we unearthed during discovery. I mentioned this to Si during one of our lunches. We were certainly relieved that he was dropping the suit. Si didn't seem to care about Fayed's willingness to restore the advertising to his European publications. But we both decided—in consultation with Henry and our lawyers—that destroying the evidence was out of the question. I wanted it available for future journalists and news outfits who found themselves in the grip of one of Fayed's blizzards of libel actions. We made an extra copy of everything and put it in storage just in case. Fayed officially withdrew the lawsuit.

Henry pleaded forcefully for us not to settle, to pursue Fayed through the courts, on the grounds that, like Robert Maxwell before him, he could otherwise continue to stifle the press with payoffs and gag orders by exploiting the British libel laws. Fayed's principal concern was that the evidence of his bullying and harassment not reach court. Indeed, according to our lawyer, Fayed was so worried that the settlement discussions might be recorded that he demanded they be held in the steam room of a London club, "with no possibility of a wire on the negotiators' unclothed torsos." Henry wanted to prepare a follow-up report that would vindicate Maureen's original story, with the mass of new evidence. It would also be about how *Vanity Fair* took on the man who was responsible for so much corruption and litigation in Britain. And it would unfurl all that we had uncovered during our discovery, including many additional details of Fayed's way of conducting business. These included Fayed ordering his security personnel to plot a break-in on a government minister's home, and members of his staff routinely bribing police officers so that they would cooperate in the arrest and intimidation of Harrods employees falsely accused of theft. These, we felt, were matters of public interest by any standard.

I agreed with much of what Henry said, but I thought a follow-up report might come off as self-serving. I went back and forth on this, worried that we could look like braggarts. In the end, the decision was sort of made for us. Two months after Fayed received our letter about the diplomat's stepdaughter came the news of the death of Princess Diana and Fayed's son Dodi following a car chase with paparazzi in pursuit through the Pont de l'Alma tunnel in Paris. Si decided that we didn't want to be in a legal dispute with a man who was grieving for his son and let it all go. In 2010, Harrods fell out of Fayed's hands when it was bought by Qatar's sovereign wealth fund. Almost three decades after our original story on Fayed ran in *Vanity Fair*, the full depths of his depravity were reported by the BBC. The number of women who have charged the former owner of Harrods with sexual offenses is now in the hundreds.

—

A couple of sentences buried within a seventeen-page story on Elaine's triggered another major libel case that would go on for more than two years. And to my mind, it should never have gone to court. The story was written in 2002 by A. E. Hotchner, the distinguished journalist and author who had been a pal of Hemingway's. Deep in his copy was an anecdote told by then *Harper's* editor Lewis Lapham, an Elaine's regular. Lewis said that the only time he remembered the place being reduced to silence was when Roman Polanski had walked in not long before the funeral of his wife, the actress Sharon Tate, a victim of the brutal Manson killings up in the Hollywood Hills in the late summer of 1969. The director, he said, had stopped in New York on his way to Los Angeles, where the funeral was to be held. Lewis said that Polanski had sat between him and a Scandinavian model who was there with his friend, Edward Perlberg. Lewis was quoted in Hotchner's story saying that Polanski had made a pass at the model, invoking the name of his late wife as he did so.

Polanski denied that the incident had ever happened. He claimed, for one thing, that he had flown directly to Los Angeles from Paris for his wife's funeral. He sued *Vanity Fair* for libel. I had met Polanski a few times before this and admired his work as a director. Warren Beatty, Diane von Fürstenberg, and Bob Evans, all friends of his, called me on his behalf. They urged me to settle the case with a correction and an apology. All argued convincingly that Polanski believed the magazine had wronged him. I met Polanski after this at a dinner, talked about the case, and thought there might be a way of resolving it.

Some cases are worth fighting, but I didn't think this was one of them. Polanski made a compelling argument as to why he would never have said what had been reported. As much as I respect Lewis's memory, most of us believe what we want to believe. And most of us have trouble recalling exactly what was said at dinner the night before, let alone three decades earlier—and in a crowded restaurant during a night of drinking. And there was this: after all that had been said against Polanski, that he took a stand on this particular anecdote gave me cause to believe he had, in my mind, a reasonable argument that he was innocent.

After a long phone conversation with Polanski, I drafted a correction and an apology based on our general agreed-upon wording. It was one paragraph long, and I was ready to send it to him. I checked first with the Condé Nast lawyers, who had told me that they wanted to see it first. They kneaded it and added clauses here and there to the point that it bore little resemblance to what we had agreed to on the phone. I knew there was no way that Polanski would sign off on it. And from that point, it all got out of control.

Polanski was—and still is, at the time of this writing—the subject of one of the longest cases in California legal history. He served time in prison in 1977 for unlawful sex with a minor, fleeing Hollywood for France only when the judge—unlawfully—threatened to reincarcerate him. The case stunned the American public even in the libertine days of Hollywood in the late 1970s. Included in the indictments were counts of sodomy and rape involving the use of drugs. Since then, and because of the misconduct of the judge, which took years for the courts to admit, the authorities have said that if he returns to the United States he would be discharged without further incarceration, having served the full sentence imposed on him. Polanski doesn't trust the courts, so the arrest warrant remains in place. As it was in place then.

Polanski sued us in the UK, and if he showed up in person, he would run the risk of extradition to the United States. His lawyers argued that he should be allowed to fight his case from the safety of France via video link. This was fairly unprecedented, and the Court of Appeal unanimously ruled against it. But his legal team appealed to the House of Lords, which in a landmark decision overruled the lower court. One other advantage for Polanski was that his past actions—the crimes in Los Angeles that he had originally been charged with—in terms of possible damage to his reputation couldn't be aired in court. Nor could Polanski be seen by those in the courtroom watching the proceedings via video link except when he was actually giving evidence, which I thought was unfair to him. Polanski is a superb actor and in court he was a forceful and disarming witness—measured and polite. And how could he not be? He directed himself in his testimony.

He called the disputed anecdote "an abominable lie" that showed "callous indifference" to his wife's murder. He also had a very good lawyer in John Kelsey-Fry, a barrister with a background in criminal law and a scrappy and eager way in court. He had prosecuted one of the notorious Kray brothers—for decades the scourge of East London. I also liked the fact that Kelsey-Fry stole outside for a cigarette from time to time.

Our own barrister, on the other hand, was the posh and laconic Tom Shields, son of the former managing director of Associated Newspapers, owners of the *Daily Mail*. I was told that he had his own cricket pitch in the country—a bit like an American having his own baseball diamond. To my mind, he was no match for Kelsey-Fry. Lewis Lapham was a long-respected editor and writer, and I had enormous admiration and affection for him. But he was a shockingly bad witness. Lewis's memory, which had seemed reassuring when the story was being prepared for publication, was, on the witness stand, shaky. His friend Edward Perlberg testified that, although he saw Polanski at Elaine's, he didn't see or hear his reported advances toward his girlfriend. The date of Polanski's visit to New York was blurry. Mia Farrow testified about a dinner she'd had with Polanski at Elaine's a few weeks *after* the funeral.

The trial, which lasted a week, took place in the fabled Royal Courts of Justice—barristers and judges wore wigs, and it was all very *Witness for the Prosecution*. On the last day, Anna and I slipped away for lunch at a locally popular pub called the Seven Stars, close to the courts. It was where the lawyers and justices often ate during long trials. As we walked in from the street, the publican, a woman of sturdy build and claret-colored hair, exclaimed to the room, "Well, if it isn't Mr. Graydon Carter himself. Welcome to the Elaine's of London."

She was indeed, as I discovered, something of an institution among the legal set. Her name, and I'm not making this up, was Roxy Beaujolais, and she waved her arm at the room and said, "Now a gentleman such as yourself will, I expect, be wanting a table."

We got a small one outside on the sidewalk. It was quite a social lunch, as it turned out. A woman I'd seen in the courtroom got out of a cab and rushed over to Roxy to give her a hug and a kiss.

"Mr. and Mrs. Graydon Carter, I'd like you to meet Marilyn Lownes," Roxy announced.

She was the wife of Victor Lownes, who had been part owner of the Playboy Club when Polanski first came to London. The three had been good friends. Roxy explained that Marilyn—who must have cut quite a dash in her earlier years—was a public figure in her own right.

Roxy expanded on Mrs. Lownes's place in the cultural firmament by explaining that she was "the first *Playboy* Playmate to go full frontal. You know, the tits, the bush, the whole thing."

The verdict was less amusing than the lunch. The jury found for Polanski and awarded damages of £50,000. Condé Nast was also on the hook for the legal costs of both sides—a penalty that ran into the millions of dollars. I was angry less with the verdict than with our own stumbling actions leading up to it. It was, I felt, a self-inflicted wound.

Chapter 20.

The Golden Age
Begins to Tarnish

I have Anna Wintour to thank for bringing me firmly into the Condé Nast fold—and also for either inadvertently or advertently giving me reason to leave that fold thirty years later. We didn't meet the way normal people do. She essentially inherited me. When Si asked her to take over *House & Garden* in 1987, she was given a magazine with a charmed history and a number of staff and contract writers, me included. Louis Gropp, the cheerful steward of *House & Garden* prior to Anna, had given me a writing contract that equaled nearly half the salary I was making at *Spy*.

I knew almost nothing formal about interiors or decorators, but the assignments I was given were more about the people than the places. Lacking the discernment of previous editors of my freelance offerings, Anna kept me on contract when she took over. I found Anna in those days to be cozy, conspiratorial, and completely enticing. My feelings toward her ran in opposition to the tagline "Nuclear Wintour," which was then at the beginning of its long run. She was a great and loyal friend, and as a result, she had a lot of close friends. Also, she had gone out with Christopher Hitchens, a big validation in my book.

Anna turned *House & Garden* into something it hadn't been— flashy and a bit obsessed with fashion and with people who were then considered fashionable. It developed the nickname "House & Garment." Within a year, she had renamed it *HG*, for reasons that I never understood, and it began a slow and steady slide off the news-stands. The magazine folded in 2007. I had always assumed that giving Anna *House & Garden* was Si's way of getting her to New York from London, where she had been the editor of *British Vogue*. It was a way station on the path to the editorship of American *Vogue*.

As much as I liked her, I found Anna's efforts to seem intimidating and powerful almost comical. Her son Charlie and my son Max were in the same class at Collegiate, in Manhattan. One year a number of their classmates decided to put on a fashion show. They went to an awful lot of effort, with a catwalk down the center and rows of chairs on each side. Like a real fashion show, but much sweeter and with young boys in place of supermodels. As a show of support, I dropped by to see it on my way out to dinner. The lights were already dimmed by the time I got there. Family members had filled out the rows of chairs, and there, in the front row, was Anna. And she was wearing sunglasses. I almost burst out laughing and had to turn my back.

Another time, she and I shared a car out to the Oyster Bay home of Condé Nast CEO Steve Florio. This was a once-a-year get-together for editors and publishers and Condé Nast executives. It was a strained affair, in that the editors and publishers at the various magazines were pitched in mortal combat the other 364 days of the year, and many actively despised their counterparts at the other titles. It was about 6:00 p.m. when we set off. We took her car, and I was surprised by how blackened the windows were. It was difficult to see outside in the back seat even with the late afternoon sun. When my eyes adjusted to the light, I was surprised to see Anna in her dark sunglasses. "You are kidding," I said. She took them off and said something to the effect of "There, Graydon, happy now?"

People who think arriving late is a power move could take a lesson from Anna Wintour. Late is not a part of her arsenal. Early is. She likes to play tennis in the morning and then get her hair done—I think I have the order right—before beginning her day. When she began to spend more time on the organization of the Met Gala, the people at the Costume Institute at the Metropolitan Museum of Art would set the first meetings for 9:00 a.m. Anna would arrive at 8:45, which would cause the Met staff to scramble to establish a quorum. When they officially changed the time to 8:45, Anna would begin arriving at 8:30. More scrambling. The times just got earlier and earlier. The meetings by now may well have been pushed back to the evening before. This was a technique she also applied at Condé Nast. I was well aware of the early-arrival act through friends at the Met. Near the end of my time at *Vanity Fair*, Anna's office called to request a meeting to discuss something. We set the get-together for 11:00 in the *Vanity Fair* conference room. At about 10:40, my assistant came into my office and in something of a panic said that Anna was already in there. I said, "Good, ask her if she'd like anything and tell her I'll see her at 11:00." I have never felt so brave and in control of a situation.

The Met Gala, held on the first Monday in May every year at the Metropolitan Museum of Art, is a must-attend obligation for most of the attendees: actors, models, and now TikTokers and assorted influencers. They and others in the sway of fashion no doubt feel they have to be there, if only to be photographed looking especially outrageous. The sponsors, who pay upward of $350,000 for tables at the affair, are essentially held hostage. It's not quite on the level of a protection racket. Fashion companies need credits in fashion magazines. The magazines get the word out and provide a form of second-party validation. Buying a table does not necessarily get you fashion credits in *Vogue*. But not buying a table does not exactly win the loyalties of the editors responsible for credits in the magazine. I doubt that a quid pro quo is ever mentioned in the negotiations over the tables. But as it is in many dictatorships, these understandings can be tacit.

A decade or so ago, Carolina Herrera realized that she needed to be in London the week of the Met Gala to attend the wedding of the daughter of her closest friend, Alexandra Theodoracopulos, the wife of Taki, the Greek shipping heir and longtime *Spectator* columnist. She called Anna to explain why she wouldn't be able to take a table. Anna said she completely understood, but that she would still like her to pay for a table—$250,000 back then—for "my charity," as she put it. Carolina explained once again that she couldn't attend and therefore she wouldn't be taking a table.

At dinner a few nights later, Carolina told me this story and asked what she should do. I told her not to send the check and just move on. Well, she didn't take my advice. She called Anna to tell her that she would take the table and that her daughter Patricia, who was working with her, would host the table. She said that Patricia and her husband, Gerrity Lansing, would invite their friends Seth Meyers and his wife, Alexi, along with Tom Brady and his then wife, Gisele Bündchen, to sit with them. Anna would have none of it. She had already assigned Seth and Alexi and Tom and Gisele to other tables. In the end, Carolina flew back the day after the wedding, and on the Monday night, there she was at the Met Gala, with her husband, Reinaldo, and Patricia and Gerrity. And seated at her table were the only two people she could corral at the last minute: my wife, Anna, and me. Loyalty can exact a high price sometimes, and it was a pretty dismal affair. Except for one thing. I noticed across the room a number of taut Upper East Side wives clustered around Donald Trump. This was before his run for the presidency. I motioned for Carolina to see this. "Interesting," I said. "No, no, no," she replied. "He likes them much younger."

I occasionally went to the Met Gala at the behest of advertisers. Often, I'd bring along a friend to ease the agony. Fran came with me a few times. And one year I brought Anjelica Huston, or she brought me, I forget which. In any event, on that night the first moment we could, Anjelica and I bolted across the street to the Stanhope Hotel. The bar was open but deserted. We found ourselves in there with a half dozen other escapees, including George Hamilton and Meg Ryan. The bartender had gone, and so George went behind the bar and pulled out a bottle of scotch. That little after-dinner party was the best part of the whole evening.

My excursions into this world were such that I got it down to a routine that made the ordeal survivable. Most attendees began to arrive at 5:30, not only to get photographed but ostensibly to see whatever exhibit the Met had done up for that year. My system was to arrive at 8:00. By that time, the photographers who lined the red carpet were gone, the crowd had thinned dramatically, and people were heading toward the dinner tables.

Anna Wintour runs the whole affair like a military operation, which is a good thing. Food on the table at 8:15, prompt. Nobody in that crowd eats dessert, but Sean Driscoll, then the chief of Glorious Foods, the city's premier caterer, served it anyway, and so the moment the dessert course hit the table, at 10:00, everyone stood up to mingle. That was the signal to escape, and my Anna and I did it with the precision of Navy SEALs. Our routine is thus: She would head to the exit first and then, about fifteen seconds later, I would follow, taking a slightly more circuitous route. No goodbyes. No obvious rushing. We would be in our car in fifteen minutes and on our way home. One year I bumped into a faintly miserable-looking Larry David. He literally threw himself on me, asking what the evening was going to be like. I gave him the key: the moment dessert arrives, you make a run for it.

Anna and I followed our plan that night. And about 10:30 I got a call from Larry on my cell phone.

"I'm out! I've done it. Where are you?" he asked.

"Larry," I said, and I felt badly one-upping him, "we're almost home."

—

Anna Wintour tends to greet me either like her long-lost friend or like the car attendant. Shyness on her part might have something to do with it. But it might also be a technique to throw the other person off their game. The trouble is, you never know which Anna you will get. Which is unfortunate. As I say, she can be a warm and loyal friend. She can also be a cold and loyal friend. Dinner with her at a restaurant is like something a McKinsey efficiency expert would admire. Seated at 8:00. No need to see a menu. Steak, rare. Not sure if she drinks. I think not. And when there are *Vogue* staff involved, the moment Anna has eaten the last piece of steak, there is a call for the check. Her dinner mates might be mid-bite. More often than not, after a meal with her, I've stopped off on the way home to get something to eat.

I attended precisely one editorial meeting at *Vogue* when I was on contract there. Condé Nast was still at 350 Madison in those days, and as I got off the elevator onto the *Vogue* floor, I could almost smell the fear. Attractive young women skittered by with terrified looks on their faces. I was ushered into Anna's office for the meeting.

The chairs were arranged in a V formation, with her desk at the point and the seats fanning out from there in a sort of flying wedge. I looked around at my fellow attendees. I've seen cheerier faces in hostage videos. I made my way to the back row and sat beside Billy Norwich, a columnist and writer who was also on contract with *Vogue*. Many of the story suggestions were met with cold stares. Billy had some very clever ideas, but none seemed to pass muster. I had come with an armful of suggestions myself, but I thought it best to keep them to myself.

After the 2016 election, Anna asked to see me. I told her I'd come to her office. I took the elevator up and walked down the long, wide, empty corridor until I got to her domain. She was behind her desk, and I was seated on a small metal chair in front of her. She said she wanted me to come to a meeting. I told her that sounded fine. She then told me it would be with Trump. I must have given her the sort of look that said "Are you kidding me?" because she told me that it was a command performance.

"We're just going to have to learn to work with him, Graydon," she said.

"Well, *you* can," I replied. "I have no interest in that. We can do just fine without his help."

But in the interest of conciliation, I said yes, I would come.

A few days later, I joined Anna and my colleagues at the other Condé Nast titles in the company's conference room. It was a long corporate table surrounded by editors with expressions that indicated a cross between forced march and this might be interesting. Kellyanne Conway was there, in the Trump camp, as was Hope Hicks. Trump came in and shook everyone's hand. He eyed me warily and then sat down. Anna introduced him. And then he began talking. The meeting was off the record, which meant that it was an essentially pointless affair. It was quite windy out that day and apparently, after he got out of his car, Trump required some fluffing before entering the building. At one point an editor who was sitting beside Kellyanne noticed the text she sent Trump, saying how great his hair looked. I did note that he kept his hands hidden and under the table most of the time.

⸺

I n the late fall of 2016, I was about to fly to San Francisco for our annual New Establishment Summit, a conference of sorts that had grown out of our New Establishment issues. Events like these were a popular sort of thing for magazines to do at the time. Ours were organized by Betsy Lack and Stephanie Mehta, along with a host of *Vanity Fair* staff members. Publishers loved such physical get-togethers because they "brought the magazine to life" and because they could reel in extra revenue from sponsorship. They were enormously labor-intensive. And for my part, they were quite stressful. I've never been comfortable in crowds, and I not only had to introduce and host the two-day affair, I had to do one of the interviews, none of which played to my strong suits.

We were packed and almost out the door when my assistant called to say that he had Anna, who by then had been appointed Condé Nast's editorial director, on the phone. As blithely as you would tell someone you wanted to change the color of their drapes, she informed me that there were going to be some changes at the company. The changes involving *Vanity Fair* that she laid out were dumbfounding. Our photo department, art department, and copy and research departments—almost half my staff—were going to be moved from the magazine to a central unit. This was serious business. I had worked with the heads of these departments and their staffs for decades, and they were the lifeblood of *Vanity Fair*. These were the people who gave the magazine its unique look and feel and the people who checked every word that went into the magazine and ensured its accuracy, both in terms of fact and usage. Inasmuch as not a word of this had ever been discussed previously, I was completely and utterly stunned by what she was saying. For a while, I was silent. But before I got off the phone, I asked who these people would be reporting to.

"To me," she said matter-of-factly. They would be reporting to her managing editor and her design director.

This left me speechless. As we drove to the airport, I tried to relay the conversation to the other Anna in my life. The foolishness of it, and the pointlessness of it, gnawed at me the whole way to the West Coast. We got through the summit, and when I returned, I gathered my staff and told them of the phone call. Chris, Aimée, Cullen, Dana, Beth, David, and Doug were all there. As were our art director, Chris Dixon; our photo director, Susan White; our legal editor, Robert Walsh; and our head of research, John Banta. I asked them for their thoughts on the matter.

With the notes from the meeting, I wrote a detailed letter to both Anna and the head of the company, Bob Sauerberg, explaining why this was an unnecessary and potentially catastrophic move. Chief among my concerns was the matter of liability for the magazine. The way it was proposed was that we would no longer have our own fact-checkers, who knew the *Vanity Fair* writers and their strengths and weaknesses. Everyone would be dumped into a pool. We could get a fact-checker from *Teen Vogue* on a ten-thousand-word story on Israeli politics. To put the *Vanity Fair* people under the direction of *Vogue* staff members seemed bizarre. And fraught with unknown dangers. Also, aside from the stories, much of *Vanity*

Fair's allure to readers and advertisers was its look—something we paid great attention to. I was not about to deal with a new assortment of photo editors and art directors.

At one point, Anna came down to my office with Raúl Martinez, her design director. She was on a mission to persuade me to see the reorganization her way. Chris Garrett joined me for the meeting.

Anna was going on about the glorious efficiencies of her plan when I got a bit heated and said, "The thing is, you never discussed this with anyone in the company—at least nobody in the editorial departments."

She admitted that this was true. "Well, I discussed it with many others," Anna said.

"Others?" I replied. "Like who?"

"People in Silicon Valley," she said.

I was almost speechless. "What the hell would they know about how a magazine is put together?"

And from there, things began a slow decline.

My contract was coming up for renewal and I said that I would only sign it if this reorganization of Anna's excluded *Vanity Fair*. She fought the exclusion for a bit, but then I got a call from my lawyer, Allen Grubman. "They're leaving things as they are," he said. "Sign the contract." And I did. But I could see the shape of things to come. You never know when you're in a golden age. You only realize it was a golden age when it's gone. And the magazine business, brutalized not just by the great recession of 2008 but also by the relentless appetite of the internet, was in the beginning of a period of rapid decline.

This great era of magazine invention and influence that had so driven the culture for the past three quarters of a century was most surely coming to an end. It wouldn't end immediately, but I thought that, like bankruptcy, it would happen slowly, then all at once. I agreed only to sign a nine-month contract. This would take me through to the end of December 2017. I would have been at *Vanity Fair* for twenty-five years, and I wanted to retire—to see if there was any fuel left for another editorial journey. By May, my decision had already been made for me. Anna and I had rented a house about a twenty-five-minute drive from Cap d'Antibes—fifteen minutes if you drive like the French. The lease started in late December. I was going to step down. And I was going to try to control the narrative of my exit.

Chapter 21.

The South of France and
One Last Swing at the Bat

fter all my years at *Vanity Fair*—where it was difficult enough to control the *daily* narrative of your professional life—I wanted to at least have a hand in directing the narrative of my tenure there and my retirement. And always in the back of my mind was the fate of my chum Art Cooper. He had been a stalwart editor of *GQ* for two decades. He stepped down in early 2003 and a few months later had a stroke after lunch at his favorite restaurant, the Four Seasons. He died a few days later.

When I was going back and forth over whether to stay or to go, a friend suggested that I see a psychiatrist who specialized in executives, mostly from the financial sector, who were about to leave the office, the perks, and the plane behind as they tiptoed toward retirement. I truly liked the man I saw, but after about a half dozen meetings with him, I decided that I was going to leave the magazine. I still had a few sessions left on the meter with him, though, and I found myself concocting arguments on both sides of the issue, just so I wouldn't bore him.

A major factor in the decision I ultimately made was a chance meeting I'd had a few years earlier. My wife, Anna, and I were in San Francisco one fall when Tom Steyer, the billionaire climate activist, invited us to lunch at his house at the foot of the Golden Gate Bridge. Anna was seated beside Jim Coulter, the cofounder of the enormous private equity firm TPG. I hadn't really heard of the company, and to be frank, I had only the vaguest idea as to what private equity was. But I had Jim's wife, Penny, on my left, and we hit it off, as did Anna and Jim. Sometime later, Jim came to see me at *Vanity Fair*, along with a deputy, Adam Mendelsohn. Adam had been Arnold Schwarzenegger's communications chief when Schwarzenegger was governor of California. Over the course of many conversations, Jim said that whatever I wanted to do after *Vanity Fair*, he'd like to be a partner. Now, I wasn't really planning much of anything after I left the magazine. My thought was that we'd settle in the South of France and I'd lie on my back and be inactive until something hit me.

At one point Jim suggested we approach Condé Nast about buying *Vanity Fair*. This I was reluctant to do. First of all, I didn't think the Newhouses would have any interest in selling it. And second, I wasn't sure I had any interest in continuing with it. But we approached CEO Bob Sauerberg, and as expected, Jim and I left with our hats in our hands. I bumped into Cullen a few days after that meeting and told him about it. He said something that stuck with me, to the effect of, in his opinion, young people are much more likely to trust the word of a new news venture over a legacy one. Cullen is liberal in attitude, but very much a conservative person in manner and dress. I thought that if he thinks this, then that's the way it is.

THE SOUTH OF FRANCE AND ONE LAST SWING

⸺

Anna and I were looking forward to living in Opio, in the hills above Cap d'Antibes. The house was a glorious find. The photographer Lartigue had lived not too far from us. Our property had been designed and built by Tom Parr, a legendary force in interiors who had been a co-owner of the British fabric firm Colefax and Fowler. Tom had decorated the house himself. It looked out over a rolling mixture of cut-glass topiary and cypress trees, with the Mediterranean in the distance. The Anglo-French couple who ran the property, James Boekee and his wife, Pascale, were among its most attractive assets. James had worked in hospitality for the British government and Pascale had grown up in the restaurant business. Her father had for years been the maître d' of the Colombe d'Or, in Saint-Paul de Vence. We enrolled our youngest daughter, Izzy, for the winter term at an international school in Mougins. The die was cast. I was going to leave this wonderful job and retire to one of my favorite spots in the world. I just hadn't informed the company yet.

Outside of my family, I had told only three people about my desire to step down: Chris, Aimée, and Beth. They had been with me throughout my time at the magazine and I trusted both their silence and their judgment. They went to work on a plan for my exit. The Brexit referendum—Britain's vote to leave the European Union— had just taken place, and so, as a joke, Aimée began referring to my leaving as "Grexit." I wanted to let the company know in early September 2017 that I would be leaving that December, in order to give them time to find a replacement. My final issue would be the March issue—the Hollywood issue—which I would edit from France. Beth approached Michael Grynbaum, the media reporter for *The New York Times*, to see if he would be interested in writing the story of my retirement. He said yes. David Kamp, Aimée's husband and a long-time colleague going back to *Spy* days, would write the story for the *Vanity Fair* website.

For the day I was to let the company know, Chris, Aimée, and Beth had worked out a complex plan. At 11:25, I would inform Anna, and then go up to see Bob Sauerberg to let him know. At 11:45, I would see Steve Newhouse, on the same floor. At noon, I would address the senior staff at the magazine, and then at 12:10, the full staff. Meanwhile, *The Times* would release Mike's story, and a few minutes later, *Vanity Fair* would follow up with David's. That was the plan. I hit my mark with Bob, who was completely caught off guard. But Anna hadn't been in her office, and neither had Steve. So I made my way down to the *Vanity Fair* floor and let the senior staff and then the full staff know. When *The Times* released their story, they also issued a news alert, and a number of friends, seeing my name pop up on their phones, told me later that they had assumed I had died.

My wife, Anna, and I had long planned to have dinner with Steve and his wife, Gina Sanders, that night at the Waverly Inn. And we went ahead with it. I worried that the dinner would be awkward, but they could not have been more gracious and indeed brought a bottle of what I later learned was insanely expensive scotch to mark the occasion. We also had a long-planned dinner the next evening with Sherry Lansing and Billy Friedkin along with Candy Bergen and her husband, Marshall Rose. Sherry couldn't get over the fact that the story of my stepping down from the magazine was on the front page of that morning's *Times*. "Graydon, dictators get the front page when they step down!" Many days I look back on her statement and take it as a compliment.

In mid-December, with Anna and Izzy standing nearby, I said my final goodbyes to the staff, and the next day, the three of us were on a British Airways flight to London, where we stayed for a week, and then flew down to Nice and went on to Opio by car. I had asked the company if Nathan King, my chief assistant at *Vanity Fair,* could come with me, and he joined us for a week and brought our dachshund, Charley. Anna's dad, Ken, and all the Carter kids joined us that Christmas. I can't recall when I've ever been so relaxed and happy. Once everybody left—minus Izzy and Charley—we settled in. First things first, I sat down and replied to the almost two thousand people who had written me upon the announcement of my retirement. We spent time tootling around the area, having lunches in the square of the nearby market town, Valbonne. I was down to about a cigarette a day by that time, and I gave that up. I swam laps every day. Louise Grunwald came for a visit, with our friends André Bishop and Peter Manning. Our dear friend from London, Lucy Cornell, paid us a visit. Bette Midler and her husband, Martin von Haselberg, spent four days with us. Aimée and David came for a visit. As did Basil Walter and Sara Marks.

After a month or two of this, I began to get a bit itchy. I'm a strange combination of inherent laziness and sporadic busyness. I can't really explain it. Anna thinks that all I do is spend hours reading the papers in the morning, have a leisurely lunch, and then take a half-hour nap in the afternoon. And she's not completely wrong in this assessment. But in my non-reading, non-lunching, and non-napping hours, I began to noodle an idea similar to one I'd had years before the internet. I was in the habit of reading the international papers in the morning, and as I went through them, I would find stories that weren't in the American papers that I thought friends back home would be interested in. I believed I could put together a weekly dispatch of interesting stories from abroad that would find a welcome audience in America and elsewhere. Jim Coulter and Adam Mendelsohn had business in Europe and dropped in on us. I told them about the idea, and Jim was enthusiastic in his support.

So I went to work drafting a plan for a digital dispatch that would be filled with what I thought were unusual and compelling stories from Britain, Europe, and beyond. It would have the same sort of mix as *Vanity Fair*: political stories, business feuds, literary finds, art-world scandals, dynastic dramas, society dust-ups, and whatnot. And cartoons. I liked the idea of having it come out first thing on a Saturday morning, when most readers want features rather than the grim news of the day. I wanted to produce a dispatch that would be like what I imagined the weekend edition of the *International Herald Tribune* would be like, if that paper was still around. And I wanted to build it so that I could edit it from France. For years I have used old airmail envelopes, with their distinctive red-and-blue borders, as bookmarks. The shelves of our places in New York and Connecticut are filled with books clamping tattered envelopes that stick out of the tops. And in *Air Mail*, I had my name for this new venture.

I drew up an editorial prospectus, but I needed someone who could help me with the business aspect of the plan. I'm fairly hopeless with numbers and had no idea what the financial elements of the prospectus should look like. I don't think I'd ever seen a proper business plan. Max, my number-two son, after going to Oxford, had settled into a career at Christie's. He took some time off to get an MBA, and then an MA in Indian history, at Columbia. One of his classmates at business school was a student his age whom I liked the look of. His name is Bill Keenan and, like Max, he'd grown up in New York. He'd somehow managed to play enough hockey in the city that he made the team at Harvard and then played pro in Europe before ending up, as so many kids do these days, at a bank. Bill wrote a book about his hockey career and one about his time at Deutsche Bank. I contacted him from France and asked if he would help me draft the business plan, and he said sure. From there, he just grew into becoming *Air Mail*'s chief operating officer.

I also wanted an editorial partner, as I'd had with Kurt at *Spy*. And I had one person in mind: Alessandra Stanley. This was to be an international offering, and I knew that she had spent a good part of her professional life abroad for *The New York Times*, as both a foreign correspondent and bureau chief in Moscow and Rome. I'd known Alessandra for almost four decades, and only through someone else did I discover that she'd gone to Harvard—a résumé gold star that you usually find out within minutes of meeting someone who went there. I discovered, too, that she spoke five languages. I asked her out to dinner at the Waverly Inn and outlined my ideas for *Air Mail*. She signed on before dessert had arrived. I do love that sort of enthusiasm and willingness to jump into the deep end.

I then went in search of someone who could help me design the platform I had in mind and someone who could actually build it. The designer I wanted was Angela Panichi. She had been a deputy art director at *Vanity Fair* but left to raise her children. She had continued to work for the magazine on the side the whole time her kids were growing up. I had long admired both her exquisite taste and her cheery collegiality. Angela signed on to become *Air Mail*'s creative director. I had at one point invested in a start-up called Zig that failed to get traction and was sold. I called one of the founders, Josh James, and asked if he knew someone with great coding skills who also spoke in plain English, not techspeak. He gave me the number of John Tornow, who had built Zig. John signed on. We've been together now going on six years, and not once have I ever had to ask him, "What do you mean?"

Emily Davis had been one of the sales engines on the publishing side of *Vanity Fair*. I was back in New York for a visit when I heard that Condé Nast had let Emily go. I called her immediately and we met at the small office on Bank Street a block west of our house that I had long rented for my restaurant and documentary work. I asked her if she'd be our chief marketing officer, and she said yes. The next day she got a call from Condé Nast saying that they had reconsidered and would like her to come back. She told them she had other plans. Chris, my longtime managing editor at *Vanity Fair*, signed on, as did Nathan, who became a deputy editor. Julia Vitale, another *Vanity Fair* hand whom I had always thought was a star, came on as a deputy editor as well.

All this happened before I'd raised a penny. I knew that I would need sufficient funding to get up and running and then a few years of what start-up people call "runway." Jim Coulter came in with a sizable investment from TPG. I twisted a few arms and Barry Diller, David Zaslav, Bryan Lourd, Louise Grunwald, and Ernie Pomerantz, Marie Brenner's husband, came in. Allen Grubman, my lawyer, got David Geffen to invest. And Aryeh Bourkoff, the investment banker, brought in Lord Rothermere, the British owner of Associated Newspapers, publishers of the *Daily Mail*. In time, an old friend, Mark Dowley, brought in RedBird Capital, run by Gerry Cardinale. And Standard Industries, an industrial company with investments in media, came in.

Jim Kelly asked if he could become the books editor, and I jumped at the offer. I had met Ashley Baker, a smart young editor and writer, when she did a story on me after I was given a fashion award. She came on as a deputy editor. As did my son Ash, who had spent a number of years at Hearst as an editor, first at *Town & Country* and then at *Esquire*. From there things quickly fell into place.

James Harding, a veteran UK newsman who had set up his own company, Tortoise, around the same time, called our group "has-beens and rookies." And indeed we were. There were cohorts from *Time* and *Spy*, and there were a good number of *Vanity Fair* hands, including our head of photo, our head of research, and our chief copy editor. We built a business with old-school values and new-school delivery. The engine of the operation, though, is a collection of incredibly smart young twentysomethings who connect us old-timers to the current culture.

With *Air Mail*, I knew that I didn't want to be dependent on Google and Facebook to drive traffic. I wanted to have a direct connection with our readers. So we set about building up our subscriber base by selling them directly on the idea of *Air Mail*—giving them a trial run before asking them to subscribe and letting the audience build organically. It was a slower way of growing, but more reliable, in that subscribers weren't taking a chance on something they hadn't tried. They were committing to something that was right in front of them. If they liked it, they signed on. The same went for the advertising. Too many websites that I had looked at were visual nightmares, with ads moving along at the top and bottom and on the sides. I wanted as pure a reading experience as is possible in the digital world. And I wanted the advertising to be as beautiful as what we had in mind for *Air Mail* itself.

Just before we launched, Jay Fielden, then the editor of *Esquire*, asked me to do some drawings for the magazine. Which I did. The drawings took half a day to complete, but it took me the better part of half a year to defang the all-encompassing forever contract Hearst sent me for those sketches. I didn't need the money at that point. But I am always mindful of the days when a check for freelance work was a vital part of survival. I wasn't going to subject *Air Mail*'s contributors to the same treatment. We have a hard-and-fast policy of trying to pay our writers and illustrators within ten working days of receiving their invoice.

As I've mentioned, I had written thank-you letters to every advertiser, every month, the whole time I was at *Vanity Fair*. So I had a pretty good relationship with the majority of these people and companies. But the sorts of advertisers that were regulars in the heyday of the glossy magazine were reluctant to advertise in digital properties. I had to convince them otherwise. I felt that if I could get Hermès on board, the others would follow. I met with the head of the U.S. company, Bob Chavez, in New York, and then flew to Paris to meet with Axel Dumas, the CEO of Hermès. I was helped in all of this by the fact that Michael Carl, who had been a number two in the fashion department at *Vanity Fair*, was by that time a popular lieutenant at Hermès. They did come in, and sure enough, that gave license for others to join us: LVMH, Ralph Lauren, Giorgio Armani, Chanel, Gucci, Brunello Cucinelli, and more. *Air Mail* is now in its sixth year. The original staff is pretty much still in place. We weathered the pandemic well—in part because the whole operation was designed around me living in France, where we still spend a part of the year.

—

I have been happily married for the past twenty years. I have five wonderful children, whom we are close to, but who, even more important, are close to each other. None of them went into banking, which I suppose is a relief. Ash, in addition to working with me at *Air Mail*, coauthored an oral biography of Mike Nichols a few years ago. Max is the vice-chairman of Christie's. Ash and his wife, Daniela (a former Boston University classmate), and Max and his wife, Sarah (a colleague from Christie's), now have kids of their own. Spike is a writer and filmmaker and lives in London. He married Izzy's former au pair, Pip Johnson, a gifted artist. Bron is a development executive at HBO in Los Angeles and lives with an accomplished young actor, Alex Akpobome. And Izzy will be heading off to college next year.

I was at Si and Victoria's one night for dinner a few years before he died. Also there were the *New Yorker* art critic Calvin Tomkins and his wife, Dodie Kazanjian. During cocktails, we were mooning over the Newhouse art collection, and Dodie, who was a magazine writer at the time, asked me if I collected art. I looked at her dumbfounded. "No," I said. "Dodie, I'm an editor with a lot of kids. I collect tuition bills." Well, yes, tuition bills and secondhand cars.

I've only glancingly mentioned this before, but I'm a car guy and have been my whole life. I got my driver's license the day I turned sixteen. That year my father bought my mother and me a secondhand 1961 Austin-Healey Sprite. It's the little sports car with the bug eyes. You still see them on the road—although this is getting rarer and rarer. Since then, by my counting, I've had upward of—I kid you not—five dozen cars. Nothing too fancy—and generally cars I could work on myself. I once paid my friend Bob Hixt $300 for his 1959 VW Bug. I took possession of the car on a Friday and spent the weekend changing the oil and spark plugs, tuning the engine, and then cleaning and sprucing the car up. When Bob came by on Monday and saw it, he bought it back from me for $600.

I've owned a half dozen of those Volkswagen Bugs and one exquisite 1960 two-toned Westfalia camper. I've had Peugeots and Renaults. I've owned a half dozen MGs (including a 1947 MG TD), three Range Rovers, three BMWs, two Saab convertibles, a Porsche, and seven or eight Volvos, including a humpback 544 and three Amazons (or 122s, as they were called in Canada). At Condé Nast, editors were offered company car leases that were renewed every three years. Most of my colleagues chose a new Mercedes or a top-of-the-line BMW. I found a 1972 Mercedes-Benz 280SL 3.5 convertible in an ad in *The Times*. It was forest green with a tan leather interior and brown canvas top. Seriously, it had pretty much only been driven by a woman on Long Island to church each week and had just 65,000 miles on it. It was the car of my dreams. I went to Chuck Townsend, then the Condé Nast CEO, and said that I'd rather lease this than a new car. Chuck was a car guy himself and, after a lot of mulling, gave me the go-ahead. That was almost thirty years ago. I bought the car when the lease ran out, and I still have it. I feel like an old-fashioned millionaire when I drive it.

Aside from the Mercedes, my current fleet is the collection of what a lower-rung screenwriter's might look like. We have a 1967 MGB, British Racing Green with wire wheels; a 1962 long-wheelbase Land Rover Series II; a 1992 Range Rover; a 1951 Chevy woody wagon that I've had since my kids were born; and a Volvo hybrid for driving back and forth to the city.

I have also loved canoeing my entire life. I gave canoe lessons at summer camp, and I still have a half dozen Old Towns, all of them more than forty years old, including a century-old war canoe, which seats a dozen people, that I had refurbished. Yes, I'm a serial collector—although that is, I will have to say, an overblown word for what I have been scrounging around for over the decades. I collect books, old cameras, felt holiday-location pennants, architectural models, old European file boxes, large airplane models, Steiff toys, and even French doors. At one point I had a 1935 double-cockpit Chris-Craft. And there is a 1950s-era hydroplane that I still have. I keep a storage facility in Connecticut near our house where the results of those errant passions are held. These include a lifetime of fly rods, flies, nets, and other assorted fishing gear; my old Anderson & Sheppard suits; hockey, football, and baseball gear used by my kids; Cherner chairs; and God knows what else. Also, a 1963 Airstream Bambi trailer that I bought on eBay one night when I'd had too much to drink.

So that's my life now. Anna and I sold our house on Bank Street just before the pandemic hit. It had five floors if you count the basement, and with four of my kids having moved out and getting on with lives of their own, it was just too big. At a certain point, all those stairs became a nightmare. If I left something on the top floor, rather than climb back up, I'd just order a new one on Amazon. We bought a duplex in an apartment building a few blocks east that we had long admired. I sold my fishing camp in Connecticut to a lovely young family who will get the kind of joy out of it that the Carters did for a quarter of a century. The Waverly Inn continues to thrive and is a five-minute walk from our apartment. The *Air Mail* offices, on the parlor floor of a once-grand town house, are a two-and-a-half-minute walk from our apartment. When we went looking for office space, I told Nathan, who was leading the search, that my one condition was that I didn't want anything that would require a swipe card to get into the building or the actual offices. The town house we have been in for the past six years has tall ceilings, marble fireplaces, French doors, and, for security, an axe given to me by Chris Dixon, my last art director at *Vanity Fair*. Chris, like me, is a Canadian. And this is the sort of thing Canadians give each other at Christmas.

I've been an editor now off and on for more than half a century. I was one of the youngest editors when I began and I'm one of the oldest now. Richard Nixon was president when I was editing *The Canadian Review*. I've been doing this same job through fifteen administrations. There were no computers when we started, and obviously there was no internet. Phones were rotary and pay was pathetic. But I fell in love with what I did and am still in love with it. Curiously, the overarching demands of the job now are not appreciably different than they were back then. You endeavor to get the most out of your staff and contributors. You try to put all their results into a package that will please the reader, and then you pray that this blessed person will come back for the next issue. Anxious editors are good editors.

Back when magazines still flourished, I could tell in an instant one edited by a complacent editor over one edited by an anxious editor. I'm proud of all the issues I put out at *The Canadian Review*, *Spy*, *The New York Observer*, *Vanity Fair*, and *Air Mail*. Some are great, a few are regrettable. But I will tell you that even getting a substandard issue out the door is the result of a lot of work by a lot of people.

In addition to the staff I worked with for two and a half decades at *Vanity Fair*, I got to coedit issues with three remarkable men. Tom Ford edited the Hollywood issue one year. He conceived and styled every photo in the issue, and we collaborated on all the stories. Another year, Judd Apatow edited a special comedy issue. And Bono and I put together a special issue on Africa. For that one, we wanted to produce twenty separate covers. The idea was to have it be a bit like the telephone game, with a figure from one cover whispering in the ear of a person on the next cover and so on. Among the people Bono booked for that issue's covers were Barack Obama, Muhammad Ali, Oprah Winfrey, Madonna, Iman, Maya Angelou, Djimon Hounsou, Warren Buffett, Bill Gates, Melinda Gates, Chris Rock, George Clooney, Alicia Keys, Don Cheadle, Brad Pitt, Queen Rania, Jay-Z, Condoleezza Rice, George W. Bush, Archbishop Desmond Tutu, and Bono himself. When I told Chuck Townsend and John Bellando, the company's CFO, about the idea to do all these different covers—which involved flying Annie and her crew on a zigzag odyssey across two continents—I thought they'd faint. But I had brought Bono along to the meeting. Never underestimate the persuasive powers of one of the world's great rock stars.

The fact is, getting a company up and running is a young man's game. I've been walking around with a tin cup, rounding up *Air Mail* financing, for most of the last six years. Friends duck into doorways when they see me coming. I can detect the fear in their voices when we chat on the phone, terrified that I am going to hit them up. The flip side is that the job itself is as enjoyable as any I have ever had. I simply love being an editor. But down here at the coal face of American publishing, the financial part has become brutal. The fact is, there are people who have money and people who *should* have money. Some mornings I just wish I had properly retired, moved to Florida, become a Republican, and worked on my golf game. But then I lie down, let the moment pass, and get on with the life I have chosen and the life I love.

Some Rules for Living

Through no definitive plan and with no particular purpose, I have developed a haphazard set of rules that helped me navigate life and not look like too much of a fool in doing so. A good number of them I received from wiser souls on the long road. Henry Porter, who has heard many of these rules, and who now just rolls his eyes when I feather one out, said that I should produce a handbook—a slim volume—called *Magna Carter: How to Be More Like Me.* I don't believe this was meant as a flattering suggestion. In any event, here is some of what would be in that slim volume.

Avoid the "Wall of Fame." In the offices and homes of people who have done relatively well in professional life, you will often find what can only be called their Wall of Fame. This is that area of the home or office where the residents are pictured in framed photos standing alongside figures much more illustrious than they are—presidents, industry leaders, actors, music stars. My rule is this: don't put the photo of you and somebody famous in a silver frame and display it for others unless you are absolutely positive that the famous person has the same photo in their home or office.

—

Be wary of calling something "the something of something else." It can apply to people and it's a cheap gimmick in the writer's bag of tricks. Saying that Herb Smith—and I'm making this name up—is "the John Travolta of Canada," for instance. You can do better than that. This also extends to cities. Beirut being "the Paris of the Middle East," for instance. I think it's fine for the lovely people of Dresden to refer to their hometown as the "Florence of Germany." Which they do, and which in many ways it is. But they should do so only if they are certain that Florentines call *their* city the "Dresden of Italy."

—

Shun ostentatious slumming when it comes to art placement. This often involves the first-floor powder room that guests will invariably have to use at some point during a visit. Here you might find the Oscar statuette propping open a cabinet, the framed letter from a world leader thanking the resident for one thing or another, or the written confirmation of their Tony win. Once, in Los Angeles, Anna, Fran, and I visited Bob Shaye and his wife, Eva. At one point I needed to use the bathroom. Bob's instructions: "Down the hall, turn left at the Picasso!"

—

Fess up and tell the truth. When you are in a conflict, try to remove yourself from the ground surface and look down on the scene from above. It is only there that you can examine the problem, if there is one, and do so objectively. This bit of advice came from one of my oldest friends, John Doran. I was editing *The Canadian Review*, my long-dying political and literary monthly, and was regularly having to go to our printer in Montreal, hat in hand, to see if they would produce the next issue before I had paid off the last one. John's advice was always the same. Don't try a "check in the mail" ploy, he said. Just tell the truth. When they ask you when you can pay, simply say, "I don't really know." "Remember," John said, "you need them. But they also need your business. And if you're straight with them, you get them on your side." Strangely enough, it worked.

Put yourself in the movie. This is an easy one—especially when it comes to dealing with others. When a confrontation arises, just ask yourself: Are you the hero in this story, the villain, or someone in between? Would you root for yourself if you saw yourself in the film? You'd be surprised how useful this is in life. I have always tried to do the right thing, hoping that my actions would cause the objective me to root for the real me. It doesn't always work, but it works a lot better than not trying it at all.

F.I.S.K.—a guide to romantic partners. I tell my kids that these are the essential ingredients you should look for in a mate: funny, interesting, smart, and kind. This is, obviously, an overlay of the physical attraction part. Funny and interesting, it almost goes without saying, are imperative. Same with smart. Kind is highly underrated. But over the long haul, it pays off in dividends.

Get two. If you really like something, always get two or more—especially if it's something that you aren't sure will remain in production. Some years ago, Lacoste came out with a plain white polo shirt with a white-on-white logo on the chest. It was sturdy pique and it seemed to mask any number of areas of my physique that were not as trim as they had once been. For some reason, they weren't offered for sale on their website, so I asked Michael Carl in our fashion department at *Vanity Fair* if he could connect me with someone at Lacoste. As it became harder and harder to get them, I doubled down on my orders, figuring they would soon stop making them. And, indeed, Lacoste did take the shirts out of production—but not before I had assembled about two dozen. I have worn one every day for much of the past two decades.

—

Make double-sided place cards. If you're giving a big, seated dinner, like a wedding or a birthday celebration, and you have place cards, make them double-sided. I came up with this back in my early days at *Vanity Fair* and I don't know why more people haven't picked up on it. For one thing, it makes it much easier for people to find their place in that they don't have to circumnavigate a round table or make two trips up and down the length of a long table. Also, it means that your guests will know the names of the people sitting across from them. Which is always useful. Cullen has suggested that I make my tombstone double-sided to facilitate family members, should they ever visit, finding me. If anybody's listening, I would like that very much.

—

It's not so much what you say yes to in life as what you say no to. Don't jump at the job opportunity simply for the money. Unless, that is, you're in a dire situation financially, in which case, by all means, jump. Back when I was struggling at *Time*, I was offered the job of being the editor of something called *Games* magazine, a venture that was owned by the publisher of *Playboy*. Despite the fact that the job paid more than three times what I was making at *Time*, and even though my future at *Time* was rocky at best, I turned the *Games* job down. I had flipped through a number of issues and couldn't for the life of me think of a way I could make the magazine better—or even keep it as good as it was. Also, I thought I would have children at some point, and I didn't think that an association with *Playboy* was the sort of image I wanted my future kids to have of me.

—

Who you *don't* invite is as important as who you *do*. Years ago, and in a moment of weakness, I said yes to sending invitations to the *Vanity Fair* Oscar party to two people who had asked to come: Paris Hilton and Pamela Anderson. The photos from the party the day after the Oscars pretty much featured only those two, who hammed it up for the photographers, with Paris autographing one of Pam's breasts. Not to cast aspersions on either of them, but it gave the party a look that didn't reflect what it was. (A few years later, I bumped into Paris Hilton at a Sheryl Crow concert. She asked me why we had called her and her sister "the axis of evil." I thought for a moment and couldn't for the life of me recall what she was referring to. So I just said, "I think you took it out of context." She nodded her head and replied, "I thought so.")

—

Stay open for business. At the Sarah Lawrence publishing course in the late 1970s, one of the speakers was the great Knopf fiction editor Gordon Lish. He was the most beautifully dressed man I had ever met up to that point. I remember he wore a tan suit, polished brown shoes, and tan wool socks with a blind cable design down the sides. (My first suit when I got to New York was a tan gabardine from Paul

Stuart on Madison. And I bought a pair of socks similar to Gordon's.) Anyway, Gordon's major bit of advice to writers—and it can be applied to anyone in any profession—was this: stay open for business. Never shut yourself completely down. This can be applied not only to writing but to life itself. Always be open to a new line of endeavor. Be willing to say, "Oh, what the hell—sure!" I have traveled with Gordon's words, and they are what got me not only into the magazine business but into the restaurant business and into the business of making documentaries.

⚊

Plan your exit before your entrance. There were evenings at *Vanity Fair* when I would have to go to three book parties and still make it home for dinner. It didn't happen often, but it happened often enough that I developed a game plan. I had a car and driver in those days, which helped considerably. The plan was simple but effective. Leave your coat in the car. (Please don't try this if you arrived by subway.) Make a beeline for the host and the guest of honor. Never pick up a drink. Never get into a conversation that could wind up being long and drawn out. Never look rushed. And never say goodbye. I passed these on to Anna and we developed the sort of hand-eye signals favored by Navy SEALs in order to coordinate our exits. I realize this is all a bit similar to Irish exits or French exits. But I do think mine is more formally thought out and executed.

⚊

Leave first. Similarly, be the first one to leave a big dinner. I remember a large, seated gathering in the New York Public Library in the late 1980s. Mick Jagger was sitting across the room from me. And the moment the dessert hit the table, I watched as he got up, casually slalomed his way through the tables, left the room, and didn't return. It is a rare instance when hanging around as the final dishes are being removed leads to anything constructive or entertaining. I do admit that I can carry this too far. When Barneys opened its uptown store in 1993, Cynthia and I went to the opening. The event included a dinner that was held in the Pierre, which had a common wall with the store. We followed my general rule and quietly left as the dessert hit the table. The next day I read in the papers that Barry White had performed afterward. He happened to be one of Cynthia's favorite singers, and I do believe it took decades for her to forgive me—if indeed she ever did. And I could hardly blame her.

Wish others well. Get any sense of schadenfreude out of your system. It's hard enough to control events in your own life—don't spend a second on the events that could affect others' lives in a negative way. David Halberstam told me to always wish for the success of everyone in your circle of friends. "There's a lot of it to go around," he would say. Similarly, John Scanlon had a form of parallel advice. He was a Falstaffian figure with a huge appetite for literature (Irish), drink (Irish), and life. On the occasion of his sixtieth birthday, he threw a dinner for about a hundred of his closest friends. Peter Jennings, the ABC evening news anchor, served as master of ceremonies. At one point John pulled me aside and said, "You know why I have this many friends, Graydon? Because they all know I wish them well."

I took John's words to heart that night and developed a corollary to them: spend as little time as possible with people you think might wish ill of you. You know who they are. They're the ones whose hearts skip a happy beat at the slightest word of your misfortune. Your good fortune can cause them to break out in a rash. Keep them at a distance.

—

Monograms are idiotic. Don't put them on your clothing unless you have two or three family members living under the same roof and you all wear roughly the same clothes and in the same size. If you aren't a Kardashian or a member of the Dionne quintuplet family, it's highly unlikely that you face such a problem. Should you have any doubts as to the wisdom of this rule, you only have to look at Donald Trump's shirts. The one exception to the no-monogram rule might be the great society photographer Slim Aarons. He had tiny Chinese hanzi stitched across the chest of his shirts. When someone asked him what they said, he replied, "No starch, please."

—

Make your own phone calls. For most of us, this sounds just astoundingly obvious, on the order of asking someone to dress themselves. In a certain entertainment sector, however, asking people to place their own calls—well, you might as well be recommending do-it-yourself dentistry.

In the movie business, where tradition generally holds that all calls must be returned by the end of working hours, there is a time of the day when assistants are told to begin "rolling" calls. An assistant might reach you and say, "Scott Rudin on line one." Being the naive hick that I am, I would generally pick up the phone and say something like "Hi, Scott." To which the person on the other line would say, "Let me get him for you." There'd be a long wait and then either Scott Rudin would get on the line or his assistant would get back on and say, "I've lost him. Can we return?" Which means that the process would be repeated. I found it almost laughably offensive.

I was new to all of this when I first got to *Vanity Fair*. A couple of years in, my assistant said that Jon Dolgen, the new head of Paramount Pictures, was on the line. I picked up the phone and said, "Hi, Jon," to which the person on the other end said, "Let me get him for you." I hung up. They tried again. I hung up again. I knew I was breaking some sort of long-held Hollywood social custom, but I was enjoying it. The Dolgen office must have tried three or four more times before my assistant whispered loudly, "It's Jon Dolgen himself!" I picked up the phone and had a lovely chat with a man who might have been one of the funnier studio executives around.

Steve Wynn's office called me once. I was out to lunch and called him back when I returned. The assistant said, "Hold on, please, I'll get him." Some Muzak came on, then Steve's voice.

"Hi, this is Steve Wynn."

"Hi, Steve," I said.

"You like pizza? You like sushi?"

I was about to say yes to both when I realized this was a recording promoting one of his casinos. When he did finally get on the phone, he asked me if I would read a few chapters of the memoir he'd been working on. I said sure. He was especially pleased with the chapter on Frank Sinatra. The next day, the manuscript arrived. I plucked out the Sinatra chapter and read it. It wasn't long. But if I can summarize it for you, it was essentially a pronouncement that Steve was the new Frank and that Frank endorsed this.

This Hollywoodization of the business call eventually filtered down through other industries and even down to journalism. Tom Brokaw, when he was still the NBC News anchor, and Steve Brill, then the editor of *Brill's Content*, a sort of media-industry watchdog, both had assistants get me on the phone. And in both cases, they were making the calls as reporters.

Luke Janklow, the son of Mort Janklow, wound up working at his dad's literary firm. He was the friend of a friend who was always saying how much I would like him. A few months after he had started working with his father, my assistant said that Luke was on the phone. With a feeling of bonhomie, and in order to welcome him back to New York, I jumped on the call and said, "Hi, Luke!"

I was shocked by the response. "Hold on, let me get Mr. Janklow on the phone."

I hung up. And regularly throughout the day, his office tried to get me on the phone. Every time I heard the "Hold on . . ." bit, I hung up. We never did talk on the phone. But my friend was right. When I finally met him, I did like Luke. But we've still never talked on the phone.

—

Whatever you do, it has to have a point. This sounds moronic and painfully obvious, but it took me a while to figure it out. The magazine I edited in Canada when I was a young man was all over the place. Neither liberal nor conservative, it was part politics, part literary criticism, part sports, part arts. It didn't have a point beyond the fact that it was a magazine and I got to edit it. Its fortunes were, alas, not commensurate with the effort that I and others invested in it.

My next magazine, *Spy*, most certainly did have a point. It was built to satirize the figures and institutions that made up the hoppy New York parade in the mid- and late 1980s. That was its point. And it thrived.

In the mid-1990s, most restaurants in the West Village were either Italian, Chinese, or bare-bones, wood-topped casual places. After we took over the Waverly Inn, a restaurant that had been around for much of the twentieth century, my partners and I wanted to create something old in feel and something new for the neighborhood: American comfort food, white tablecloths, great cocktails, a mid-century jazz soundtrack, flattering lighting, red banquettes—and a mural that evoked the Village's bygone years as the epicenter of New York bohemia. This all added up to having a point. And the Waverly Inn still has a point and continues to do well.

A few years after we opened, one of my partners, Emil Varda, got the keys to the Beatrice Inn, a few blocks north. It had been a pleasant family-run red-sauce restaurant for decades. We redid it a bit. White tablecloths, great cocktails, mid-century jazz soundtrack, flattering lighting, and *green leather* banquettes. It did well at first— as so many new restaurants do in their early months—but then the business just drifted away. People looking for a Waverly-like experience went to the Waverly. The Beatrice, as shiny and as lovely as it was, simply didn't have a point beyond the fact that it was like the Waverly but wasn't it.

—

You never learn from success, only from failure. I tell my kids this all the time. Just try to keep the failures small and the successes big, or at least big-ish. Nobody ever mulls over a success to figure out how it happened. But a failure can become a thinking field for years. Just make sure something good comes out of all that stewing and worry.

—

Your time is valuable. Let's say you're fifty. If you're an American male, actuaries give you another thirty-one years. That's a little over 11,300 days and includes around 3,200 weekend days—1,600 Saturdays. It sounds like a lot, but they go by faster than you might think. Do you really want to use up one of those Saturdays with someone you'd just as soon not see? Do you want to blow one of the 1,600 Wednesdays on a dinner you could do without? As the days and years progressed, I bundled friends into groups. Lunch friends. Dinner friends. Weekend-together friends. Family-vacation friends. Lunch friends who are wonderful company can be upgraded to dinner. Dinner friends who leave you feeling better about yourself can move into weekend or vacation slots. Similarly, people can be downgraded. Dreary dinner dates who talk only about themselves often get moved to the lunch bin. Trust me, it works. And your life will be the better for it

⌁

Always carry a handkerchief. I haven't left home without one since I was in my twenties. I find myself using it almost hourly.

1. It's not just for blowing your nose. Although it serves that purpose wonderfully. Also, if you have a cold, it's much easier on the nose than any form of paper tissue.

2. Hang it on your driver's-side door handle for highway assistance.

3. Tied in the corners, it makes a serviceable sun hat.

4. Workable as a mopping-up rag in an emergency.

5. Whatever you're wearing, you will look a bit more dapper if you tuck your hankie in your breast pocket. And if you're a man and you have a hangover, this makes you look crisper on the outside than you are inside. Combine it with a bow tie and your boss will see past the hangover. In his eyes you will positively shimmer with promise as a young go-getter and someone destined for great things.

6. Good for dabbing your eye, or that of your loved one, at weddings, funerals, breakups, and so forth.

7. Brow mopper in hot weather.

8. Good hobo-style sack when fastened to a long stick.

9. Eyeglasses cleaner.

10. Bird-droppings remover!

11. Can handle the services of a do-rag in hot weather or at an E Street Band concert.

12. Tourniquet.

13. Pandemic mask.

14. Holdup mask.

15. Good for close-at-hand party tricks.

16. If you get desperate on a cold night: kindling.

17. Wonderful for holding a chilled cocktail in your hand.

18. A splash of water and it's a fire mask. Remember, most people die of the smoke inhalation, not the flames.

19. Serves as a notebook in a pinch.

20. Jaunty kerchief if you're in a Picasso-ish mood.

21. Invaluable for replacing a hot light bulb.

22. For fathers (and mothers): good for cleaning up baby vomit.

23. Ditto: a serviceable bib.

24. Napkin. Especially in the United Kingdom, where they are rare at dinners cooked at home. Saves on the sleeves.

25. And when all else fails, something to wave in the air when it's time to surrender.

Acknowledgments

Sorry, I'm not quite done yet.

There are a number of people I must thank who played their parts in the procession of better souls who molded this lumpen mass of frostbitten Canadian eagerness into the still eager, but slightly less lumpen mass I am now. I should start with my parents, obviously. They were hopeless on any sort of career advice. But they had strong moral cores and taught me the difference between right and wrong. They also read constantly, and my mother was a gifted Sunday painter—two activities that I have inherited and that have all but made my life. If I'm going back that far, I do have to tip my hat to the overall Canadian education system. I don't know what it's like now, but when I was a kid, it managed to drill enough English, history, and rudimentary Latin into my numbskull brain that I became a functioning member of the brotherhood of the written word.

New York, the most welcoming of cities, took me to its bosom and gave me a life—a life that I, like so many foreign urchins, had only dreamt about. I would be nothing without this calamitous, glorious city.

In my partnerships with others, I've always endeavored to be the dumbest person in the room. And in this goal, I have, for the most part, succeeded. I mean, what is the future in being the smartest person in a working group? Who are you going to learn from? Through Graham at *The Canadian Review*, Kurt and Tom at *Spy*, Aimée at *The New York Observer*; and on to Sean, Eric, and Emil at the Waverly Inn; Annabelle in our little documentary unit; Chris and a series of gifted editors and publishers at *Vanity Fair*; and Alessandra at *Air Mail*, I've been blessed with partners who typically knew a lot more about whatever it was we were trying to do than I did.

I picked up elements in taste and social interaction from the objects of my romantic passions, notably my wives, Marie, Cynthia, and Anna. Especially Anna.

I love having a partner as one embarks on a new adventure. Even with this slim volume, I wouldn't have written a word without James Fox's wise hand guiding me along the narrative path. We were having lunch one day in London about six or seven years ago, and he mentioned that should I ever decide to write a memoir, he'd love to work on it with me. He was just coming off the success of *Life*, the Keith Richards memoir that he had a major hand in. It was the first time I had even thought of writing anything about myself. Without James's suggestion and later encouragement, I never would have given it a try. I had known and worked with him for years, and aside from his brilliant newspaper and magazine journalism—some of it done for *Vanity Fair* during my time—there were his books, *White Mischief* being at the top of the list. Unlike Keith, I write for a living and therefore my partnership with James was different. The writing is mine, but so much of the order and narrative pace were in good part thanks to James. Nobody would have continued reading this book had it started with my birth in Toronto's General Hospital and continued in a linear fashion from there. I've mentioned earlier that I'm inherently both busy and lazy, and James kept the boiler stoked on this project, at the same time digging through the hoard of archives and tapping the memories of friends and colleagues. We worked on the book in New York, London, Connecticut, and the South of France. When we were apart, we worked on it long distance over Zoom. We were assisted by Hannah Lack, a relentless and unflappable researcher, who had helped James on the Keith Richards book.

My agent, Bob Barnett, is a man whom I had known from the other side of the desk. A litigator at Williams & Connolly in Washington, DC, who also handles the affairs of a stable of esteemed writers, Bob would come to the *Vanity Fair* offices to make sure that Chris and I were taking proper care of his clients on the masthead. I came to realize that he was a full-service representative for his authors. As a result, Bob handles the literary affairs of former presidents and first ladies on both sides of the aisle. He also handles the work of arguably the biggest nonfiction author in the country (Bob Woodward) and certainly the biggest fiction author (James Patterson). When he offered to represent me, I leapt.

Once James and I had a serviceable manuscript, I asked Cullen Murphy to join the group. Cullen and I have worked together for almost two decades. He edited my copy when we were at *Vanity Fair*, and he edited this book. There is nobody better in this regard.

I was under the impression that book editors no longer actually edited the books they commissioned. That was not the case with this one. Ann Godoff, an old friend going back forty years and the head of this imprint, gave the manuscript a skilled and spirited edit and polish. I must thank her and the wonderful assembly of talents at Penguin Random House for making this such a pleasant experience.

You can reasonably say that editors are only as good as their assistants. And in this area, I've been blessed with several supportive hands who have made me look better than I am and have gotten me to wherever I was supposed to be going to, and on time. From my very first assistant at *Spy*, John Brodie, I've been skillfully aided by

ACKNOWLEDGMENTS

Aimée Bell, Dana Brown, Pat Kinder, Punch Hutton, Matt Trainor, Liz Welch, Jon Kelly, David Foxley, Tony Rotunno, Nathan King, and Carolina de Armas. There were others, and many were great, but these were the all-stars.

I'd like to thank the readers of *The Canadian Review*, *Spy*, *The New York Observer*, *Vanity Fair*, and *Air Mail*. You yourself might well be one of them. Without those readers—without you—I wouldn't have had the long ride that I've had.

You simply cannot invest too much time in your children. I carved out as much time for them as humanly possible given the constraints of trying to feed them, educate them, and keep a roof over all our heads. We filled the house with books, music, movies, and art supplies. And these elements became significant elements in their lives. The result is that I get the great pleasure of their company as adults. And aside from the joy of being with these incredibly interesting family members, I get touchpoints into aspects of the culture that I'm not particularly interested in or simply not aware of. This has been a boon in my day job. I may have had a hand in making them. But they surely had a huge hand in making me.

I owe a special thanks to Si Newhouse. In addition to keeping me around for a quarter of a century, he taught me so much about not only the magazine business but about life. I have great affection as well for so many other Newhouses, including Si's wife, Victoria, his brother Donald, his cousin Jonathan, and his nephew Steven.

Some of you will recognize the title of this book. It also happens to be the title of Evelyn Waugh's collected travel writing. He's not around to thank, but I'm sure some family member will appreciate the credit. It came out a few years before I was born. I reread it recently, and I have to say, the book has aged better than I have.

Okay, that's it, I'm quite done. As I'm sure you are.